The Reality of School Management

Derek Torrington and
Jane Weightman

Blackwell Education

First published 1989

Published by
Basil Blackwell Ltd
108 Cowley Road
Oxford OX4 1JF
England

British Library Cataloguing in Publication Data

Torrington, Derek, *1931–*
The reality of school management.
1. Great Britain. Secondary schools.
Management
I. Title II. Weightman, Jane
373.12′00941

ISBN 0–631–16331–X
ISBN 0–631–16332–8 Pbk

Typeset in 10/12 pt Symposium
by Colset Private Ltd.
Printed in Great Britain by T.J. Press (Padstow) Cornwall

Contents

Introduction

The Management and Organisation of Secondary Schools: The Search for Better Ways

Traditionally the core professional task of teachers was to manage their relationships with children: their new core professional task is to manage their relationships with a wider constituency of children, parents, advisers and – above all – each other. The 1980s have seen a shaking of the foundations that few teachers have welcomed – and a scenario for a future for which few teachers are prepared. For many, the future seems to hold the prospect of less autonomy, declining professional independence and little social status. We disagree.

There is also a widespread belief that the art of the teacher is no longer required; that instead of winning a response from children and developing their capacities through such qualities as enthusiasm, selflessness, empathy and skilled encouragement, the teacher will become the operator of administrative procedures, as the child becomes a pin cushion on which a variety of labels are progressively stuck to indicate relative achievement. Again, we disagree.

The reason why we disagree with these glum prophecies arises from our observation of the integrity and commitment of those who make them. As much as any other professional group – and more than most – teachers are dedicated to their mission. Some will give up the struggle, some will not be very successful and a few will withdraw into a cynical shell of 'going by the book', but the great majority will continue to commit their time, skills and enthusiasm to the flowering of the talents possessed by the children in their care. The satisfaction that teachers derive from the varied achievements of their pupils is so profound that it will continue as their prime motivation. The means to that end will, however, change from 'managing' children only to 'managing' a wider constituency.

We make these bold assertions on the basis not of conviction but of evidence. We make the claims not from within the teaching profession but from outside, after 700 days of empirical research in two dozen schools, interviews with over 1000 teachers, attendance at 400 meetings and structured observations of 90 teachers through the varied incidents of their working day. This information is summarised in Table 1.

Table 1: Breakdown of research

Number of days spent by researchers in schools	733
Number of interviews carried out (teaching and non-teaching staff)	1,065
Number of structured observations of individuals	90
Number of meetings attended by researchers	431

Interest in management ideas grew steadily among teachers through the 1960s and 1970s, yet there was little reciprocal interest shown by management researchers in the processes of schools. Research based in departments of education was conducted by some highly skilled and imaginative investigators and advice on how to manage was provided from many quarters. This book describes a piece of research carried out from a university management department and based on a belief that the application of management ideas in education was flawed by the taken-for-granted assumptions of the existing advocates and by the lack of comprehensive empirical evidence and analysis of current practice.

We do not claim that everyone else has previously got it wrong and that we have effortlessly produced a string of right answers. We do claim the perspective of those disciplined within the framework of management research and working in a community of researchers studying issues of organisation and management in situations as diverse as psychiatric hospitals, retail stores, central government, financial services, the armed forces, manufacturing, medical practice and many more. We also claim that this perspective can enhance the understanding of management in education when added to the insights of those whose discipline and experience is within schools, faculties of education and educational administration.

The nature of the investigation

The research was supported by a grant from the Education and Human Development Committee of the Economic and Social Research Council, and we are most grateful for the confidence shown by members of that committee in enabling us to carry out the work.

Our brief was to study management and organisation within English maintained secondary schools; this produced the shorthand of MOSS to describe our project. Our objective was to develop materials that could be used to assist teachers in the running of their schools. We began, therefore, with the assumption that management and organisation in schools was something undertaken by all, or most, of the adults within them. The study was not directed specifically at the work of the Headteacher, or the governors, or the local authority, since these groups have either been studied recently, or were outside the immediate school environment.

Our specific objectives were:

a To describe alternative styles of organisation and methods of management practice for secondary schools against a background of rapid change.
b To provide these descriptions after empirical investigation in schools of varying size and type that are regarded as being relatively successful, and by reference to research on management and organisation being conducted in other types of organisation.
c To interpret the research findings by blending the expertise of those having experience in education with those whose experience lies in management and organisation behaviour.
d To disseminate the results of the research widely by publications and by developing materials that could be used in any secondary school to assess organisational effectiveness and produce improvements.

Jane Weightman and Kirsty Johns were employed full-time for two years to work on the project from the spring of 1986 to 1988. Derek Torrington acted as director of the programme while a permanent member of staff in the Management Sciences Department at UMIST. We were all management specialists, as Jane had gained a master's degree and a doctorate in the Department at the same time as Kirsty was completing a bachelor's degree. There was also familiarity with school processes through Jane having previously been an education adviser and Kirsty having spent two years as an administrator in a faculty of education.

A key element of the research strategy was the recruitment of research associates, both to extend the range of the fieldwork and to ensure the in-school credibility of our conclusions. After approaching various local authorities, we secured a twelve-month secondment to our project for six practising teachers. They were all men, which eventually led to them being described as 'The Moss Bros.':

Philip Adams, Head of Modern Languages, North Chadderton School, Oldham;
Roger Clark, Deputy Head Teacher, Irwell Valley High School, Salford;
John Davnall, Chemistry Teacher, Hadfield School, Derbyshire;
Roy Harris, Deputy Head Teacher, Purbeck Upper School, Wareham, Dorset;
Peter Reid, Deputy Head Teacher, Tiverton School, Devon;
Ray Sylvester, Head of English, Kirk Hallam School, Ilkeston, Derbyshire.

The team was completed by Pat Loftus as secretary and administrator.

After a pilot study and intensive preparation during the summer of 1986, fieldwork began in the autumn and continued through the following school year, working in maintained secondary schools in Cheshire, Derbyshire, Devon, Dorset, Manchester, Oldham, Salford and Stockport.

Methods of investigation were:

a Non-participant observation Researchers acted as 'flies on the wall' at schools to which they were attached, being on the premises from some time before the school day began until shortly after it had finished. They talked informally to many people, observed the manifold incidents of the day around them and came to understand the atmosphere and culture of the school.

b Semi-structured interviews In addition to the informal conversations mentioned above, most members of the school staff were also interviewed more formally. Interviewing included all the senior staff and most of all members of staff at other levels, including non-teaching staff. The purpose was to find out how the management elements of jobs were actually done, the view held of the school organisation, and its effect on the interviewee; and to identify examples of good practice.

c Structured observations 90 members of staff were also observed throughout a working day, while the researcher recorded and analysed the nature of the work being done at each time. This produced detailed understanding of how management and administrative work was done by people holding widely differing responsibilities.

d Meetings Researchers attended a variety of meetings as observers, ranging from the formal meetings of boards to short meetings of members of a single department. This added a further dimension to our understanding as so many innovations and procedural matters are mediated by meetings.

e Documents Researchers scrutinised documents such as the timetable, staff handbook, bulletin, staffing details, capitation figures and minutes of meetings.

f Workshops Throughout the collection and analysis of data the research team met for regular workshops to compare experiences, share understanding, further develop the research materials, analyse the data and derive tentative conclusions. These lasted for periods varying from three weeks to a single day. One feature of the workshops was the discussion of papers produced by researchers writing up issues that were emerging from the research. The model of description – analysis – evidence was used and it is from these issue discussions that the framework for this book has been derived.

g Feedback discussion From the early summer of 1987 onwards draft materials were taken back to the schools for discussion with members of staff who had co-operated in the early fieldwork, so that the evolving ideas and prescriptions could be tested against their shrewd common sense and comments about priorities. Finally these discussions were widened to include local authority officials and other academics and researchers.

Researchers worked in 24 maintained secondary schools in eight different local authorities. The full-time researchers worked together spending four weeks in each school; the research associates worked alone, spending seven weeks in each school. They included schools in city centres as well as leafy suburbs, and in local authorities of varied political persuasions. There were two single-sex schools, including one with some boarding places, and three that were voluntary-aided. The main details of the schools studied are shown in Table 2. We have used pseudonyms instead of the real names, as we are seeking to emphasise the general nature of our conclusions rather than features of individual schools.

The period of the empirical work, from the summer of 1986 to the summer of 1987, included widespread industrial action, the change of teachers' terms and conditions produced by the new contract of 1987, and a host of other initiatives such as national curriculum, city technical colleges, staff appraisal, TVEI, TRIST, GRIST, and 'opting out' at various stages of development between tentative proposal and general implementation. We realise that the nature of the changes facing schools will be different in later years, but we were focusing our attention, not on the changes themselves, but on the processes whereby the schools handled them. These processes change much more slowly and will make our findings relevant to school organisation and management for many years to come.

Theoretical background to the study

The methods of investigation had been used previously in two pieces of work studying the activities of middle managers in a wide variety of occupations (Torrington and Weightman, 1982; Torrington and Weightman, 1987; Weightman, 1988). There was also the benefit of prescriptive work on management practices (Torrington and Weightman, 1985; Torrington, Weightman and Johns, 1985). The research thus had the benefit of relevant comparative empirical study both as an important precursor and as a concurrent activity. The study was grounded in recent British and American research into the nature of management work and was influenced by British research on the running of schools. The main British source on management work was Stewart (1976 and 1982), who has developed our understanding of the variety of work to which the term 'manager' applies, and who has shown how managers can make choices within the constraints upon them in order to improve both their effectiveness and their job satisfaction. Other British sources have been Alistair

Table 2: Schools studied

Name of school	Group of school	Total number of teaching staff FT	PT	Total number of pupils 1986/87	Age range	Sex of pupils	Split site Yes/No
Hall End	10	52	4 (half time)	750	11–16	Mixed	No
Oakhill	Protected 10 (would be 4)	44	1	360	11–16	Mixed	No
William Barnes	11	60	3	1,083	11–18	Mixed	No
Westcliffe	12	80	11	1,401	11–18	Mixed	Yes
Summerfield High	10	44		800	11–16	Mixed	No
Jackson	11	77	5	1,221	11–18	Mixed	No
Renold	10	47		694	13–18	Male	No
Churchbrook	10	39	2	682	11–16	Mixed	No
Hillside	8	36		535	11–16	Mixed	No
Montgomery High	10	67	4	1,052	11–18	Mixed	No
Pennine End	11	64	11	1,204	11–18	Mixed	No
Francis Bacon	11	84	7	1,388	11–18	Mixed	Yes
Ridley	8	28	4	410	11–16	Mixed	No
Francis Drake	12	87	5	1,498	11–18	Mixed	Yes
St Elmo's	9	40	2	720	12–16	Mixed	No
Lodge	10	42	2	606	13–18	Female	No
Park	10	49		758	11–16	Mixed	Yes
Abbey	9	33		570	11–16	Mixed	No
Kirkside	10	40	8	723	11–16	Mixed	No
The Ridgeway	11	63	6	1,174	11–18	Mixed	No
Valley High	10	43	14	741	11–18	Mixed	No
Central High	11	65	11	1,083	11–18	Mixed	No
Southern High	10	64	12	1,007	11–18	Mixed	No
Ferndown	11	64	10	1,090	11–18	Mixed	No

Mant (1979 and 1983), who has questioned some of the conventional status-conscious views about management and placed fresh emphasis on aspects of leadership, and Charles Handy (1984 and 1985), who has been a powerful influence because of his publications on management and organisation in general as well as his work on schools.

The main American source is Henry Mintzberg (1973 and 1979), who has carried out analyses of managerial work that are similar to those of Stewart, but who has also developed some new ideas on organisation design and structure. John Kotter (1982) provides us with the idea that management work is essentially the setting of agendas for action and developing networks to implement those agendas. Ed Schein (1985) and Peters and Waterman (1982) have been our main sources for explanations of organisational culture.

The studies we have consulted about the running of British schools were mainly carried out in a different social and economic context. The writings of Richardson (1973), Lyons (1974 and 1976) and Rutter *et al.* (1979) are all based on the situation before the rolls began to fall, while career advancement for teachers was a more realistic prospect than at present and before performance appraisal had been extensively canvassed. We hope to make a useful addition to this particular literature. We have also been influenced by the POST project of Morgan *et al.* (1984), which includes detailed consideration of the generic features of the work of Headteachers, and the work of Walsh *et al.* (1984), with its attention to problems of contraction. In the latter book we find the comment:

> Too little serious attention has been given to the nature of management roles in schools and how they may vary with size, and perhaps more particularly as schools go through the process of decline . . . headteachers and their senior staff need help and training in the management of contraction.

During the course of our work we have also been assisted by the studies of Reid, Hopkins and Holly (1987), Morgan and Hall (1986) and Murgatroyd (1985).

The management background I – The recent past

Management thinking in commerce and industry has been dominated by the 'factory' concept, whether people are employed in workshops or offices. This concept has been implicit in the operations of the insurance company, the newspaper, the airline, the hotel. Places of work have been utilitarian organisations to which people came because they needed the benefits that their wages or salary would provide; if they found their work interesting or helping towards their personal fulfilment, that was incidental. Also the employer engaged people only because they were a necessary means of production. This concept has underlain all general employment, with the implicit assumption that employee and employer are exploiting each other. The way in which schools are different will be considered in Chapter 2.

Some of the effects of the factory concept as the main constituent of business life have been as follows:

a There was a sharp division between 'us' and 'them': wage earners and salariat. Wage earners were seen (and saw themselves) as doing a tightly specified job, with their contribution measured in hours ('I get £X an hour') and not having anything to do with the management process. The salariat were seen as doing a part of the proprietor's job, closely identified with management and making a non-specific contribution measured in years ('my salary is £Y a year').
b Many managers saw their job as to be in charge, rather than to control or lead. The main emphasis for managers was on: Are you a good leader? Have you leadership potential? There was much less concern with how leading was actually done and with the quality of the performance.
c Union organisation as reaction to weak, inadequate management made the situation worse. Union membership and local organisation grew as a result of 'them and us', as well as because of the lack of interest and shortcomings of management. Union representatives achieved significant influence within individual firms, controlling piecework schemes and restrictive practices, and inhibiting change.
d Because of their limited interpretation of the management role, managers in firms reacted defensively and resentfully. There was much talk about the right to manage, but litte about the ability to manage.
e As the union movement is the opposition that can never become the government, it needed effective management with which to interact. Despite some isolated examples of effectiveness, management generally conceded rather than negotiated, providing a poor management service to employees, who became more dissatisfied rather than less, receiving more money but less dignity. Union representatives seldom won an argument, they were merely bought off and resented.
f The working relationship was construed almost entirely in commercial terms that were collectively determined. There was some focus on people's individual problems, but only as an exercise in welfare. There was relatively little attention to the work that people had to do, the social organisation of which they were a part and the physical environment in which they worked.

These six points are no more than generalisations, but they are listed here as a caution. All of these problems were apparent while British industrial performance was in slow but inexorable decline. Some of these problems can be perceived in vague outline within the schools we have studied. There seems often to be a 'them and us' divide between the teaching staff and the non-teaching staff. Management roles are widely misconstrued, although not always in quite the same way as among industrial counterparts. Much of this book is taken up with various aspects of managing the adults in the school, as there seems generally scant attention paid to the detail of what people's jobs are, how they fit in with the work of other people, whether the jobs make sense and how they can be developed. The 1985/87 industrial action undoubtedly broke the mould of industrial relations in schools, often giving lay union officials an unprecedented degree of influence. Seldom are school Heads able to cope with this change, and there is the danger of a Pyrrhic victory for union members if this situation is not well managed.

The management background II – The evolving present

In the world of general employment outside schools there have been a number of changes in emphasis since approximately 1980. The main trend has obviously been greater efficiency and profitability, both as criteria and as outcomes. These were initially generated by large-scale redundancies, reducing the size of most organisations, but there have been a number of other effects:

a Trade union influence has been much reduced. There is less use by managements of trade union channels of communication with their employees and greater reliance on managers and supervisors to manage the day-to-day work of the business. There has been an associated increase in responsiveness of those at the top of the hierarchy to those at the bottom. This has been stimulated by the decline in union influence, but also made easier by a reduction in the number of middle managers and the number of tiers in the organisational hierarchy.
b There has been some shift of emphasis in the preoccupation of individual managers away from being a manager and towards getting the job done. Associated with this has been a change in relative status between management jobs. Those that are outward-looking and concerned with doing business in the market place are now more significant than those concerned with looking inward and managing the firm, so that management as a job of being in charge of others and being responsible for internal affairs is less important.
c The closed 'factory' thinking is breaking down. Businesses have become less inward-looking and less anxious to have all necessary resources under direct control under one roof. Although the number of employees in most businesses has been reduced, this has been accompanied by sub-contracting many of the activities. There is also widespread adoption of the idea of two broad categories of employee: core and peripheral.
d Individual managers have acquired greater independence, but more accountability and less security. They have been given more rope, but sometimes it has proved sufficient to hang themselves, due to an emphasis on results and achieving specific objectives.

e There is great interest in developing organisational culture as a form of cohesion that is more effective than supervision and more feasible than relying on loyalty to leaders. Here, of course, education is far ahead of the business world. The idea that a school needs a distinct ethos to provide cohesion is well established and has been aided by the idea that a school is a community. It is difficult to establish in a conventional business because of the 'factory' tradition described above.
f Thinking on leadership is altering, reducing concentration on the qualities and style of the individual in charge and looking more closely at the needs for leadership of both the working group and the tasks to be accomplished.

General conclusions

The outcome of our work is a number of detailed points about the running of schools which are set out in the following pages, but here is a sample of what we consider to be the more important of our findings.

a Effective schools deploy time and initiative towards the management of the adults in the school. In many ways the aspect of school organisation that strikes the outside observer most forcibly is the *neglect* of this aspect. Adults are the taken-for-granted resource, with their contribution organised through basic departmentation and the timetable. Where a school is organised to foster the development and motivation of the adults as well as of the children, then there are considerable, tangible benefits to the school as a whole. This includes the non-teaching staff, who are often an under-utilised resource and badly treated by their teaching colleagues. In 1988 there is at least one school librarian – a magistrate and local secretary of a national charity – who has to drink coffee sitting on a chair beneath the stairs because of not being allowed in the staffroom.
b One of the greatest traditional strengths of school organisation is the culture of community that is found. This is a strength that many industrial and commercial organisations labour in vain to achieve. The turbulence of recent years means that great care has to be taken to nurture that culture and, particularly, to ensure that it is appropriate to the changing organisational structure and mission of the school.
c All members of school staffs need valuing and rarely have this experience. The introduction of formal performance appraisal schemes *may* assist this process, but it is ideally the product of the patterns of social intercourse between all adults in the school; frequently, however, they devote such energy to valuing the children that there seems nothing left for their colleagues. Our observations show that there is not only a need for valuing from those senior in the hierarchy towards those below, but a need for valuing from all directions. This enhances performance.
d Various jobs in schools provide their holders with problems of personal credibility in the eyes of their colleagues. A lack of credibility produces

ineffective performance. This is a particular problem for Deputy Heads and rarely a problem for Heads of Department. It can be overcome by careful attention to distributing responsibilities logically and clearly.

e Management jobs frequently have too great an emphasis on administration instead of management, with the administrative emphasis leading to inefficiencies elsewhere. Analysis of how time is spent can always improve effectiveness. Is it an appropriate use of resources for a Deputy Head to spend all afternoon arranging the chairs in the hall?

f Organisation can often be improved by considering the lay-out of the school, and the use of different rooms. The hub of the school is the staffroom, which is the communications centre for staff and children, and which provides the best arena for the social interaction and valuing that are so important. All too often the staffroom is underused by the staff because it is squalid or in the wrong place. Most schools now have reduced rolls and spare rooms that would enable a reorientation of the school around a functional and attractive staffroom.

g Our key conclusion is about management and organisation style, a topic explored in the closing chapter of the book. Despite a general belief in educational circles that effectiveness is a product of good leadership, with everything depending on the Head, we have found three different approaches that can produce effectiveness: prescription, leadership and collegiality. Although most Heads favour the leadership style and most other members of staff favour the collegial style, we find that each of these can lead to effectiveness, providing first that the style is clear and not dithering, and second that the style is appropriate to the prevailing context in which the school is operating. There is no single 'best' way.

The structure of this book

This is not a textbook, nor a work of reference, so we hope that readers will resist the temptation to start at the end. The book is an entity and we would like you to read Part I first, as the material at the end does not make sense without the earlier material.

Management is not a box of tricks with a nice drill to suit any eventuality: it is an art that requires clear understanding of issues before the performance can be produced. We have identified seven central issues which are set out in Part I. It is only by understanding the nature of these seven issues in the school that anyone can hope to find appropriate management practice for a situation. Part II contains a great number of practical suggestions, based on what we have observed in schools and compared with aspects of management practice in other types of organisation. Effective management and organisation in schools are delivered by the means described.

References

Handy, C.B., *Taken for Granted? Understanding Schools as Organisations,* Longman, York, 1984.

Handy, C.B., *Understanding Organizations*, 3rd edition, Penguin Books, Harmondsworth, Middlesex, 1985.

Kotter, J.P., *The General Managers*, Free Press, New York, 1982.

Lyons, G., *The Administrative Tasks of Head and Senior Teachers in Large Secondary Schools*, University of Bristol, 1974.

Lyons, G., *Heads' Tasks*, NFER, Slough, 1976.

Mant, A., *The Decline and Fall of the British Manager*, Pan Books, London, 1979.

Mant, A., *Leaders We Deserve*, Martin Robertson, Oxford, 1983.

Mintzberg, H., *The Nature of Managerial Work*, Harper & Row, London, 1973.

Mintzberg, H., *The Structuring of Organizations*, Prentice Hall, Englewood Cliffs, New Jersey, 1979.

Morgan, C. and Hall, V., *Headteachers at Work*, Open University Press, Milton Keynes, 1986.

Morgan, C., Hall, V. and Mackay, H., *The Selection of Secondary School Headteachers*, Open University Press, Milton Keynes, 1983.

Murgatroyd, S., 'Management Teams and the Promotion of Well-being', in *School Organisation*, Vol. 6, No. 1, 1985.

Peters, T.J. and Waterman, R.H., *In Search of Excellence*, Harper & Row, New York, 1982.

Reid, K., Hopkins, D. and Holly, P., *Towards the Effective School*, Basil Blackwell, Oxford, 1987.

Richardson, E. *The Teacher, The School and The Task of Management*, Heinemann, London, 1973.

Rutter, M., Maughan, B., Mortimore, P., Ouston, J. and Smith, A., *Fifteen Thousand Hours*, Open Books, London, 1979.

Schein, E.H., *Organizational Culture and Leadership*, Jossey Bass, San Francisco, 1985.

Stewart, R., *Contrasts in Management*, McGraw Hill, Maidenhead, 1976.

Stewart, R., *Choices for Managers*, McGraw Hill, Maidenhead. 1982.

Torrington, D.P. and Weightman, J.B., 'Technical Atrophy in Middle Management', in *Journal of General Management*, 1982.

Torrington, D.P. and Weightman, J.B., *The Business of Management*, Prentice Hall International, Hemel Hempstead, 1985.

Torrington, D.P. and Weightman, J.B., 'Middle Management Work' in *Journal of General Management*, 1987.

Torrington, D.P., Weightman, J.B. and Johns, K., *Management Methods*, Institute of Personnel Management, London, 1985.

Walsh, K., Dunne, R., Stoten, B. and Stewart, J.D., *Falling School Rolls and the Management of the Teaching Profession*, NFER-Nelson, Windsor, Berkshire, 1984.

Weightman, J.B., 'Effecting Change in Schools: Working in the Organisation', in *Planning for Special Needs*, Thomas and Feiler (Eds), Blackwell, Oxford, 1988.

Part One: The Central Issues

Chapter 2
The Culture and Ethos of the School

In contrast with the traditional concept of the factory which has been dominant in most large, commercial, employing organisations, the traditional concept of the school is of a community, with the associated emphasis on ideas like ethos, spirit and individual commitment. There is concern with the process as well as with the content of the work that is done. There are people with posts of pastoral responsibility as well as those with academic responsibilities. There is discussion of the 'hidden curriculum' and a belief that the school cannot achieve its objectives unless the whole is much more than the sum of the parts.

Factory thinking, as described in the opening chapter, is alien, and recent use of terms like 'product' and 'customer' make most teachers wince because they run counter to the ideal of an integrated community seeking the welfare of all members. Even such a shrewd commentator as Charles Handy makes suggestions which seem to undermine the integration that most teachers regard as essential:

> . . . the great fallacy of comprehensive education was to think that it had to be done in comprehensive institutions. Why can't they go to different places for different skills, including a work organization, with the school being the central hub, tutor-in-chief, counsellor and mentor . . . The different bits would be smaller, more specialized institutions, language schools for instance, independently run but paid for by the local authority . . .
>
> (Handy, 1987, p. 521)

Teachers believe in the integration of education, with much of the emotional and intellectual development of their pupils coming from the wholeness of the school in which they are set. As was indicated in our opening chapter, we believe that teachers do not realise how much their own needs must be attended to if the integration is to be complete.

Wholeness is created and maintained by the ethos, the spirit or – in our language – the *culture* of the school. Much of the agony that schoolteachers have experienced in the era of falling roles has come from the reorganisations that have justified the destruction of school cultures by economic expediency. Amalgamating schools is seldom successful and usually disastrous unless there is a powerful engine for growth and progress. Attaching the front of an aeroplane to the back of a train does not make a super-vehicle; it makes a nonsense.

It is ironic that commercial thinking is developing in – or being foisted on – schools at the same time as commercial organisations are endeavouring to overcome the deep-rooted problems engendered by the factory concept. Commerce and industry have only just begun to examine and discuss the culture of organisations, in works such as those of Handy (1978), Peters and Waterman (1982) and Schein (1985). Now there are determined attempts to overcome problems such as 'them and us', alienation and lack of commitment, with the development of organisational culture being the method most frequently chosen. In many ways schools accomplish with ease that which other organisations find extremely difficult, partly because excellent culture can seldom be developed quickly; culture and tradition are closely intertwined.

Ethos and culture in schools

The concepts of ethos and organisational culture are very similar but there is a slight difference. Organisational culture is the characteristic spirit and belief of an organisation, demonstrated, for example, in the norms and values that are generally held about how people should treat each other, the nature of working relationships that should be developed and attitudes to change. These norms are deep, taken-for-granted assumptions that are not always expressed, and are often known without being understood.

The history and traditions of a school tell one something of a school's culture because the cultural norms develop over a relatively long period, with layers and layers of practice both modifying and consolidating the norms and providing the framework of ritual and convention in which people feel secure, once they have internalised its elements.

The ethos of a school is a more self-conscious expression of specific types of objective in relation to behaviour and values. This can be in various forms, such as a formal statement by the Headteacher, and in such comments as 'we don't do things that way here'.

The word 'culture' is more common in management circles whereas 'ethos' is used more often in education circles, particularly when referring to the children in the school. We are concerned with both culture and ethos but only in relation to the adults in the school, and we therefore normally use the word 'culture'.

Traditionally the culture in schools was one of high consensus, often centred on strong loyalty to a Headteacher who was expected to symbolise and expound the culture of the school, rather like a monarch, through such ritual devices as social distance, taking school assembly, wearing a gown, having a veto on major decisions and running staff meetings in a magisterial way.

In the mid-1970s doubts crept in as the aims for schools became more diverse and the organisation more complex. In some cases this led to increased managerialism, an interest in management for its own sake rather than as a means to an end. Through all employing organisations there is inevitably some witholding of co-operation by staff, even where they accept the authority of managers and their right to manage (Anthony, 1986, p. 41). This is, in part, because managers have an unrealistic expectation about co-operation and in part because of the limited extent to which the authority of position can be excercised. If a school culture is long established and widely accepted by staff, the authority of position may be effective. Once change becomes necessary the authority of position becomes insecure, unless the person in authority is a charismatic polymath.

It is axiomatic that schools have had to cope with a great deal of change in the last decade, but much of that change has involved teachers working in different ways, especially working more closely with each other and across the boundaries of disciplines. It would not be an exaggeration to suggest that this has been the real shaking of the foundations of recent years. Not only has it made great demands on individual teachers, it has also made inoperable a culture of consensus based solely on loyalty to the head. Debate increases as a necessary prelude to action, uncertainty becomes more commonplace, the nature of individual autonomy is being reconstructed.

It is important that those in schools should try and understand the culture they share, the extent to which it can be changed and how the changes can be made, even if the changes may be much harder and slower to make than most teachers believe.

As we have already said, culture is often not expressed and may be known without being understood. It is nonetheless real and powerful, so that the enthusiasts who unwittingly work counter-culturally will find that there is a metaphorical but solid brick wall against which they are beating their heads. Enthusiasts who pause to work out the nature of their school culture can at least begin the process of change and influence the direction of the cultural evolution, because culture can never be like a brick wall. It is living, growing and vital, able to strengthen and support the efforts of those who use it, as surely as it will frustrate the efforts of those who ignore it.

Current practice – four contrasted cultures

To understand the culture of a school fully requires longer than our stays of four to seven weeks, but we feel we got under the skin of the schools by being present all day, every day of our visits. We noticed increasing levels of trust from members of staff, who talked with us very frankly and often articulated in their conversations with us feelings and attitudes that they had never previously understood.

As culture is such an individual cloak we have included four rather long examples here to demonstrate the nature of culture and ethos. The first two examples are of cultures that, in general, assist staff commitment, co-operation and self-renewal. The second two are of cultures that are rather discouraging for staff. Like all real examples, they contain inconsistencies.

Valley High: An example of staff commitment and cohesion

One of the striking features of this school is the level of staff commitment and the quality of staff cohesion. The extent of these interrelated characteristics is indicated by the frequency and attendance at departmental and other meetings, the range of extra-curricular activities, the provision of lunchtime lessons and tutorials, and the vitality of the curriculum. Not all the teachers are equally committed, but overall there are more 'keen' staff then elsewhere. As a result of attending INSET meetings elsewhere they were aware that in some way they were 'different', but they had not given much thought as to why they were so committed and worked so well together. When asked to do so they produced a range of answers which many of them had not previously considered.

The most frequent response to any question about commitment was that it had something to do with the Head. Members of staff perceived him as a person who, when he was in school, was constantly involved with children and the general affairs of school life, rather than sitting remote in his office.

Many teachers commented that they could talk very easily to the Head, although it was not always easy to get in to see him. He was always prepared to listen to them and took a genuine interest in their problems and plans. Most felt that, where he could do so, he had recognised their efforts with internal promotion. For his part the Head professed to making his appointments 'with an eye on the future'. In this way he could be sure of having a Head of Department 'in waiting' in the event of a Head of Department gaining promotion.

Another reason for their loyalty lay in the fact that he appointed them. Only two teachers in the school pre-date the Head, who took up his appointment in 1971. He talked about the care he took to appoint teachers with the 'right' philosophical commitment, 'outstanding candidates' with a strong pastoral orientation and potential for growth. He admitted consciously appointing people in his 'own image' and believed that he was able to select the best candidate almost intuitively.

Many of the staff had only worked in this school. Even the Head was surprised to learn that 24 out of 43 full-time staff had only ever worked in this school. One of the most important reasons is that they believe in what they are doing there. Many of the staff are trapped in the school as a result of these beliefs, with the obvious disadvantages of professional narrowness, complacency and staleness.

Those staff who operate in departments meet formally at least once a week. In fact they spend almost every break and lunchtime in each others' company. This intense interaction with colleagues creates a collegial atmosphere in which the departmental curriculum is constantly under review and pressure is all-pervasive, not coming from one direction or another. If you do not work hard then you let down your colleagues as well as the children.

Most staff gain great personal and professional satisfaction from working closely with colleagues and being seen to be committed. They also feel themselves to be members of a team which is contributing to the growth of the school. Not all individuals fit into this pattern, and some departments are livelier and more cohesive than others. Nevertheless, the departmentalisation of the school has helped in the development of team-oriented individuals who are generally well motivated and prepared to work hard for the department and the school.

The whole-school and inter-disciplinary meetings which operate within the school also contribute to the pattern of team building and commitment. There was less apparent inter-departmental sniping, territoriality and stereotyping than in most schools. It seems that being closeted with all your colleagues in a series of curriculum meetings, or meeting them on a regular basis to develop inter-disciplinary courses, breaks down the traditional barriers between departments and makes for greater staff cohesion and solidarity.

House staff have the opportunity of meeting each other during some afternoon registration periods and over lunch. During the course of these interactions (particularly with the Head of House) they exchange ideas about how different pupils should be handled and enabled to absorb the House ethos. Conversations in the house areas at lunchtime serve to reinforce the individual's commitment to a particular way of handling children. The regular group support of other house staff and the departmental meetings help teachers maintain their belief in an enlightened approach to managing children despite the everyday pressures of the classroom.

The school is losing some of its middle-class pupils to other areas because of the zoning policy of the local authority. Teachers know they have friends amongst the councillors at County Hall but fear the drift from the smarter villages in the locality will affect their intake.

Their Sixth Form is barely viable and their intake down to four-entry. The staff feel unloved and misunderstood by the outside world and seem to be drawing even closer to each other for mutual support. Many talk openly of their fears for the future under a new regime because, although the Head is only 48, he is not a well man and could retire early. Perhaps it is this fear which makes them want to protect him and complain that he does not get enough support from his Deputies!

So here we have a school with a culture that has developed staff commitment and cohesion. This is largely due to the Head, who has worked hard to develop opportunities for the staff and to take a positive interest in their work and ideas. It is also due to the stability of the staff who have grown up together in the school and have been appointed by the Head 'in his own image'. Despite the risk of narrowness, and the feeling of dependence on the Head that gives rise to fears of the future, the cohesion is a valuable benefit to the school and its staff. Other aspects of culture are those of mutual support within departments and cohesion through committees and the House system. These three organisational devices have become much more than means of making decisions: they have become interdependent processes by which members of staff maintain their commitment, develop fresh ideas, find emotional support, renew their understanding of the shared mission and ensure that the sum is greater than the parts.

Summerfield High: An example of how co-operation, trust, cohesion and a sense of wholeness are maintained by small things

Of all the schools visited this had the calmest, most co-operative atmosphere. The staff seemed genuinely to like the pupils – which was not always apparent among the teachers with whom we spoke in other schools. There were many extra-curricular activities outside school hours, staff were very friendly and helpful to each other within school as well as at friendship/social gatherings outside school. The Head and Deputies were rather remote from this.

There was less expressed irritation over cover, rooming, finances, registers and duties than we found elsewhere, although there were complaints about decision making and communication with senior management. Both children and adults were trusted. A small example of this was when two boys asked to go home at break to change for a theatre performance; permission was readily granted. A more significant example was the way in which the Finance Committee of Department Heads organised the distribution of GCSE money in the most amicable way, deciding both weightings and distribution.

As both adults and children passed each other around school they gave eye contact, smiled and said something. 'Thank you' was a common phrase in both private conversation and public gatherings.

A number of factors contributed to this atmosphere of wholeness. First, the school is organised round open-air quadrangles, so that people are constantly aware of each other. The movement of people in circles and squares rather than in lines down corridors both generates and underpins the sense of oneness. The quadrangle makes possible a feeling of community in the same way as a cloister or a courtyard. The exceptions are the Headteacher, the office staff and PE staff, all of whom are located away from this set of quadrangles. PE staff made special efforts to come over to school before school started, but the Headteacher remained remote.

Second, there is thoughtful use of catering facilities, with tea, coffee, toast and cereal available on arrival and at break time, provided by dinner staff in a very pleasant hall. Most children and several staff use this facility, responding positively to the civilised way in which they are treated.

Most staff came into the staffroom before the school day began to look at the cover list and to check their pigeonholes, so there was the usual brief social gathering for jokes, chat and the sense of cohesion that such occasions provide. Senior staff were rarely seen here at this time.

A block timetable enables departments to organise their own groupings of pupils, teachers and what is taught. Departmental staff are also free at the same time for meetings, with the opportunity for all members of the department to be involved in decisions. Subject groupings – such as humanities, science and craft – are relatively large, tending to increase the general level of co-operation within the school.

Academic and pastoral structures are not separated. Heads of year are subject specialists with one extra free period. By this arrangement the Year Heads do not become a repository for every pastoral problem. These are left for individual members of staff to handle, with the co-operation of the Year Head when there is some particular crisis. All the pastoral staff are located in one room to ease their interaction and exchange of information.

There are several reliable senior staff, who deal with the main day-to-day difficulties with children and variations on routines and check up on what is happening without a lot of fuss, keeping everything on an even keel. This frees other staff to try new ideas, develop their teaching and discuss longer-term changes, with the reassurance of a 'safe' environment.

Of particular interest were the position and attitudes of the senior staff. The Headteacher was away for a term, although frequently mentioned by members of staff in our interviews. He and the Deputies were seen as being very closely knit and rather remote from the rest of the staff. Although it may seem unsatisfactory for the senior management team to be remote, this did help to unify the rest of the staff. This point about the roles of senior staff is developed in Part III.

The school had frequent contact with people outside, with industry, the feeder schools, advisers, the Sixth Form College, College of Further Education and so forth, so that teachers could compare their own understanding and performance with others and have the confidence of judging themselves as doing a good job.

Summerfield High had a culture of trust and co-operation that was maintained by a number of features of school life, from aspects of established behaviour, like the smiles and 'thank yous', to aspects of the use of the buildings, like the quadrangles and the staffroom, and the sensible academic and pastoral organisation. There was nothing dramatic and no overriding formula; just patient, thoughtful attention to the small things that make all the difference.

William Barnes: An example of low morale and poor self-image in a school

Low morale was indicated first by feeling among the staff that they had stagnated. The school's Headteacher from 1974 until 1984 had not, apparently, allowed any new blood in or anyone out. Many staff members felt they, and many of their colleagues, had been in the school too long, many for 20 years, or their entire career. Believing they would get neither jobs elsewhere nor promotion, they faced a depressing prospect of a further 20 years without change or fresh opportunity.

A frequent comment was that the school had few signs of achievement and a bad image, due to bad pupil behaviour and poor examination results. Staff felt ignored by the LEA and advisers, and also felt that the problem of declining rolls was exacerbated by parents preferring to send their children to the neighbouring ex-grammar comprehensive school, even though reorganisation was in 1974.

Some comments were made about things being sloppy and that not everyone was pulling their weight. Nothing was done properly in this view because of lack of time or poor discipline.

'Blockitis' was felt to be a problem, as people worked in one of three blocks and the only time staff came together was for ten minutes at a Monday-morning meeting, which had been introduced by the present Headteacher, and at half-termly staff meetings. The local joke was that you needed a passport to go to the other blocks, although several individuals explained how they, of course, did know folk throughout the school because of their jobs.

Coming from outside, we saw a different reality. Several people had been in their jobs for a long time but no more than at many other schools. The general standard of pupil behaviour and attainment seemed perfectly reasonable, compared with other schools, although not many stayed on for 'A' levels. There were as many cross-school operations and groupings as in many other schools. In other words, William Barnes was a perfectly ordinary, good school. So why should staff suffer from low morale?

Like many other schoolteachers, members of staff did not like the ongoing industrial action of the time. Also they were isolated from other schools because of the previous Head's staffing policy, so few of them had worked in or visited other schools and had no idea of prevailing standards. The LEA had a policy of devolving autonomy, so there were very few visits from advisers. No senior member of staff had responsibility for seeing individual teachers formally about their work unless secondment or re-deployment or discipline was involved.

In this school 33 members of staff have telephones in their classrooms, and all lessons are frequently interrupted by phone calls or by messages taken round by pupils. Most communication is done this way and we observed as many as 20 interruptions in a single lesson. There is no tradition of waiting until breaks, lunches or using pigeonholes. This means teaching is undervalued, only traditional methods can cope, and people have an excuse to give up. One example was from a teacher who said in her previous lesson a phone call was about a boy not wearing a tie and this completely disrupted her fourth-year French lesson.

Some male members of staff maintained a very heavy-handed 'macho' attitude to discipline, including yelling at children. Caning had only been abandoned in the previous year, when it became illegal. Many teachers were unable to adopt this macho approach or disliked it.

So William Barnes was a school in danger of fulfilling its own prophecy. Morale was low despite a lack of objective indicators to justify the poor self-image. Staff did not believe in themselves, each other or the children in their charge. Although they believed they had stagnated, there was no will to overcome the resultant self-doubt. The school was isolated from the educational community at large and divided within its own blocks, while the extraordinary system of communication and the reliance on 'tough' discipline militated against wholeness and any sense of caring community.

Ridley: An example of a senior manangement team lacking cohesion and beginning to disable a school where consensus might be expected

Recruitment of staff to this voluntary-aided school was constrained by the wish to maintain a 'Christian ethos', so producing a further variation of the normal ethos and culture theme. In addition to the normal extramural calls on the Head's time, there was involvement with the Church authorities at both local and diocesan levels.

Pastoral management was through Year Teams, co-ordinated by Heads of Year and the Second Deputy. Heads of Year had, in official guidelines for staff, an important disciplinary function. However, staff did not consistently follow those guidelines and problems arose from that failure. The generally helpful and supportive attitude at the bottom of the pastoral hierarchy was not found at the Deputy Head/Head of Year level. There was an undercurrent of antagonism directed towards the Deputy, who did not receive wholehearted co-operation.

Eighteen months before the study, the First Deputy Head had retired and been replaced by internal promotion. The Head had offered one of the unsuccessful internal candidates a new senior post of 'Curriculum Head' and revised the job descriptions of the Deputies. The job of the Curriculum Head was real, but the status (Scale 4) was not a fair reflection of the work compared with that of the Deputies. The one other Scale 4 teacher had, through being Head of RE, accumulated responsibilities peculiar to a denominational school.

The senior management did not meet as a team during the study. The Head had weekly scheduled meetings with the Curriculum Head and frequently met both him and the First Deputy (their offices were close together). On one occasion a meeting of all three, called to discuss 'Curriculum Planning' as one of a regular sequence of weekly meetings on the topic, discussed matters of a pastoral nature without any note of concern that the Second Deputy was not present. In scheduled meetings observed between the Head and the Second Deputy, there was a sense of minds not meeting. The Head, First Deputy and Curriculum Head made remarks critical of the Second Deputy and his work.

It is a small school in which everybody knows everybody else; the whole school can, and does, assemble. Its mission gives a purpose to assemblies and might have been expected to promote more unity of purpose among the staff. It is selective in a way which should generate parental support and interest. But its size means that staff challenge each other little; many staff members have been there a long time and are set in their ways. There seems to have been a peculiar bitterness during the industrial action and both the Head and a union representative blamed each other for unnecessary aggravation.

The position of the Second Deputy was disturbing. Of foreign extraction, his command of English was insufficient for him to express himself and to understand diplomatic turns of phrase. The Second Deputy did not organise his time well and was inclined to unnecessary interference in the detailed work of colleagues.

The senior management seemed to be struggling. Two had only been in post for four terms and a third was widely disregarded. The Head himself still felt, after several years, that he had not been accepted in 'a tightly-knit community' and was frustrated: 'We can't look to the future because of the history.'

Here was a school that ran smoothly, but did not provide the culture in which staff could review their progress and create their future. There was no openness and confidence among the members of staff, and the senior team were not able to find a way out of the collective difficulties, with one of their number being isolated by his colleagues.

Conclusion: culture and the school

The culture of the school needs to be understood because a mismatch of action and culture can produce ineffective action. The Second Deputy at Ridley was acting counter-culturally by undue interference in the work of colleagues who were accustomed to greater autonomy. Other members of the senior team were acting counter-culturally in tending gradually to isolate him, which was not an acceptable pattern of behaviour in the ethos of that school. At Summerfield High a tendency to isolate the senior management team from the rest of the staff appeared to increase the cohesion and trust between other members of staff.

So far we have used the word 'culture' in the singular. We find, however, a need to emphasise that each school has at least two: one for adults and one for children. The school is an integrated community, but cultural norms for children are different from those of adults, and perhaps the greatest misjudgement of the cultural match is to develop procedures, practices and behavioural expectations for adults that are only suitable for children. However obvious a point this may seem, our observations show this type of cultural mismatch to be a commonplace. A further variant is where there are separate cultural assumptions about adults in the school who are not teachers. This is discussed in Chapters 18 and 19.

The most penetrating analysis of organisational culture is by Schein (1985). He distinguishes between the ways in which an organisation needs to develop a culture which enables it to adapt to its changing environment (pp. 52–65) and, at the same time, to build and maintain itself through processes of internal integration (pp. 65–83).

How do cultures change? How do they become consolidated? The remainder of this book is largely concerned with answering those two questions. The general comment of Schein is that there are primary and secondary mechanisms. The primary mechanisms are (pp. 224–37):

a what leaders pay most attention to;
b how leaders react to crises and critical incidents;
c role modelling, teaching and coaching by leaders;
d criteria for allocating rewards and determining status;
e criteria for selection, promotion and termination.

We note two difficulties for schools here. First, such emphasis on 'leadership' implies that a school can only succeed when led by a Great Person on whom everything depends and to whom everyone else responds (see HMI Report, *Ten Good Schools*), Second, it is too easy to confuse cultural leadership with position leadership; those who are most effective in setting the tone may not be the senior staff even though they are well placed for this.

Focusing on the Great Person as the key to school success also emphasises hierarchical principles of organisation. There are limits to what can be achieved by hierarchical means and some radical views of organisations, such as Hyman (1977), criticise all hierarchical forms of organisation as preventing their members giving of their best. Organisational culture is the concern of all members and change in a culture is effective and swift only when there is wide agreement, 'ownership', concerning the change to be sought. In a school, wide agreement about important aspects of its culture seem to be best obtained, paradoxically, through a recognition and toleration of a legitimate plurality of views and styles on less central matters. In such a school, differences will not be resolved by the Great Person's exercising 'the right to manage', but through 'the collegiate approach' – discussion amongst all parties concerned.

Elevated position in a hierarchy, though possibly helpful, is not a guarantee of effectiveness in the pursuit of, or opposition to, cultural change. Many Heads will have noticed profound cultural changes in their schools following the recent prolonged pay and conditions dispute. Despite their efforts, the changes are deep-seated because they are owned by the staff. This is an unusual example, but we know of schools where Heads have been unable to effect cultural change (whether for good or ill) and of schools, often the same, where change has flowed from those in less exalted positions. 'Staffroom credibility', a combination of evident experience with persuasive personality, and patience seem to be the attributes, rather than formal positions, which help effect change.

A third difficulty is the assumption in much of the theory that the stamp of its culture leaves an identical mark across all of an organisation. We refer above to a 'legitimate plurality of views and styles' as a counterweight to the Great Person. In fact, we have to go further because schools contain teams of staff, each of which will have its own culture drawing on its members' views, the nature of its subject (if a teaching team) or tasks (if a non-teaching team), its history, its location in the school and so on. A visitor walking round a school will notice different cultures in different areas; where this variety is respected across the school, the culture of the school as a whole will be quite different from that in a school where such variety is suppressed.

If we now consider Schein's secondary mechanisms for the articulation and reinforcement of culture, we see they are (pp. 237–42):

a the organisational structure;
b systems and procedures;
c space, buildings and facades;

d stories and legends about important events and people;
e formal statements of philosophy and policy.

This introduces a wider range of possible actions, but notice what comes last! So often we have found in practice that attempts to develop aspects of culture actually begin with formal statements of policy, or that cultural inertia is attributed to the lack of such statements.

Without a central sense of unity, schools, like all other organisations, are no more than a collection of people who would rather be somewhere else because they lack effectiveness and conviction in what they are doing. The effective school has a few central ideals about which there is a high degree of consensus and those ideals are supported and put into operation by simple rules and clear procedures. The organisation that depends principally on rules for its cohesion is in the process of decay.

HMI pointed out a decade ago the key to success:

> The schools see themselves as places designed for learning: they take the trouble to make their philosophies explict for themselves and to explain them to parents and pupils; the foundation of their work and corporate life is an acceptance of shared values.
>
> (HMI, 1977)

Do It Yourself

Here are a few questions to ask about your school. These can be answered by you alone or used as the starting point for a group discussion. Groups of more than six would probably not work for this type of discussion. But feedback from each group could be worthwhile for a whole school INSET.

1 What are the central two or three ideals of your school? Go on, be cynical.
Identify three ways in which each is demonstrated.

2 *a* Give three ways that staff co-operation is promoted in your school.
b Give three ways that this co-operation is undermined.
Choose one of these.
What can be done about it?
Who do you need to work with to make this change?
Do you think they share your perception?
Do you think that together you could effect the change?
If yes, how? If no, why not?

3 How does your school evaluate its own performance?
Try to think of three devices your school uses for each box in the

following table. If you cannot think of any, what do you think would be useful?

	Things done well	Things done badly
Formally		
Informally		

4 How does a new member of staff, including non-teaching staff, learn to be part of your school? What are the important behaviours? What are the important attitudes?
5 An exercise developed by Harrison and Handy looks at an individual's preference for club, role, task or person culture and compares it with their understanding of where they work. It is described and explained in Chapter 7 of Handy (1985). In our experience it works well with groups and is a good starting point for discussion about cultures.
6 Schein (1985) has structures for group interviews to uncover cultural assumptions about organisations, on pages 128–35.

References

Anthony, P.D., *The Foundation of Management*, Tavistock, London 1986.

Handy, C., *The Gods of Management*, Pan. London 1978.

Handy, C., *Understanding Organisations*, 3rd edition, Penguin, Harmondsworth, 1983.

Handy, C., *Understanding Schools as Organisations*, Penguin, Harmondsworth 1986.

Handy, C., 'The Future of Work; The New Agenda', in *The Royal Society of Arts Journal*, Vol. cxxxv, No. 5371, pp. 515–25, June 1987.

HMI, *Ten Good Schools*, HMSO, London: 1977.

Hyman, R., *Strikes*, 2nd edition, Fontana, London: 1977.

Murgatroyd, S., 'Management Teams and the Promotion of Well-being', in *School Organisation*, Vol. 6, No. 1, 1985.

Peters, T.J. and Waterman, R.H., *In Search of Excellence*, Jossey-Bass, San Francisco 1982.

Schein, E.H., *Organisational Culture and Leadership*, Jossey-Bass, San Francisco 1985.

Chapter 3
Control and Autonomy

For many of the senior staff in the schools we visited, running a 'good school' had become entwined with the idea of '*being a good manager*'. This they frequently interpreted as setting up procedures and control systems, compliance with which could be measured to see whether or not they were '*doing good management*'. The procedures and controls were often met with hostility and resentment by the rest of the staff, who complied reluctantly and inefficiently. Commonly even more control devices were introduced because managing had been understood to be controlling other people. This is a dangerously narrow and blinkered view of the management process.

In a school some monitoring of what people are doing is required, to ensure sufficient consistency and common purpose for the children to benefit from their education. Further, staff may welcome standards to guide them, methods on which they can rely and the satisfaction of getting things done in an orderly manner. Few people can cope with a situation of corporate activity where individuals follow their own paths.

However, too much control makes monitoring spurious as people spend time in circumventing the rules rather than following them. Participation and innovation are discouraged and organisation members make the minimum contribution. A further twist is the question of what is controlled. Managers need to be clear about which behaviour, activities and outputs they wish to control. A teacher's behaviour may need controlling (for instance, they shout too much in a quiet school); activities are controlled by specifying standards (all books to be marked at least once a fortnight) and procedures (all tutors must accompany their forms to assembly). Control of outputs involves determining the objectives to be achieved and emphasises ends rather than means (an Integrated Humanities course to be operating in eighteen months' time). Clarity is difficult to achieve (is 'No smoking in classrooms' aimed at behaviour or activity?) but important, because different sorts of control attract different reactions from teachers (as well as from pupils). Most people find control of behaviour oppressive; many attempts to control the activities of teachers are regarded as denying professionalism, experience and competence; but control of outputs is often acceptable, especially when those who have to meet an objective have shared in choosing it. The art of the successful manager lies in determining which outputs to control and in controlling them efficiently.

The effectiveness of individuals and the whole school is enhanced where control is balanced by autonomy. Peters and Waterman's (1982) study of excellent American businesses found that the 'simultaneous loose–tight properties' of autonomy and control were one of the keys to excellent organisation. Handy (1984, p. 33) argues that 'schools are not *that* different [from businesses], or they need not be.' An example of 'loose–tight' from our research was of the Headteacher who took a two-stage approach to spending the school's GRIST allowance. The Head gave clear guidelines on what INSET was needed (tight), and remitted to a small committee full authority to decide exactly how the money was to be spent (loose).

The danger of the blinkered view mentioned at the opening of this chapter lies in the misconception that management equals control. Control is only a small part of management, and slackening control by providing more autonomy for individuals and groups is a major element of effective management. There is also the misconception that control is done by a small number of people at the top of the hierarchy: it is what 'they' do to 'you'. However, as autonomy extends, 'you' develop your own control of your outputs: if 'you' don't, then control moves rapidly back to 'them'.

We are not advocating a free-wheeling, *laissez-faire* style of management, which is simply an abdication of responsibility; but autonomy seems an important feature of school management to emphasise because it causes so much uncertainty. Discussion among schoolteachers is replete with terms like 'participation' and 'collegiality'. Headteachers feel overwhelmed by the number and complexity of changes they have to introduce in their schools and frequently adopt centralised initiatives with strong control features in order to cope with these demands. But initiatives will only succeed when they are widely owned by the school staff and to own an initiative one also has to own control of that initiative. However, individual staff members have to be willing to sacrifice a degree of *individual* autonomy for the benefits of *collegial* autonomy.

Many people in schools nurture the belief that management in the commercial world is much more tightly controlling than in schools, but Peters and Waterman found differently in *excellent* companies. Another American, James Stoner, provides an apt summary:

> At a time when the legitimacy of authority is being sharply questioned, and when there is a growing movement towards greater independence and self-actualization

for individuals, the concept of organizational control makes many people uncomfortable . . . excessive control will harm the organization as well as the individuals within it. Controls that bog down organization members in red tape or limit too many types of behaviour will kill motivation, inhibit creativity and damage organizational performance.

(1986, p. 577)

The issue of control and autonomy is demonstrated in school in such areas as:

- How much should control of *resources* be centralised or decentralised?
- How much *financial* autonomy have departments got?
- How much does the *timetable* limit a department's freedom to assign staff to particular classes?
- Are there *whole-school policies* on teaching methodologies?
- Is the holder of a *post of responsibility* given a job description which comprises a list of tasks or one which delineates the areas for which they are responsible?

Current practice

An example of control and autonomy in a department

Ken (Head of Art) puts an emphasis on quality, both in the work of the children and that of his staff. In this he tries to lead from the front, spending considerable time each year preparing for the year to come. He regularly reviews the syllabuses and changes elements from time to time to stimulate and motivate his staff, with whom the changes are discussed – 'I plant a lot of seeds and lay a lot of hints' – but he says he decides in the end. He prides himself on being well organised and having a clear idea of what he wants. He produces policy documents, syllabuses and schemes of work which express a clear concern for quality in their content, style and presentation. They usually have the distinctive Art Department logo at the top of each page. 'There's a conscious department style', he says.

Tom, with an MA in Fine Art, says of Ken, 'He goads you, but he doesn't brutalise. When I started I really appreciated the amount of structure provided.' He finds Ken's thoughtful, well presented policy documents very useful. 'It's much better than the back-of-an-envelope approach.' Tom says that it is unusual to find that degree of structure in an Art Department. But he says that Ken emphasises the amount of flexibility that is possible within the structure. Tom thinks that he puts more of himself into the work now, and has gradually taken on more responsibilities. All members of the department were involved in drawing up a self-assessment questionnaire for GCSE, which Tom thinks is already working very well. Ken has told him he is more or less in charge of his own part of the department now. He orders his own materials and has a good share of the Sixth Form work. Tom talks about the advantages of being well prepared: 'It's a very calm department. We don't rush for deadlines, it's all paced.'

Susan, the pottery specialist, has her own section at the far end of the large, open-plan Art area. Her expertise means that she has a great deal of autonomy within Ken's overall scheme. She says that it compares very favourably with her previous school. 'It's well organised; we get damn good work out of the kids.'

Examples of types of control

a One school's detailed departmental handbooks which, with prescriptive lists of readings, activities and materials, were more than just source books. This over-emphasised control, as the scope for individual teachers to develop their own ideas and methods was limited.
b A very detailed staff handbook with procedures for, amongst many others, room bookings, sick children, students on TP, pastoral matters. Although this initially sounded to be heavy-handed control, with a great deal of central specification, it was welcomed by staff as it provided a ready source of reference without curtailing the scope of the individual.
c A detailed analysis of each department's exam results so that comparisons could be made about how a particular child had done in different subjects, how this year compared with last, and how individual teachers in a department compared. This was an excellent example of monitoring output to achieve good management because the comparisons were all internal and were always used in a constructive way, for seeking ways to assist teachers and to develop effectiveness, rather than punishing people by disapproval or silence.
d A Head of Department's list of the department meetings issued at the start of each term, itemising which agenda items were to be dealt with on which date. This provided a clear and useful framework, which would not become a straitjacket unless matters could *only* be discussed on the prescribed date.
e Central monitoring of expenditure, with 'chaser notes' to spend up towards year end. Here is an example of the bureaucratic malaise that is widespread in public sector administration. Money is allocated to be spent in a particular financial year and if it is not spent by 31st March it cannot be transferred (without superhuman effort over a long period) to the next financial year.
f Half-termly scrutinising of work records/mark books, Heads of Department of their staff, senior staff of Heads of Department. This can

be useful provided that the scrutiny is directed at matters concerning the education of the children. All too often the comments relate to matters like neatness and orderliness, which are likely to infuriate those to whom they are directed. Also the hierarchical emphasis is inappropriate; it is more productive if teachers scrutinise the books of other teachers with the same specialism, regardless of rank. If the scrutineer changes on each occasion, all members of a department rapidly become familiar with what others are doing and pick up useful tips.
g Common periods of non-contact time to encourage holding of departmental meetings.
h The Headteacher who asked that all minutes of departmental meetings be sent to her, with the minutes to include starting and finishing times. This was much resented as needlessly tight control.

Examples of developing individual and group autonomy

a Block timetables granting departments the autonomy to decide which and how many teachers should be with a particular year group. This helped to integrate the work of departments and increase the amount of flexibility available.
b The Lower School of a split-site school having developed different financing through its own fund-raising attempts. This strengthened the sense of community on the site and prevented it from being seen merely as an outpost of the main school.
c A school had developed an integrated curriculum for Humanities, English and Maths for the first two years that was separate from those departments. This gave some new, young staff the opportunity to be autonomous.
d Responsibility for capitation decisions devolved to Heads of Department or Faculty.
e Departments choosing their GCSE boards and syllabuses with little or no reference to senior management.

Examples of good practice

We also found example of how the loose–tight balance was sustained across a school through its culture in a way described in Chapter 2.

1 An example of a school having strong control structures at the centre coupled with autonomy to participate

> The staff of *Hillside School*, as a group seen for the first time, certainly suggest a co-operative team who appear to relate very well to each other. There is no obvious awareness that cliques or

dominant sub-groups exist nor could it be seen that any individuals were outside the common social structure of the group.

Research over the period of seven weeks largely confirmed this impression. That is not to say that there is no conflict over resources, influence or power but there is a very high degree of loyalty and commitment to the organisation as an entity and very little feeling of alienation.

It is a highly structured school in the sense that roles and practices are very well defined. It is progressive and outward looking and is involved with many current initiatives.

Decision making tends to be the result of consultation and participation at many levels, but policy making in a general sense is largely seen to be the prerogative of the Headteacher.

Members of staff feel secure within the organisation and this is reflected by the nature of their involvement in the staff developement and appraisal programme. Perhaps it is also the reason they have not felt it necessary to replace the two major union representatives who have left.

To understand how the rather interesting mix of involvement, commitment, autonomy and acquiescence has come about, it is necessary to understand the history of the 'givens' of the present culture.

The school has changed in a relatively short period of time from a formal, traditional girls' grammar school to a larger, co-educational, comprehensive school with a school population skewed towards the lower end of the ability spectrum.

One 'given' from the former grammar school days, which has been carried through by remaining staff (and passed on by those now in senior positions) is a traditional, unquestioning view of the legitimacy of the power of the Head.

A second 'given' is the wartime effect of the fusing together of the staff through the common experience of adversity during the period of far too many changes in a relatively short period of time.

Third, after this period of great change there has been relative stability of staff and many have been promoted.

Fourth, the Headteacher was an internal candidate and she had taken the opportunity to consolidate the changes that she had begun to introduce under the former Head, who had responded very little to the staff's demands for order and structure.

2 'Laid back' but 'hard working' – an example of loose–tight as part of the culture of a school

The frequently mentioned comments to us in *Jackson School* were:

- 'It's a very laid-back school.'
- 'We work longer than any other school.'
- 'No one wants to come here because we work too hard.'
- 'It's a very lively place to work.'

There was thus a combination of a relaxed social situation, which was generally described as 'laid back', and an atmosphere of industry and diligence: 'hard working'.

Examples of their laid-back nature are:

a A relaxed attitude to time keeping. For example, at the end of breaks they sat in the staffroom, then drifted off to lessons.
b An informal, chatty style in their dealings with the children.
c Encouraging the children's awareness of the natural world by the unusual device of keeping domestic animals on the premises. A cow, pigs, rabbits, hens, geese and ducks were all to be found in the school quadrangles.
d One-and-a-half-hour lunch break so that games could take place.

Examples of their hard work are:

a A long school day of 8.55 am – 4pm, with various meetings until 6pm on three nights a week.
b Taking on a number of new initiatives and carrying out pilot schemes for TVEI and NPRA.
c Constant revision of procedures.
d Vigorous support for industrial action.
e Extensive extra-curricular activity, with sport outstanding, as well as a number of clubs and activities, such as computing and music.

Most teachers felt they were working in an exciting school where many of them had developed personal friends. This seems to be an example of the 'loose–tight' method working.

The interesting questions are: how has this come about and how is it sustained? Several of the older staff mentioned a Headteacher who retired seven years previously and who was a quiet, thoughtful person scattering ideas and waiting for them to take root. This might account for a large number of senior and middle staff who are keen. They, in turn, provide sufficient security for the ardent young thinker to have a go. Before any of the older teachers became too set in their ways or embittered through lack of progress, new jobs had been found for them by the present Headteacher. These usually were across-school responsibilities, to enable younger staff to move in and get on.

3 Valley High School – loosely coupled or simultaneously loose–tight

Valley High has many of the characteristics of a loosely coupled organisation. This is a term invented by Weick (1979) to describe a situation in which there is constant experimentation and 'retrospective sense-making' in choosing between a number of alternatives as the experiments proceed. This is similar to what James March has called 'organised anarchy' (1980).

Departmental autonomy, for example, is so pronounced that the school has virtually fragmented into a number of sub-units. This is reflected in the fact that most teachers only visit the staffroom to collect their mail. Tea and coffee are taken in their own departmental offices or 'prep' rooms. Only the smokers use the staffroom on a regular basis. Departments are trusted to get on with their work with the minimum of interference from senior staff. There is no evidence of any systematic 'top–down' monitoring or evaluation of the performance of individuals or departments. The administrative 'slackness', which is at times all too apparent, was exacerbated by the fact that the school was organised into vertical tutor groups and three discrete 'Houses', each having its own dining facilities.

The benefits of this loose structure are apparent in the commitment and energy of the teachers and the lively innovative curriculum. But this is not at the expense of institutional cohesion. Valley High, in a phrase, 'hangs together'.

Interviews with the staff show very clearly that there is a shared sense of purpose. Despite the lack of both directive management and regular informal contact between teachers from different departments, the staff still rally around the same flag. The glue which seems to hold this loosely coupled 'system' together is a commonly held set of mainly, but not exclusively, pastorally oriented values and beliefs. These are readily articulated by teachers at all levels, who maintain that the culture of Valley High serves to reinforce rather than diminish the idealistic notions with which they might have started their careers. There is little doubt that these values provide a 'tight' ideological core which counteracts the forces for disintegration in what would otherwise be a fragmented school. In this sense the organisational structure of the school is both 'tight' and 'loose'.

This value-driven cohesion has a number of origins. The main source is undoubtedly the Headteacher who, as the embodiment of the school's culture, regards his primary task as one of defining, promoting and protecting the central core of values which hold the school together. He takes every opportunity to communicate and reinforce these values by leaving his room as often as he can and becoming directly involved with the pupils and teachers. This provides him with the opportunity to talk about his 'vision' and to set an example in an active way. No one accuses him of mouthing hollow, 'do as I say, not as I do', platitudes.

This cohesion is further enhanced through staff involvement in 'open access' participative forums. These not only provide the Head with important corporate opportunities for infusing the staff with a common sense of purpose, but also help to achieve greater staff 'ownership' of agenda and outcomes. Regular cross-curricular contacts of this sort, as well as various working parties, engender a marked degree of team-bonding across departments in what appears to be a heavily departmentalised school.

Conclusion

The balance between control and autonomy will vary between schools. What is controlled makes for different types of school culture. We use the word 'control' not just for the administrative, monitoring devices: it is more than that. It is about who decides which things should be done, how they are done and the amount of checking.

Only one of our schools has systematically decided what needs to be controlled and what can be left free. Monitoring and control systems are introduced when some new device is happened upon or some disaster has occurred. Consequently, extraordinary mixtures exist where 'how' things are done is centrally controlled but 'what' is done is not. Handy (1984, p. 33) makes the distinction that:

> . . . it is important to distinguish between the 'what' and the 'how' and between 'policy' and 'execution'. The centre needs to keep a close eye on the 'what', on the key objectives, the key values and key standards of the different parts of the operation. The details of the 'how' can be delegated. As long as the key standards are maintained the individual units should have as much freedom as possible in attaining those standards. It is another version of after-the-event permissions. Too many schools find it too tempting to control the 'how' centrally and delegate the 'what'.

The argument is just as valid for the parts of a school, such as Faculties, Departments, Houses or Years, as it is for the whole school. Control systems are only needed to monitor departures from standards. This does not, however, mean that the centre should ignore what is happening in the units. This is done through other management activities, such as communication, dealing with personnel issues, meetings and administration; but formal control is counter-productive when it is of the 'how' rather than the 'what'.

The examples we have quoted of the loose–tight culture in three schools all emphasised the key role of the Headteacher. We do not wish to over-emphasise this, but the traditional power of the Headteacher has a vital impact in the area of control and autonomy. Heads need to relinquish some of their power and then play a central role in nurturing staff to take more responsibility.

One of the problems for those with a management role is that their power often rests on their perceived *control* of resources, monitoring systems, agenda and so forth. It is not easy to relinquish this part of their work. There is, however, a great variety of sources of power (see Figure 1) and generally the most effective, as well as the most legitimate, is that based on expertise or skill.

One of the problems with *autonomy* within a school is that individuals have to take responsibility for their own work. This requires confident professionals. Where particular staff have not been trusted to behave in this way they may be uncertain and unsure how to react. No organisation can move rapidly from centralisation to decentralisation without dire consequences. Staff will need training to communicate with and meet colleagues as well as children to learn to participate. This takes careful handling and is discussed in our training materials.

There are advantages and disadvantages associated with both the very controlled school and the very free school. Trying to achieve an appropriate balance between control and autonomy is one of the exciting management and organisational issues schools have to face. Each school needs to consider its own position and culture but our advice would be to err on the side of looseness, freedom and autonomy whenever there is a doubt. Few schools appear to be suffering from too much autonomy, but many are suffering from too much control of the wrong things.

A balance between a tight central mission of a school coupled with a loose, decentralised, autonomy of how to put that into practice seems to make for effectiveness. How this can be achieved in practice is the subject of our training materials; but the hotch-potch of control systems in many schools is frequently counter-productive, as it produces a minimum rather than a maximum contribution from the adults who work in the schools and, consequently, from the children. For schools to be effective they need simultaneous loose–tight properties. To have these many managerial roles will have to be re-interpreted and many teachers will need to have the confidence to take responsibility. As Weick (1979 p. 60) says:

> . . . it is easy to over-manage an organisation . . . it is an excess rather than deficiency of intervention that lies at the heart of many organisational problems.

Figure 1: Sources of power

1 **Position**

Resources Control access to what others keep; whether subordinates, peers or superiors. It includes the following: materials, information, rewards, finance, time, staff, promotions, references.

Delegation Whether jobs are pushed down the hierarchy; with rights of veto retained or not.

Gatekeeper Control information, relax or tighten rules, make life difficult or easy depending on loyalty of individuals.

2 **Expertise**

Skill Being an Expert. Having a skill others need or desire.

Uncertainty Those who have expertise to deal with a crisis become powerful till it is over.

Indispensable Either through expertise or being an essential part of the administrative process.

3 **Personal Qualities**

Motivation Some seek power more enthusiastically than others.

Physical Prowess Being bigger or stronger than others....... Not overtly used in management except as controller of resources. However, statistically leaders tend to be taller than the led.

Charisma Very rare indeed. Much discussed in early management literature as part of leadership qualities, but usually control of resources can account for claims of charismatic power, as many ex-headteachers have found.

Persuasion Skills Bargaining and personal skills that enable one to make the most of one's other powers, such as resources.

4 **Political Factors**

Debts Having others under obligation for past favours.

Control of Agenda Coalition and other techniques for managing how the issues are, or are not, presented. Being present when important decisions are taken, control of minutes.

Dependence Where one side depends on the other for willing co-operation, the power of removal exists. Strikes, or threatening to resign *en bloc* are two examples.

Adapted from Torrington, Weightman & Johns (1985, p. 110).
See also Pfeffer (1981, Chapter 4).

Do It Yourself

1 Is there a control mechanism in your school for:

a How each department's budget is spent?
b Who teaches, what, to whom?
c Comparing/analysing examination results of individual teachers' classes?
d Marking of books?
e Next week's schemes of work?
f When teachers can leave the premises?
g When Departments/Years/Houses should meet and what they should discuss?
h Breaktime duties?
i Approval of letters to parents, outside agencies, etc?

Now look through the list and mark with 'what' or 'how', according to whether the control is of what is being done or how it is being done.

Which of these controls could be tightened, relaxed, or made more efficient? How?

2 What do you as a teacher have autonomy to decide in your school? Would you like more or less autonomy? In which areas? Why?

3 What do the answers to question 1 tell you about the assumptions your organisation makes about the adults? How would you like to see those assumptions altered? Why?

References

Handy, C., *Taken for Granted? Understanding Schools as Organisations*, Longman, York 1984.

March, J.G., 'The Technology of Foolishness', in Leavitt, H.J., *Readings in Managerial Psychology*, 3rd edition, University of Chicago Press, Chicago 1980.

Peters, T.J. and Waterman, R.H., *In Search of Excellence*, Harper & Row, London 1982.

Torrington, D.P., Weightman, J. and Johns, K., *Management Methods*, IPM, London 1985.

Weick, K., *The Social Psychology of Organizing*, Addison-Wesley, Massachussetts 1979.

Further reading

Pfeffer, J., *Power in Organisations*, Pitman, London 1981.

Stoner, J.A.F., *Management*, (3rd edition) Prentice Hall, Hemel Hemstead 1986.

Chapter 4
Valuing

Teaching staff generally feel unappreciated and misunderstood, not only by the world outside their schools, but also by senior managements within schools. There may be a relationship between the two: as the appreciation of teachers by the world outside diminishes, so teachers' self-image wavers, and requires more support and confirmation from those in authority within the school. Where this support is felt to be lacking, morale plummets. Senior staff are of course suffering a similar lack of appreciation but this does not remove the expectations their colleagues have of them and could indicate a need for senior staff to delegate more responsibility and do less routine administration.

To get the most out of our work we all need to feel that some inner need, or motivation, is being met. This can vary from the most basic physical needs to such culturally determined needs as achievement and fulfilment. Appreciation by others of our efforts and social approval are widespread, but not universal, motivators to put in extra effort. Our analysis of the situation in schools matches the well-known explanation of Maslow (1954), who grouped needs into a five-step hierarchy. Only when needs in the lower stages are satisfied does the next stage become potent. Once a need is satisfied it is no longer a motivator unless it returns. The five stages are explained in Figure 2.

Most professional or white-collar employees in Western societies do not seek the satisfaction of lower-order needs at the place of work. Arguments about teachers' pay, for instance, deal more vociferously with aspects of status relative to other groups than with how much food and drink the salary will purchase. The higher-order needs of esteem and self-actualisation are largely satisfied by what happens at the place of work and few people have other arenas in which these needs can be satisfied.

Being appreciated or valued satisfies a combination of Maslow's social and esteem needs. Appreciation is shown in a wide variety of ways, reflecting the differences between organisations' cultures and their behavioural norms. To complicate matters, individuals feel valued in

Figure 2: Motivational theories

a Maslow's model

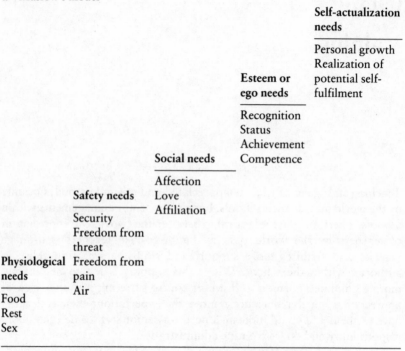

Physiological needs	Safety needs	Social needs	Esteem or ego needs	Self-actualization needs
Food	Security	Affection	Recognition	Personal growth
Rest	Freedom from threat	Love	Status	Realization of potential self-fulfilment
Sex	Freedom from pain	Affiliation	Achievement	
	Air		Competence	

Primary needs	Secondary needs

Herzberg developed this hierarchy as it affects the motivation of people at work. Hygiene factors lead to dissatisfaction if they are not up to standard, but increases above this do not give more satisfaction. In contrast, the satisfiers can motivate beyond the basic level as people want more of these regardless of how much they have.

b Herzberg's model

Hygiene factors	Satisfiers
School policy and administration	Achievement
Supervision	Recognition
Working conditions	Work itself
Salary	Responsibility
Relationships with peers	Advancement
Personal life	Growth
Relationship with subordinates	
Status	
Security	

different ways. In parts of some commercial undertakings individuals are valued by their colleagues for their defiance of management interests; elsewhere in the same undertakings people value each other for closely identifying with management interests. Within schools teasing is seen as appreciation by some and criticism by others.

Making others feel valued is a complex social interaction requiring the others' views to be considered at all times. It is their needs as people, not just as job holders, that have to be met, because the job is held by a complete person, not the part which comes to school; the normal complement of personal needs is not left at home to be picked up again in the evening. Even the most alienated teacher, having lost enthusiasm and feeling socially or emotionally crippled by the job, has salient personal needs which can be satisfied through the everyday processes of teaching. Most of such satisfaction will come from the children (as will some of the cruellest pain), but the adults can add greatly to this and may transform a working experience from a tedious routine into a source of psychological well-being.

In the late 1980s most teachers feel undervalued by their fellow citizens. Partly they are sharing in the situation of all employees, as there has been a general levelling out of status differentials, if not of pay differentials, but the particular situation of teachers' low self-esteem has been aggravated by the acrimony of long-running industrial action and widespread dissatisfaction with government policies on education. This feeling of low appreciation from outside makes it much more important for teachers to be valued by their colleagues inside the school.

At the same time as teachers feel less appreciated by the world outside, the innovations to which schools are being required to respond, generated largely by that same world outside, have multiplied in recent years. Bolam (1986) listed as many as 40 'current changes (innovations, policy initiatives and developments) which have to be managed'. Seldom will all these apply simultaneously to a school, but never before have secondary schools had to cope with so many changes, many of them major. The fact that most of these changes are landing on schools from outside means that staff feel little or no 'ownership' of them. This not only reduces the likelihood of changes being implemented effectively, it also demoralises by creating a sense of being at the mercy of others. Many of the changes require staff to adjust their working practices, and nearly all of them are generating increased workloads. Most schools are suffering from innovation overload, at the same time as their staffs' morale is generally at a lower ebb than it has been for a long time.

Staff are responding to this situation in different ways; some by withholding commitment, some by withdrawing from out-of-school activities, some by increased militancy, some by reduced militancy, some simply bow their heads and resolve to work harder – again – like Boxer the horse in *Animal Farm*. We encountered many staff who seem to have stoically decided to concentrate on doing their best to tackle the major, inescapable tasks that face them.

Current practice

We found four types of valuing that needed to be examined in discussing adult relationships within schools; consideration, feedback, delegation and consultation.

Consideration

It is surprising how often in schools the basic etiquette of smiling, asking others how they are, saying 'thank you', 'well done', 'that's great', is ignored. We frequently heard from staff that they wished those senior to them in the hierarchy would take an interest in them. When pressed, this often meant just the small things listed above though not in a mechanical, 'painting by numbers' way that is meaningless. Two typical teacher comments were:

> The children are not motivated to work and teachers get disillusioned. There's no help from senior staff. If we got more support such as 'homework in lower school must be done' it would be better.

> No one supports me here. No one talks to you in the staffroom. It is not friendly with folk across departments. I'd rather go and read a book.

It may be that these acts of consideration are not common because senior staff feel it would be condescending and counter-cultural to the idea of the independent, professional teacher. But our evidence suggests that most teachers would welcome more of these small gestures, that there is a lack of this type of consideration and that it is important in the school setting. To the outsider it may seem a minor issue, but to the teachers themselves it is clearly very significant. The American researcher Herzberg (1968) made the shrewd observation that those aspects of the working situation which *dissatisfy* us are what he called 'hygiene factors' in that they infect the whole working performance. When, however, they are removed, then other features of work may motivate us. Lack of consideration in schools seems to be the biggest of all 'dissatisfiers'.

> Consideration is appreciated. Vicky, a young Music teacher, found herself making all the arrangements for a visiting band of professional musicians. In conversation with the Head, she realised that her front-of-house arrangements were not as thorough as was

> needed. The Head suggested ways in which she could make improvements and she believed that helping her in this way was an indication that he valued her. He also made a point of coming in to her classroom, taking an interest in what she was doing with the pupils and talking about the concerts she was staging: 'I like the way he puts himself about. It makes you feel important.'

Another aspect of consideration is in housekeeping matters, such as the state of the staffroom, coffee facilities, whether there are social activities, the cleanliness of the staff lavatories and so forth. Living in squalid surroundings undermines self-respect and detracts from personal dignity: one feels undervalued. We found many of the people with whom we spoke apologetic and defensive about their circumstances, feeling that torn curtains, dilapidated furniture and evil-smelling coffee was in some strange way an indictment of them rather than of their employer.

Feedback

The second type of valuing is concerned with feedback, evaluation and appraisal. The teacher, in company with many other professionals, lacks tangible indicators of success because the output of 'a good teacher' defies measurement, just as 'a good school' defies definition. A company director can refer to the annual profit figures, the barrister can refer to the number of cases won and lost, the entertainer can look at the size of the audience and the writer can look at the level of sales, but the teacher does not have even such simple, if misleading, yardsticks of personal achievement. All too often the enormous contribution and exhausting effort seems to lack any perceptible output. Like anyone else the teacher wants an answer to the question. 'How am I doing?' There are many instances when the children provide much-cherished valuing through their spontaneous warmth or sudden spurts of progress, but these have to be balanced against instances of rudeness, boredom and sullenness. Few human groups can be quite so unexpectedly brutal as a group of children dealing with an adult.

Teachers need feedback from other teachers. But they have ambivalent attitudes towards it. They have seen that it can provide reassurance and encouragement, or it may destroy self-confidence.

Many staff we interviewed said that they did not see enough of the boss, no-one seemed interested in what they were doing and that if appraisal was positive and supportive, in a climate of trust, they would welcome the chance to let the world know what they were doing. Some find teaching to be a lonely job and need reassuring that they are working appropriately despite their own worries and sense of insecurity.

One example of positive feedback was in the English Department at William Barnes. It was well established, many of its members having been in post for 20 years. The Head of Department was described as a gentleman. He systematically saw each member of this large department for a period each half term to talk about their classes and what they wanted to develop in the future within the department.

Although we have separated feedback from consideration in the last few pages, in practice they are inter-dependent and one is of little value without the other. Blake (1964) suggested that managers can be characterised by their location on a two-dimensional grid, one axis of which is labelled 'concern for people' and the other 'concern for production or task'. According to a hypothetical position on this grid he differentiated various management styles, of which three will suffice to illustrate our point.

- A 1.9 manager has little concern for task (1) but high concern for people (9), leading to a comfortable, friendly organisation and a relaxed work tempo.
- A 9.1 manager has the priorities reversed, so that the task is made as efficient as possible but there is no consideration for the people.
- A 9.9 manager gives high priority to both task and people, producing work relationships of trust and respect and a high degree of effectiveness in attaining task objectives from committed people who have a common stake in the purpose of the organisation.

In the quarter century since Blake set out his thesis, we have seen a change in attitudes that does little to reduce the value of his model. In the 1990s people in all employment will want their organisations to be efficient, not only to secure their personal position but also because the efficiency of the organisational context enables the individual to be efficient also, gaining the satisfaction of a job well done and the possibility of doing another job even better.

Teachers are remarkably keen to win the approval of the boss:

> I like the way he pats you on the head. I suppose there are times when he over-praises you, but you can't accuse him of being insincere.

but they also need to win the approval of themselves:

> There's nothing quite as satisfying as knowing that a lesson has worked . . . that's magic.

Nias (1980) has something to contribute here, but her oft-quoted study was of graduates who, after a specialised, one-year PGCE, had taken jobs in infant and junior schools. That her sample was thus rather untypical is not always mentioned by those who have used her to support their views, but the following comment seems absolutely right:

> The teachers in my survey felt that Headteachers should be seen to be involved in the life of the school. In the same way, they wanted their Heads to monitor the

work that was being done . . . it seems that many teachers, even those described in glowing terms by their Heads, do not appreciate the extent of the professional freedom offered them by 'passive' Heads. On the other hand, there was no mention among factors contributing to job satisfaction of the obverse of this. Like inefficient administration, the absence of monitoring is a 'dissatisfier', but its existence does not serve as a 'satisfier'.

(p. 263)

Delegation

The Head of Department is very appreciative of what I do. So is the Head. He sends me little notes occasionally. Recognition of this sort is important because teaching is such a lonely job, but the most important sort of recognition is being given real responsibility.

Members of staff are valued when responsibility is delegated to them, but this involves delegating *responsibility* down the hierarchy, not just giving people jobs to do. Teachers must be trusted to make decisions about whether, what and how to do things, not just given the work of filling in lists or teaching new courses. Also responsibility cannot be delegated and then taken away without devaluing the person and destroying their confidence and future effectiveness.

Among teachers a common complaint about Heads is 'the SHAM (Staff Hoodwinked by Administrative Mechanism) Working Party'.

We spent hours in discussion and came up with a set of proposals on which we were unanimous, but the Head did not like them and did what he had decided on beforehand.

In situations like that the Head will explain that the members of the working party had failed to appreciate all the nuances that had to be considered, or were not bold enough, or imaginative enough, or knowledgeable enough. Despite all this members of the working party feel humiliated that their time has been wasted and that they have been cynically manipulated, when the course of action to be followed was decided before their deliberations began. If working parties are set up they need to be fully briefed and kept informed of developments. If there is doubt about their ability to come up with viable proposals, they may need assistance with their discussions: anything rather than repudiation afterwards.

Delegation is not an easy option for the delegator. It requires careful judgement. What can be delegated and who is the right person? Then it requires trust of, and support for, that person while the assignment is carried through. In the early stages it will probably take more time than if the delegator kept the task, but later that investment pays off in the confident, reliable, sustained and developing performance of a valued colleague whose capacity is enhanced.

In some ways the most important aspect of delegation is that it is as necessary for the delegator as for the person to whom the responsibility passes. If there is to be consideration and feedback within the school, then the senior members of staff make space for it by delegation. They also channel people's energies.

> The Head of Pennine End held interviews with members of staff on scale posts to discuss the targets they had set for the coming year. The reason for this initiative was a belief that the industrial action had distanced the Head from many of the staff and he now needed to bridge that gap by meeting them on an individual basis. One of the interviews was with a teacher of Physics who had been given responsibility for theatrical lighting. He was encouraged to look for other talent in the school to help him with productions. The Head of Chemistry was encouraged to forge links with the Chemistry department in another local school, to look for ways of furthering integration within lower-school science and consider the feasibility of modular science courses. Not only were these important matters needing attention, it also enabled the Head to divert an interest which the teacher had displayed in profiling that would probably 'generate loads of data which may or may not be used.'

Consultation and participation

In view of the innovation overload referred to already, it will be difficult to create the conditions in which teachers can respond to changes with much enthusiasm. However, if they wish to respond with commitment rather than mere stoical compliance, there is scope within schools for a participative style of implementation that creates a sense of ownership of the 'how' of innovation even if there is no sense of ownership of the 'what'. Too often the Head and close colleagues react to innovation overload without offering participation and it is likely then that change will be implemented formally. There is precise specification of what everyone else should do from the in-school innovator, who will have acquired some ownership of the change at the same time as denying ownership to colleagues.

Most teachers we interviewed felt there was insufficient consultation in their schools. Lack of consultation seems to be a dissatisfier. This feeling can be partly interpreted as a product of the long period of union action which involved a ban on formal meetings. Yet during the period of our study, there was a revival in the holding of meetings in all schools; we observed no less than 431 in 733 days spent in 24 schools and we found staff still dissatisfied. There is, therefore, a need to examine the structures in existence, the processes involved, and the consultative performance of individuals in key strategic positions.

Existing hierarchical structures, no matter how designed, are not appropriate to a period of rapid change and new demands, since they 'freeze' roles, attitudes and expectations at a particular time. When we look at a formal structure of a school, we learn more about its past than about its present. The contraction of the profession and the consequent slow-down in teacher movement only serve to aggravate this problem. Nevertheless, there is no obvious way that a hierarchy can be dismantled in the immediate future with pay allowances geared to hierarchical prescriptions for staffing structures.

As with structure, so with culture and style. It can be argued that a participative culture in schools is not only desirable but essential. There can be no more self-evident truth than that the staff are a school's most important resource, but a resource which will remain largely untapped as long as each member is squashed into his or her limited role in a hierarchical, bureaucratic structure. If schools are to have the best chance of responding in an organic, adaptive way to the pressures being imposed on them, the particular talents and interests of every member of staff need to be identified, nurtured and appropriately mobilised, through a participative, collaborative, collegial climate and style of management.

Notwithstanding our earlier comment about sham working parties, some working parties were used skilfully. When members had been co-opted, not just allowed to volunteer, they felt valued and recognised, especially when they found that membership encouraged personal development by making new demands of them. When working parties are always made up of the same trusty handful of stalwarts, the recognition of a few can lead to the undervaluing of the many.

Conclusion

Undoubtedly, many teachers feel undervalued and unappreciated. The difficulty for senior staff is not knowing what they can do about this. A solution is to articulate and promote the idea that the school is one happy team pulling together. This emphasises leadership and responsible control with appeals to loyalty, but it can lead to condescension or patronising behaviours and there is inevitably some conflict from those whose loyalty has been lost or never won. The united team all pulling together without any dissension is an ideal seldom realised because of the plurality of interests represented on any school staff.

By recognising that all schools are plural communities, senior staff can increase the openness and trust within their own and, consequently, the degree to which individuals feel valued. Trust is increased where individuals have discretion in their job and are able to participate in the total process of decision making (Fox, 1974, p. 97). Superiors attract little trust when they direct individuals to pursue ends they do not fully share;

there will be mutual suspicion, bargaining, gamesmanship, defensiveness and distorted communication (Fox, p. 30). Fox's high trust is interlinked with our valuing.

The staff in most of the schools that we researched is an aging population, stuck in a situation of little movement and growth. Increasingly these people are demanding a greater say in 'their' school, as are the younger staff who are not being promoted quickly. Despite the difficulties of changing to participative managerial styles, the risks of persisting with a strongly centralised style are great. Handy (1977) described it well:

> . . . morale is lowered, secrecy and subversion mount, energy and commitment reduce. Lonely and anxious, management then too often responds with more controls and checks, more assumed rights. Self-fulfilling, the organisation begins to respond only to whips and spurs and everyone wonders what went wrong.

It can no longer be a question of a school having to adopt the Head's preferred style of management; it is too late for such luxuries as 'preferred style'. The schools which will adapt successfully to all the pressures identified above, which will survive and eventually thrive, are those which will adopt a participative approach where all members' contributions are valued. As Stephen Murgatroyd (1985) says:

> . . . a school which fails to care for its staff is not likely to be caring effectively for its pupils.

The final word, however, is that valuing of colleagues is something for *all* the adults in the organisation to offer each other; it is not just for the mighty to confer on the lowly. The probationer who says, 'I wish I could do that', will make somebody's day. Teachers perhaps hesitate to praise the work of colleagues through diffidence, feeling that the comment would be out of place or meaningless or misconstrued, yet a moment's reflection would convince them otherwise.

> Ron Grainger was a teacher of Physics who had spent most of his working life in the engineering industry before making a late career change to teaching in his fifties. He was not ambitious for promotion but enjoyed teaching Physics; he had a calm cheerfulness throughout the working day and was splendid at putting things in perspective. When the Head of Science was infuriating the other scientists by making unreasonable demands, Ron would stay calm, asserting 'it'll all look different on Monday.' His enjoyment in teaching Physics extended to enjoying the achievements of colleagues. He was regularly picking up comments from pupils and trying to learn from them in discussions with other teachers: 'How do you get through to Peter Robinson? I can't get anywhere with him, but yesterday he said that you . . .'

Do It Yourself

1 In the next week, see if you can find opportunities at work for saying:

- 'Thank you.'
- 'Well done.'
- 'That's great.'

  at least five times.

2 Look in the staffroom; are there dirty cups, untidy papers, squalor? Could these be tidied up in half an hour? Why not do it?

3 When delegating work to someone else, ask yourself:

- Am I allowing them to make decisions about this?
- Can they decide whether to do it or not?
- Can they decide what to do or not?
- Can they decide how to do it or not?
- Are there any variations that they cannot decide to opt for?

4 In meetings do you ask for everyone's opinion? How do you hear the views of the quiet members of the group?

References

Blake, R.R. and Mouton, J.S., *The Managerial Grid*, Gulf Western, Houston, 1964.

Bolam, R., 'School Improvement: The National Scene', in *School Organisation*, Vol. 6, No. 3, pp. 314–20, 1986.

Fox, A., *Man Mismanagement*, Hutchinson, London, 1974.

Handy, C., 'The Organisations of Consent', in *The Changing University*, Piper, D. and Glatter, R. (Eds), NFER, Windsor, 1977.

Herzberg F., 'One More Time: How Do You Motivate Employees?' in *Harvard Business Review*, Vol. 46, pp. 46–52, 1968.

Maslow, A.H., *Motivation and Personality*, Harper and Row, 1954.

Murgatroyd, S., Management Teams and the Promotion of Well-being, in *School Organisation*, Vol. 6. No. 1, 1985.

Nias, J., 'Leadership Styles and Job Satisfaction in Primary Schools', in *Approaches to School Management*, Bush, T., Glatter, R., Goodey, J. and Riches, C. (Eds), Open University/Harper and Row, 1980.

Chapter 5
Co-Ordination and Cohesiveness

The work of individual teachers needs to be co-ordinated within a cohesive school culture if the variety of classroom practices is to provide a successful educational experience for pupils. When the non-teaching staff are also included in the co-ordination and cohesiveness there is a greater chance of being an effective school. Co-ordination is achieved by a series of organisational and administrative devices: group cohesiveness derives from a feeling of solidarity and common purpose. It is an essential management task to install the necessary co-ordinating mechanisms, so that individuals and groups maintain their sense of place within the whole school and direct their efforts towards the whole-school objectives. An associated, but more subtle, management task is to develop the sense of joint enterprise.

Not all systems of co-ordination are thought through with sufficient rigour to ensure the required result, and not all attempts to foster common purpose are consistent with both the distinctive culture of the school and the overall values of the teaching profession. Some of the organisational tinkering in schools whereby faculty systems, for instance, have been installed, modified, discarded and reintroduced may make sound resources sense, but can wreak havoc with co-ordination. Effective teaching depends on the enthusiasm and commitment of the teacher, and those qualities can only be produced voluntarily. Teachers work within the tradition of autonomy typical of British schools. In accepting the central values and mission of the school, teachers deliver the high level of commitment that can come only from autonomous responsibility. Attempts to achieve solidarity that are heavy-handed or autocratic will destroy rather than create cohesiveness.

Current practice

An important co-ordinating device is the *organisation structure*, with its allocation of responsibility and distribution of authority (see Figure 3).

Figure 3: An example of an organisation structure (Southern High)

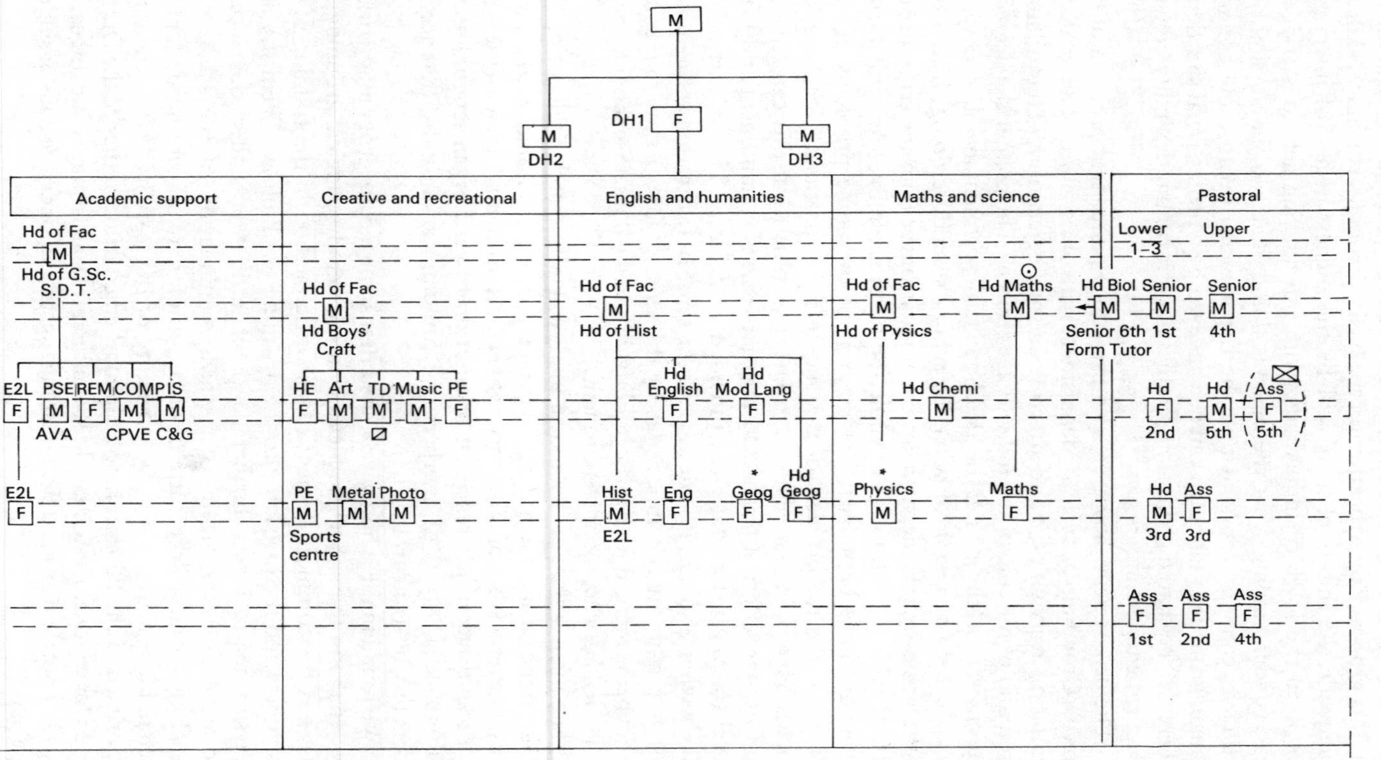

The main co-ordinating element here is the subject department or faculty, as this groups people together on the basis of common technical skill and language. At this level there will be the highest degree of integration between the work of individuals, with interlocking activities and with each understanding what the other is doing. There is the possibility of efficient communication within the department, because the common language means that much can be conveyed by a professional shorthand; there will be shared professional values and maximum flexibility between departmental members.

The department, however, also presents a permanent problem of balance. Grouping people in departments involves more than a differentiation in activities; it also affects values and perceptions of the organisation and of the role of the individual within it. The greater the degree of specialisation, the greater the likelihood of department members developing their own version of what the school should be doing. The group cohesiveness of the department becomes stronger than the sense of solidarity with the school as a whole. Some of the moves towards faculty structure have been partly an attempt to overcome problems of such diversity and the problem of the one-person department. Small departments have been assimilated into larger faculties, but this can have the unfortunate effect of teachers losing that sense of commitment at the first level that departmentation is intended to achieve. This is particularly likely when a subject is in decline, as the sense of frustration at the subject losing popularity is compounded by the sense of lost identity that comes from being merged with those holding different values. (See the chapter on The Head of Faculty or Department.)

The main source of theoretical analysis and research evidence on this issue in the business world comes from Lawrence and Lorsch (1967), who found several types of difference between departments. In school the types we found were: differences in orientation toward organisational goals, differences in styles of interpersonal communication and differences in formality of structure.

We found in the schools we visited that some faculty groupings worked better than others. Science faculties are generally a logical grouping, as there is the common element of scientific method in the training of all members and the division into the disciplines of Biology, Chemistry and Physics maintains a further level of affiliation under the faculty co-ordination. As the move towards combination of the sciences in teaching develops, this form of organisation may be reinforced. A more debatable practice is to have a Faculty of Recreational Arts, where the approach of the PE staff may be in marked contrast to that of the Drama and Dance staff. Design faculties can be rather amorphous and appear to be no more than an expedient pushing together of odds and ends of subject specialists.

Another co-ordinating device is the *pastoral structure*, where an individual member of staff co-ordinates the activities of many colleag they impinge on the welfare and development of children in a part year or years. This usually proves to be a more difficult form of co-ordination, as it lacks the advantages of a common language and set of values with which subject departmentation begins. (See the chapter on The Head of the Pastoral Team.)

In our schools *other co-ordinating roles* had emerged, such as those responsible for TVEI, Special Needs and Multicultural Education. As is discussed in our chapter on Change, such posts are associated with innovation and are made problematic by the basic departmentation of the school. This role was studied by Lawrence and Lorsch, and Handy (1985) draws on their evidence to formulate his own advice on this most difficult of situations.

> 1 [The co-ordinator] must have position power and appropriate status . . . One way to achieve this is to move into the post a demonstrably successful individual who will carry some of his previous position power with him. He must also have the information appropriate to his position . . .
> 2 He must have expert power, and be perceived to have it by all the groups or individuals with whom he is co-ordinating . . .
> 3 He must have the inter-personal skills necessary to resolve conflict in a problem-solving mode.
>
> (p. 210)

(See our chapter on Personal Credibility and Effectiveness for more on these posts.)

The members of *the senior team* in a school also provide a co-ordinating element, and the effectiveness with which this role is established depends on the way in which expert power is deployed. This is discussed more fully in Chapter 10: Technical, Administrative and Managerial Work, but it is interesting how often school Heads value Deputies more than do other members of staff. This seems to stem from the extent to which some Deputies are seen to be assisting the Head rather than deploying expert power and skill in the general affairs of the school. The importance of a Deputy controlling the timetable is often because of the co-ordinating role that that carries with it.

A co-ordinating device that has developed rapidly in schools is that of *meetings* (see Table 3). Although staff meetings have been held since time immemorial, their frequency has increased and many smaller meetings have been set up. These also contribute to group cohesiveness. Anthony Jay (1972) made this comment:

> . . . corporation man needs to come together regularly with other members of the species – operational objectives can always be found to justify this deeper need. I suspect that meetings are most frequent and most enjoyed by men whose work keeps them solitary or in very small groups for most of the week . . . There is a

Table 3: Co-ordinating meetings in the MOSS 24 schools

	Senior staff meeting	Head of department/ Faculty meeting	Head of Year/House meeting	Other
1	Weekly	Weekly	None	
2	Daily	None	Weekly	
3	Weekly	None	Weekly	
4	Weekly	Half-termly	Half-termly	
5	Weekly	Half-termly	None	
6	None	None	None	Four-week cycle, Management Organisation open to all
7	As required (Academic Board)	None	As required (Pastoral Board)	Weekly Senior Management Team, 2 ad hoc Working Parties on curriculum, Faculty teams
8	As required	None	As required (weekly more or less)	2 per Week Senior Management Team, 1 Standing Committee on curriculum, 2 Working Parties, Faculty teams
9	Monthly	None	As required (without Head!)	Full staff – open agenda, open interest meetings, 2 Working Parties, Faculty teams
10	Weekly Head + 3 Deputies Weekly 3 Deputies 2 Senior teachers	Monthly	Monthly and 2 briefing meetings per week	Staff Consultative Committee and Staff Management
11	Weekly, incl. Union reps.	None	None	Staff Development Committee and ad hoc Working Parties
12	Weekly with 2 Deputies	None	None	Full staff meeting monthly and new support team meetings

13	Weekly Head + 2 Deputies	Monthly	As required	Termly staff meeting
14	Weekly Head, Heads of Faculty + Heads of Year	None	1 as required but none while there	Full staff meeting, 2 per term
15	As required	Monthly	Monthly	Full staff meeting, 2 per term
16	Weekly	None	None	Weekly staffs briefing – school teams, e.g. Expressive Arts, Lower School Unit
17	None (but three-quarters met weekly)	None	2 per term	
18	Weekly	None	2-weekly but flexible	Senior Staff Meeting – open attendance, Heads of Faculty/Department/Year expected to attend weekly briefing
19	Weekly	Monthly	Monthly	Curriculum Working Parties Half-termly
20	Weekly	Half-termly	Half-termly	
21	2 per week	Half-termly	Half-termly	Curriculum Working Parties monthly or ad hoc
22	Most mornings	As and when necessary	None	2 Working Parties, 'Open' Curriculum meetings
23	Weekly	None	Head of House – occasional	Working Parties
24	Weekly	Half-termly, more often if necessary	Half-termly	None

need to feel the security of the group around you, even if you do not belong to a real or effective one.

(p. 217)

There are many *administrative devices* to aid co-ordination. The timetable is the most obvious, but there is also the array of rules and procedures that are designed to get people to do things consistently and keep their colleagues informed, like guidelines on sending letters, staff handbooks, noticeboards and many more. For example, see Figure 4, which is a very detailed flow diagram we found in one school; many would see it as over-elaborate.

Conclusion

There can be no doubt that the need for co-ordination is rapidly increasing in schools, especially with the cross-school or whole-school initiatives that appear to be proliferating. The obvious danger is that the methods of co-ordination become burdensome, with so much time spent on them that the main task of teaching is almost overwhelmed, especially when the emphasis is on *administrative* mechanisms.

Co-ordination is more likely to succeed when group cohesiveness is maintained, and this sense of solidarity is going to operate mainly at two levels; the department and the school. The solidarity of the teaching profession is also important, though there is little that those running schools can do about it.

For cohesiveness to exist, group members have to spend time together and groups have to be of a viable size. Previous successful group activities and the existence of external threats both increase cohesiveness.

It is only as people spend time together that they become more friendly, as they talk and respond, and discover common interests and values. This obviously requires proximity, so members of a staff group have a better chance of developing cohesiveness if they work near each other, as most art teachers do, than if they work in differing locations, like many history teachers. The staffroom provides an opportunity for whole-school cohesiveness, but sharing cups of coffee in the stock room may be the best opportunity for departmental cohesiveness.

The problem of group size is described in the following quotation.

> As group size expands, interaction with all members becomes more difficult, as does the ability to maintain a common goal. Not surprisingly, too, as a single group's size increases, the likelihood of cliques forming also increases. The creation of groups within groups tends to decrease overall cohesiveness.
>
> (Robbins, 1986, p. 195)

This type of difficulty has been seen in many of the very large schools that were more common in the 1960s and 1970s than today, but the recent

Figure 4: System for a combined concern/information slip

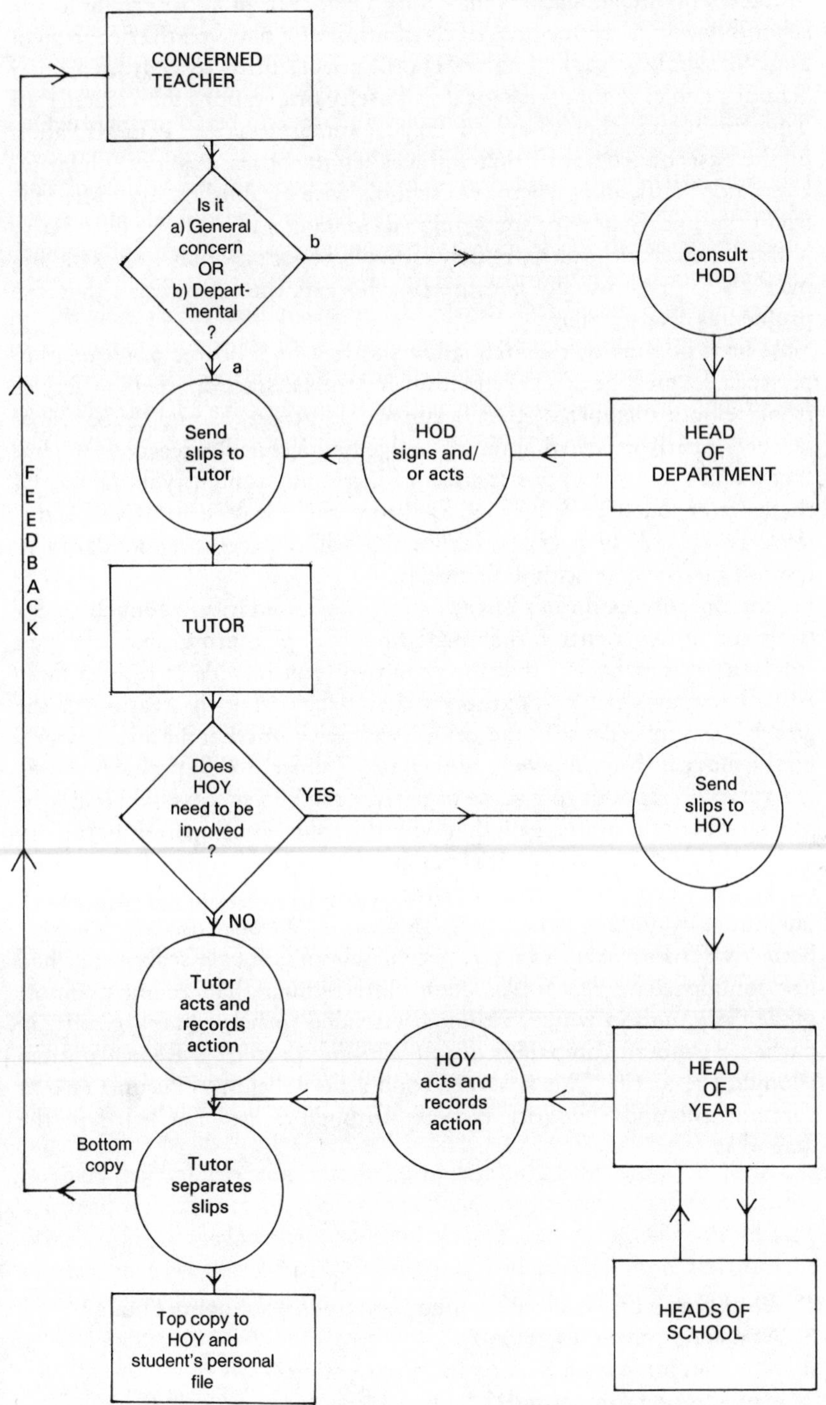

problems of amalgamations may have been even more severe. Split-site schools develop intermediate levels of affiliation between the department and the whole school. 'Lower School' people drift away from 'Upper School' people, so that the logical and useful orientations for a teacher, of department and school, have an illogical and useless overlay of affiliation on the basis of geography that will weaken the other senses of solidarity. Even more difficult is where two schools with established, but different, traditions and values are amalgamated, making a new sense of solidarity within a new institution extremely difficult. If one school is seen as 'taking over' the other – usually because of who gets the key posts – then the problem is even greater.

At least one major research study shows a high degree of correlation between the prestige of an occupation and the satisfaction a person derives from being a member of that occupational group (Kahn, 1973). Most teachers clearly believe that their prestige has declined in recent years, but this can produce the opposite effect of increasing solidarity in the face of threat from outside (Stein, 1976). From the whole-school perspective there is the risk of a group within the school increasing solidarity in opposition to whole-school objectives.

External threats do not always strengthen solidarity, as much recent trade union experience has shown. Members of a group may not gain solidarity if they believe that the group will not be able to resist attack. Also they may abandon a group if they believe that the reason for the attack is simply because of the group's existence and that the attack would not be made if the group were broken up (Zander, 1979, p. 436).

Everyone responds to a sense of participating in success, whether it be as a member of a sports team that wins the championship or as part of an activity that produces deep satisfaction for non-competitive reasons. With the lack of adequate criteria to define 'a good school', much depends on qualitative evaluation from a range of sources. We once used the phrase 'a perfectly satisfactory, ordinary, decent school' about a school that had lost confidence in what it was doing. Interestingly that comment almost made the situation worse, although intended to help. Many Heads, in particular, mount campaigns of self-fulfilling prophecy. Repeated often enough, the words 'This is a very good school' begin to become true as commitment and solidarity increase through a growing belief in the diagnosis.

Do It Yourself

1 What type of co-ordinating meetings does your school have?
2 Who is permitted to attend?
3 Who can put forward ideas for the meeting?
4 Is everyone represented?

5 How are the information and decisions from these meetings fed back to those who did not/could not attend?

References

Douglas, quoted in Mars, 1982.
Handy, C.B., *Understanding Organisations*, 3rd edition, Penguin Books, Harmondsworth, Middlesex, 1985.
Jay, A., *Corporation Man*, Cape, London 1972.
Kahn, R.L., 'The Work Module', in *Psychology Today*, February, 1973.
Lawrence, P.R. and Lorsch, J.W., *Organization and Environment: Managing Differentiation and Integration*, Harvard University Press, 1967.
Mars, G., *Cheats at Work*, Counterpoint, London 1982.
Robbins, S.P., *Organization Behaviour: Concepts, Controversies and Applications*, 3rd edition, Prentice Hall International, London, 1986.
Stein, A., 'Conflict and Cohesion: A Review of the Literature', in *Journal of Conflict Resolution*, pp. 143–72, March, 1976.
Zander, A., 'The Psychology of Group Processes', in *Annual Review of Psychology*, Rosenzweig, M.R. and Porter, L.W. (Eds), Vol. 30, 1979.

Chapter 6
Resources

Schools are expected to achieve extraordinary results with only limited resources. Given that the level of most resources available to schools is determined elsewhere, for example, in the LEA or DES, the limits mean that schools have to make choices about:

- making better use of what is available;
- raising additional resources, through PTAs, from local businesses, etc;
- doing less than they would like;
- cutting corners on the quality of what they do.

These choices are not mutually exclusive and they call for constant revision as circumstances change.

Types of resources

People are a school's principal resource. This *human* resource is delivered through the time and skills of, among others, teaching, non-teaching and ancillary staff, support personnel, such as advisers and welfare officers, and parents. Some time and some skills are paid for through salaries and wages, but a school benefits greatly when more are given voluntarily.

A school also has: *physical* resources, which include buildings, grounds, furniture, equipment and books; and *financial* resources which comprise, primarily, capitation and equipment allowances and, secondarily, special 'occasional' grants and the results of local efforts by, for example, PTAs. The curriculum and the timetable involve the use of all these resources and the way in which they are brought together, arranged and distributed, affects the way the school operates.

Current practice

The following are examples of how schools managed their resources. They have been grouped into sections by type of resource – human, physical, time and financial.

Human resources

a Pennine End keeps a register of parents who have particular skills or abilities to offer the school and are willing to be called upon to provide assistance.

The Librarian at Pennine End School maintains a 'Directory of Human Resources'. This is a file and index of parental skills based on a questionnaire sent out to parents of all new pupils. The variety of expertise potentially available to the school is enormous – from bell-ringing to shark-fishing, from matchbox collecting to parachuting. The occupations represented are also wide-ranging – farmers, architects, dentists, printers, vets and many others. The majority of main local employers are represented in the Directory, and in many cases visits to workplaces are welcomed. Some parents are able to talk about life and work in foreign countries, including Egypt, the USA, Pakistan and Ghana. Many of these parents are willing to share their skills and experiences with the school by coming in and talking to pupils and staff.

b William Barnes employs two non-teaching staff as Resource Technicians. They are long-serving clerical assistants, who do typing, secretarial, reception and reprographics work. Unlike most clerical staff in schools, each is located separately in an office some distance from the General Office. They each provide general assistance with the business of the school (as well as specific assistance to two Deputy Heads) and are focal points for staff in each location. They have their own budgets and spending powers.

c William Barnes participates actively in a CPVE consortium, consisting of five schools in the locality. Besides co-ordinating lessons, with pupils being bussed to other locations for lessons which would otherwise not be available, the consortium co-ordinates activities such as industry visits, work experience, and assessment. Members of the consortium also exchange information on staff training opportunities and local courses.

d A CDT department has built up a good reputation locally and has become the local centre for A-level graphics, with pupils from other schools attending graphics lessons there. Other schools in the area specialise in the art and design areas of CDT, and pupils from this school attend those locations.

e At Oakhill a member of staff has been encouraged to develop Integrated Curriculum modules for the Lower School which reflect his personal interests. This has been done partly by the Head of Department providing a small amount of money, some donated by other departments or from tuck shop money, but mainly in the form of time and a large amount of individual leeway. Personal interests which are now part of the IC curriculum include amateur radio, graphic design and word processing. This was considered to be a method of releasing energy and ideas in a way that could not always be achieved by just providing finances, and in this case has revitalised a demotivated member of staff.

Physical resources

a Summerfield High frequently makes use of the regional resources centre, via a free weekly delivery/pickup system, to provide a changing variety of books and materials for departmental and central use. An item borrowed recently by the Art Department was a stuffed fox!
b At Westcliffe it was commonly agreed that a Head of Year needed an office, but no 'spare' space was available. Another member of staff identified a windowless storeroom which was full of redundant papers. These were sorted and cleared out, and the room converted into an office.
c Five years ago, one member of staff was put in charge of co-ordinating school resources, including printing, AV and photographic equipment, cassettes, etc. One of his first jobs was to collect together all the equipment then lying in classroom cupboards and storerooms – some of which was unused – so that it was available to anyone in the school who needed it. The school now has an extensive and competently run resources centre, which includes a useful video cassette catalogue for easy reference, and comprehensive information for the benefit of teaching staff on the cassette labels, as well as a log of equipment's location.

Financial resources

a At Summerfield High discussion in a Finance Committee regarding the equitable distribution of capitation has revealed a need to know, in detail, the components of each department's spending to see, for example, how much is spent on 'consumables', how much on 'non-consumables' and how much on individual elements of the syllabus, such as particular science experiments. The Committee feels that this information will lead to better decisions about future allocations.
b At Westcliffe the Head of Lower School, on a split-site school, works hard at making finances available so that local initiatives in the Lower School are made possible and can be developed quickly, without any call on whole-school or LEA finance, and sometimes without special permission from higher levels. The money is raised through the personal efforts of Lower School pupils and staff, often during school time, by the organisation of activities such as sponsored reads, illustrated lecture evenings, etc. It is spent on financing such things as equipment for the chess club, curtains for the dining and staffrooms, paint for furniture and general facelifts, overtime for ancillary staff and, most recently, the development of a resource-based learning suite.

Resource objectives

Many schools do not think about the use they make of, and their organisational attitudes towards, the resources available to them, and can be tempted to blame lack of resources for deficiencies in their operation. As educational issues have been under increasing scrutiny, it has become even more important that schools establish and justify their resource objectives.

Hall End school has in its policy 'ongoing evaluation . . . and . . . the need to continually appraise, assess and evaluate our performance since the school is 'an accountable insitution'. This is unusual, since we found few schools putting into writing aims that were not just concerned with the pupils. We rarely found any objectives written down about the development of the adults in the organisation. Westcliffe School, unusually, states that it seeks to 'identify the needs of both children and staff so that they may derive satisfaction from their work'. In general staff are not the subject of any organisational aims. Raising and maintaining the well-being of all adult members is a vitally important organisational objective for schools.

In addition, few schools articulate any aims about making maximum use of the resources available. Staff who are new to a school, whether probationers, supply staff, new teachers or new clerical assistants, are rarely given any information about the availability or use of resources. Summerfield High has details in its staff handbook of the use of the resources bank, and the availability to staff of reprographic and photographic resources.

The schools which have formalised any sort of objectives about the use of their resources also seem to put them into practice – it is, of course, little use having objectives if these only exist on paper.

The actual task of taking an overview about the use of resources seems rarely to be undertaken by any member of the school. Specific people may be in charge of staff development, finance, timetable and buildings, for example – usually at Deputy Head or Senior Teacher level – but this is normally the 'nuts and bolts' practical side of things, rather than any opportunity to stand back and consider the overall management of resources. Time must be devoted to planning their use. This is expensive in manpower terms and, as events rarely run exactly to plan, some cynicism about the planning process is not surprising. Rickards (1985, p. 83) points out that:

> the benefits of planning may arise through the learning that is acquired in the process, rather than in establishment of a totally accurate plan of where the organisation is going.

At William Barnes a meeting on the dispersal of some DES funds for scientific and technical equipment took place between the Heads of the

Physics, CDT and Home Economics Departments, so that the use of these funds could be linked with planned departmental developments and the availability of other funds.

The effective use of resources needs careful thought. As Paisey argues (1981, p. 33), resource objectives are concerned with the current use of resources, the changes which might be made in them, and the future uses to which they might be put. A school should, therefore, be considering such things as:

- the use made of every member of teaching and non-teaching staff's experience, abilities and interests;
- the way that time in the school is used (such as the length of the lunch break);
- the use made of rooms, halls, store cupboards. Are all those store rooms and offices really necessary?
- how equipment and materials are utilised;
- what capitation is really spent on;
- whether the information coming into, or held within, the school is used effectively.

Objectives should set the task of considering how both qualitative and quantitative improvements can be made in the use of all the resources available, including those outside the school itself, in order to achieve its educational objectives.

Such objectives should be reviewed frequently, so that they can be adapted to the changing environment of the school. They should also be as specific as possible to the situation of the school. For example, a school in a large city may be backed up by easily available support services such as educational psychologists, advisers, training centres, audiovisual resources, libraries and transport. It will, therefore, have different resource objectives from a rural school whose network of such services is much looser.

It can be seen that schools need to take a long-term view of resources. The ability to do this with school capitation is not, of course, helped by LEAs disallowing any carry-over from one financial year to the next, since this makes it more difficult to 'save up' for a particular item, and often results in a frantic spree of spending on non-essential items in March. We found that schools sensibly found unofficial ways of getting round this problem, such as getting advance dummy invoices from co-operative suppliers, or swopping funds or equipment between departments. It would seem undesirable that such activities are the only methods of providing the necessary flexibility.

Once equipment is purchased, or expertise utilised, on which the school comes to rely, the problem of its replacement must be considered if a crisis is to be avoided. This is currently applicable, for example, to the use in schools of computers, which have a limited life in terms of spare parts. It is going to take schools a long time to become accustomed to 'throwaway technology'.

Centralisation of resources

Schools vary widely in the extent of resources available to them centrally, whether between schools within a district or, more immediately, within an individual school. Co-ordinating area resources can, in many instances, be of positive benefit to an isolated school, which might neither justify nor make effective use of individually held resources. In addition, staffing and equipment needs for certain curriculum elements are often best met by groups of schools, brought together for specific purposes as a result of deliberate foresight and planning by teachers with a wider vision. Within the school, a centralised stationery store may, or may not, get round the 'hoarding' instincts of individual teachers!

Control of resources

If there is formal hierarchical control over the availability, exchange and allocation of resources, the chances of innovative developments at the 'chalkface' are reduced. Making resources of funds of time available to Heads of Department by, for example, giving them a development budget of their own or encouraging team teaching, may make it easier for ideas to proceed without needing clearance from higher levels. Certain freedoms are vital if a school is to be in a position to respond to needs in an individual and innovative manner. With safeguards built in via governing bodies and auditing systems, the decentralisation of certain resources can create an enabling, innovative and motivating environment. These things are also applicable within the school, for example at departmental level.

We were struck in our research by the importance for the effective use of resources of the ownership of resources and their use. Hofstede (1968) suggests that an 'optimal' balance is needed between, on one hand, the control of resources for organisational effectiveness and, on the other, autonomy to satisfy democratic ideals and opportunity for innovation.

Resource culture

Schools should be sensitive to the likelihood that demands for resources will be pitched at levels which are likely to be fixed whether against the background of conditioning against 'extravagance', or encouragement of improvement and innovation (Byrne 1974). A constant refusal of resources will, in the long run, have the effect of depressing the demand for resources, leading to comments such as 'there is no point asking for that, you will never get it.' Where less-than-honest efforts to get round this are seen to be successful, however, there is the risk of artificially inflating demand – 'I always put in for more than I need.' A system where the assessment of future allocation tends to be carried out on the basis of past need, not on present or future needs, only serves to perpetuate this.

Conclusion

In most schools, the deployment of resources is too often a reactive activity. We recommend a proactive approach.

First, schools should exploit their resources, making the best possible use of them and constantly reconsidering how they can be better used. Effective exploitation of human resources is also a form of investment because it increases value and potential. Poor exploitation or neglect dissipates such investment at great human cost.

Second, resources are what schools invest in, both in the long and short term. People in schools should consciously decide how to utilise their money or their time, and then work hard to make their investment more valuable, concentrating on development, improving and making it more appropriate to changing needs.

Third, a positive view of resources, as those things which we can control, exploit and invest, leads to the sense of ownership that will produce thoughtful use. It does not matter how limited the actual amounts of money, time or space are, it is the attitude to their availability and use which is important. Quoting the shortage of resources and lack of money becomes an automatic reaction to every problem and a simple excuse for not being able to cope.

Do It Yourself

1 List all the types of human resource, internal and external, available to your school.

2 Draw up resource objectives for your school, to include use of staff, time, space, equipment, materials, information, capitation and other finance.

3 Make a list of the people who have control of the time resource in the school. What other power do they also hold (eg hierarchical, expert)?

4 Make a case out for the school to have centralised (or de-centralised) stationery storage, with recommendations about who should be in charge. Consider who might be against your proposal, and who might be most affected by it.

5 Think about any innovations/initiatives which could be developed by releasing resources other than financial ones.

6 What is the cultural expectation regarding the level of bids for financial resources? Is it 'normal' for departments to bid for more resources than they need? Why should this be so?

References

Byrne, Eileen M., *Planning and Educational Inequality: A Study of the Rationale of Resource Allocation*, NFER, Windsor, 1974.

Hofstede, G.H., *The Game of Budget Control*, Tavistock, London, 1968.

Paisey, Alan, *Organisation and Management in Schools: Perspectives for Practising Teachers*, Longman, Harlow, 1981.

Richards, T., *Stimulating Innovation: A Systems Approach*, Francis Pinter, London, 1985.

Chapter 7
Participation

'Participation' is a word much used currently in education circles; it even appears in the 1987 teachers' contract. The meanings attributed to it vary enormously. We restrict ourselves here to discussing participation by the adults working in a school, in decision making which affects the whole school.

The ideal of participation is fundamental to Western political structures, partly because it is seen as a means towards fairness between all members of society and partly because it is seen as a way of delivering effective government. Management, like government, depends on both efficiency and justice, neither of which can be pursued at the expense of the other. Concentration on efficiency and the neglect of justice leads, at best, to the under-utilisation of people's skills and potential; at worst, to debilitating stress for individuals and the loss of that collective consent from the majority which is needed to maintain the effectiveness of those in senior posts. Concentration on justice and the neglect of efficiency leads to organisational inertia and individual frustration. As with most other aspects of the art of management, success and effective performance lie in finding and maintaining a viable balance between justice and efficiency.

Participation: a model of staff involvement

There is a continuum of participation, which is set out in Figure 5. None of the positions is 'correct', as their appropriateness varies according to the situation. They are seldom found in a pure form, but they are described here to show the elements of a model or continuum of participation categories. When teachers say they would like more or less participation in the running of their school, a useful starting point is to determine the level of participation that already exists.

1 *Coercive:* A regime which depends on penalties to maintain social control. A prison is the obvious example.
2 *Normative:* Here there is a strong sense of moral obligation on all

Figure 5: The continuum of participation

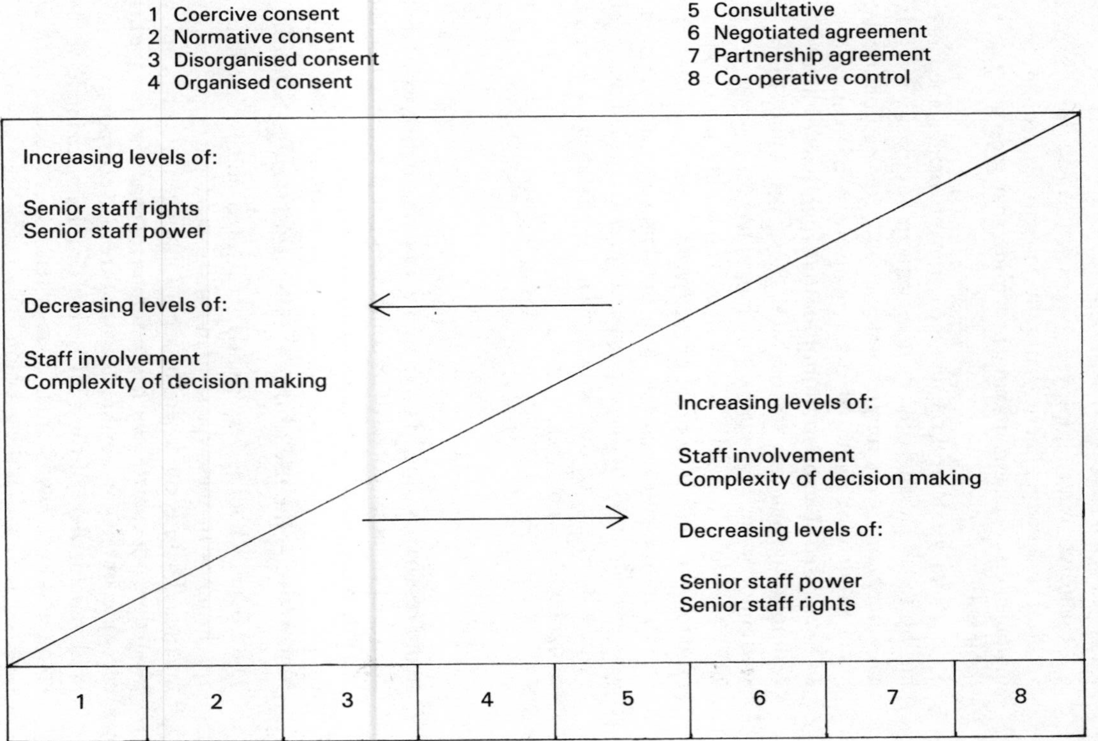

1 Coercive consent
2 Normative consent
3 Disorganised consent
4 Organised consent
5 Consultative
6 Negotiated agreement
7 Partnership agreement
8 Co-operative control
Increasing levels of:
Senior staff rights
Senior staff power
Decreasing levels of:
Staff involvement
Complexity of decision making
Increasing levels of:
Staff involvement
Complexity of decision making
Decreasing levels of:
Senior staff power
Senior staff rights
1
2
3
4
5
6
7
8

organisation members to accept the values that those in authority represent, so any challenge to authority implies a refutation of the shared norms. A religious order could be an example.

3 *Disorganised:* Here there is acquiescence simply because there is no focus for a challenge, despite discontent.

4 *Organised:* When employees organise to resist some aspects of hierarchical authority. There is usually no involvement in any aspects of management decision making providing that individual grievances are dealt with.

5 *Consultative:* Here is the first incursion into management decision making by those lacking official management responsibility. Management asks other employees for an opinion about proposals before decisions are made, though the right to decide remains with the management.

6 *Negotiated:* Negotiation implies that both parties have the power to withhold agreement, so decisions rest on some form of mutual accommodation. Management no longer has the sole right to decide.

7 *Partnership:* Authority is now shared on a more formal basis. There is a fundamental shift in control of the organisation as all the staff (or staff representatives) now share in the general management decision making.

8 *Controlling:* When the employees acquire control of the organisation – as in a workers' co-operative – then the managers are subject to the control of the employees.

Current practice

In our research we found no examples of participative styles that could be described as either coercive or controlling, but there were schools which broadly represented each of the other six styles.

Normative – the use of moral obligation (Lodge School)

The Lodge School is very tightly structured and is, in many ways, an anachronism in these days of increased staff participation in decision making. There is no aspect of school management or policy which the Head does not control. She freely admits that she likes to have her finger in every pie, but maintains that decisions are made corporately, although the predominant view of the staff is that decisions are made at the top and communicated downwards. Even when issues are discussed with staff, there is a feeling that the decision has already been taken.

Many staff said they had no influence over school policy and not one of them could cite an example of policy emanating from the staff.

There are no regular Heads of Department's meetings and none took place during our research period. The Head feels that she doesn't need to meet Heads of Department regularly because she meets the Faculty and House Heads once a week and has a full staff meeting once a month.

Although this system works efficiently, it is resented by some Heads of Department.

The venue and layout of the monthly staff meetings hinder full and free expression of opinion. They are held in a classroom, with the Head and Deputies seated at the front facing the staff who sit at desks. The staff feel that if they say anything unpopular or which appears to be critical of the Head they will be sternly reproved ('the Head talks and we listen'). Thus, the staff meeting is used mainly for the dissemination of information.

The idea of secret management is nourished by the fact that there is no published timetable other than that in the Head's study. Staff are only given a copy of their personal timetable, so that they have to make a conscious effort if they wish to know what anybody else is teaching. Minutes of meetings are not circulated and, in most cases, not even taken. There is no published list of the allocation of scale points.

Disorganised consent and how discontent can become organised when things go badly (Francis Drake School)

The new Head has been in post two and a half years. The pattern of decision making revolves around a weekly meeting of the Senior Management Team consisting of the Head, four Deputies and the three Senior Teachers who are Heads of Maths, English and Science.

Under the previous Head staff felt manipulated and threatened. They had formed a Common Room Association, open to all teachers not on the Senior Management Team, which held well attended meetings to discuss school policy. The chairman was always a respected member of staff, who met with the Head to inform him of the decisions of the Association.

A new Deputy Head, appointed in September 1985, was given the brief 'to improve the lines of communication between the Head and his staff'. This was widely known in the staffroom. In July 1986 the two union representatives not already on the Senior Management Team were invited to join their meetings. (The AMMA representative, Head of Maths on Senior Teacher scale, was already a member.) At first the NAS/UWT representative refused, but the successor agreed when the meeting's name was changed to Management Team.

Union representatives raised important matters in the first five months after attending the meetings. They vetoed a proposal for a new position of responsibility as assistant to the Deputy Head in charge of the main school site ('a training post'). They instigated the setting up of a committee to look at the amount of free time Senior Heads of Department had. On several occasions one representative drew the attention of the meeting to legal pitfalls that staff might fall into by releasing children from lessons early, or sending children outside the classroom as a punishment.

Increasingly staff have become aware of opportunities available to them to be part of the decision-making process, and union representatives have used their membership of the Management Team meeting to feed back to staff information about things affecting the school.

Organised consent – where grievances are dealt with (Francis Bacon School)

The school operates Faculty and Year systems, with regular meetings of the Heads of these sections. Departments meet regularly and there are also less frequent Faculty meetings. At the time we visited the school, the Head met the Deputies once a week for an hour in school time. He also met the Deputies and two of the three Senior Teachers for a shorter meeting. Every morning there was a short meeting of the Head, Deputies and Year Heads. When we joined the school in September, each Year Head also held a daily meeting after this first meeting with the Year Tutors and Associate Tutors to pass on information. During our time at the school these five meetings a week were reduced to two.

There was a monthly Staff Consultative Meeting chaired by the Deputy with responsibility for staff development. In theory, items for this meeting were provided by the staff. Full staff meetings, chaired by the Head, were also held once a month. Agendas for these meetings were generally provided by the chairmen or, in the case of the Heads' meeting, drawn up by members of the meeting at the beginning.

Although this school operates a more extensive structure of meetings than some others, there was little evidence that meetings are used to allow staff either to express dissent or to pass ideas up through the system. The first two meetings of the day were largely information-giving – 'cascade' meetings – and were dominated by short, often trivial items (on one occasion a Year Head invited his colleagues to pass on to all 80 staff the fact that Jenine, a pupil in his year, spelt her name in this unusual way). Although the Head invited staff at the first of the morning meetings to say something, none of the Year Heads observed ever invited Year Tutors to do the same at the subsequent meetings although, of course, people could interject if they wished.

The Head deliberately kept away from the Staff Consultative Meeting since he felt his presence there would prevent colleagues disagreeing with him or putting forward new ideas. Nevertheless his presence was felt, and the Deputy Head, who chaired the meetings, said in response to one suggestion, 'You'll never get that one past.'

The Consultative and Staff Meetings operated in a large Fifth Year Common Room, with staff sitting in rows before the chairman who sat behind a table. Both this layout and the way that the agenda was drawn up prevented people from feeling any ownership of the meeting and they often felt that decisions had already been made.

Consulative – where staff are asked their opinion before decisions are made (Hillside School)

Hillside School's fact sheet for job applicants reads, in part:

> The management policy of the school is based on maximum consultation with and involvement of staff in the running of the school. Great stress is laid on ease of communication and Senior Staff are as accessible as is practicable.

An attempt to translate this policy into practice is made by providing all members of staff with access to a series of meetings. The framework of meetings to assist the formulation of policy and to aid the dissemination of information is as folows:

- Heads of Department meetings, for all major subject Heads and those teachers who are in charge of a particular subject;
- Heads of Year meetings, for Heads and Deputy Heads of Year;
- Curriculum, for all those who have opted to be involved in the particular business in hand;
- Staff meetings, normally one long meeting once a term and a mini-meeting every Friday morning for 10 to 15 minutes;
- Department meetings, scheduled after Heads of Department meetings and as needs arise;
- Year Tutors, to follow Year Heads and as needs arise;
- Senior Management Group, Head/Deputies weekly during shared free time and after school if needed.

We believe that the following features of the organisation helped in turning lofty intentions into effective practice:

a A clear timetable for meetings was known and the sequence facilitated multi-directional movement of information.
b Agendas were published in advance and minutes were taken and circulated widely.
c The small size of the school and the involvement of many staff in more than one subject meant that no powerful cliques formed. An open policy towards the composition of certain groups also encouraged wider participation.
d As it was the practice of the Head to respond to matters arising from the minutes, staff felt that there was value in being part of the process.
e There was a recognition that meetings for meetings' sake served no good purpose, and if progress was not being made other machinery could be tried.
f Meetings with clearly defined objectives and participants at ease with their 'expert' knowledge were better organised and managed than those

where 'authority' status was in doubt (for example, the English Department coming to terms with standardising for GCSE, compared with a CDT meeting with the newly promoted Head of Department struggling to bring together traditionally independent subjects).
g Some effective meetings rotated chairing and minuting and this seemed to lead to greater commitment and involvement.
h Senior management recognised that meetings did encroach on an individual's time and were irksome to some. The overall pattern of meeting was set so as not to overburden individuals and senior management expressed their appreciation of those who did participate.

Negotiated – where both staff and management have the power to decide (Valley High School)

The formal arrangements for consultation and participation are more extensive than we found in many schools.

A significant feature is the Curriculum Committee. Strictly speaking it is not a 'standing' body since it is only called into existence when major curriculum issues concerning the whole school need discussing. A post-industrial action curriculum review, initiated by the Head, has resulted in the Curriculum Committee meeting once a fortnight in the early part of the autumn term and then more often. The issues which have been discussed in this period include multicultural education, gender, and personal and social education – all resulting from County initiatives. In addition the Curriculum Committee has considered a move towards a 25-period week, and modifications to the core/option arrangements. Decisions on these last two matters had become urgent, leading to the cancellation of a Finance and Consultative Committee.

The Curriculum Committee is an open forum which is chaired by the First Deputy and supported, on the occasions observed, by about 60 per cent of the staff. Although the proceedings were dominated by a few participants, our records indicate that most people had something to say in each meeting. Although it was clear that the Chairman had preferred directions for change he did not overtly promote them and, on occasions, seemed to play the devil's advocate with his own arguments in order to stimulate those with opposing views to develop their position.

If this was his intention then it was not always successful. On one occasion he made a presentation which was designed to prove that the costs, elsewhere in the school, of running an 'Alternative Curriculum' for 45 Fourth Years were prohibitive. The idea for such a curriculum had been proposed by a Head of House and widely supported by staff at a previous meeting as a means of coping with a particularly difficult year group. The staff at the subsequent meeting were not prepared to let their idea disappear and, aided and abetted by the Head, proceeded to 'find' staff and time which would make it possible. The exercise was slightly unreal since the extra staffing which would be required could only come from a curriculum-staffing 'bonus' (which the County had not yet granted) and staff opting to teach in the 'Alternative Curriculum' at the expense of their own more academic teaching. The possibility of this extra 'Curriculum' staffing was just the sort of straw which the Head and many of his staff were happy to grasp in order to realise their ideas. The staff also said that they would all be willing to 'do their bit' in the Alternative Curriculum. At a later meeting it became clear that the staff were not, in fact, prepared to opt in, and in doing so face up to the implications of their collective decision to establish an Alternative Curriculum.

Partnership – involving fundamental change in control of the school (Jackson School)

Over the previous 18 months the school had moved towards what it called 'open management'. This meant that all policy-making decisions were to be taken in meetings which any member of staff could attend. In September a structure of nine different meetings with sub-groups was initiated. A timetable of these various meetings was drawn up and agendas posted; minutes went to those who attended. By the end of February it was clear that there were far too many meetings with a great deal of overlap between them. It was also felt that the same 10 to 12 people were usually the attenders.

A revised structure was proposed by a Senior Teacher and a Scale 4 teacher and accepted by the Management Committee at the end of February 1987. This structure (see Figure 6) was being tried for the first time whilst we were there.

Each week had one of the three main meetings (management, organisation or curriculum) with the fourth week free; then the cycle re-started. They were trying two cycles and then reviewing at the beginning of May. Minutes are now distributed to all staff via the pigeonholes.

Figure 6: Committee Structure at Jackson

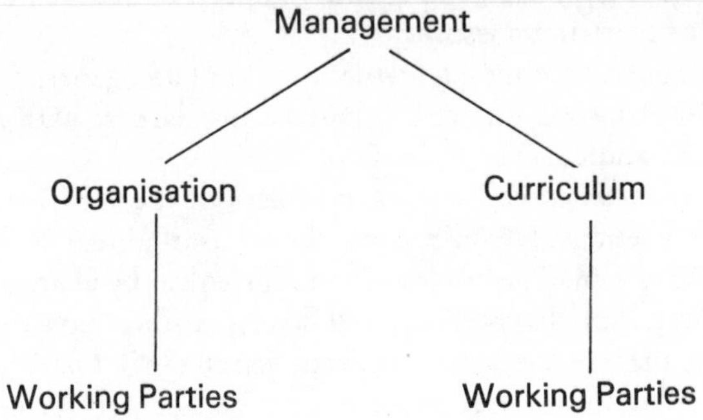

Management

Organisation | Curriculum

Working Parties | Working Parties

Senior staff were concerned that junior staff did not attend these policy meetings and sent out a questionnaire asking for views. Assorted other questionnaires were being distributed on such matters as the school day, finance and special needs. Discussion documents were also circulated, for example on the management structure: the Headteacher's vision for the future, called 'I have a dream'; the record of achievement scheme.

The quality of chairmanship was seen as crucial, particularly to ensure that meetings did not drag on. For this reason the management meeting was chaired by someone with experience of chairing union meetings.

The advantages and disadvantages of increased participation

As the various examples demonstrate, increased participation is not universally beneficial in practice, however attractive it may be in principle. We list here the benefits and drawbacks.

Benefits

a It meets the felt need of teachers to be a *college* of professionals, with all able to air their views. Although seniority and experience give weight to expressions of opinion, a valid argument from a junior member will win the day.

b It is a very good *staff development* device for those seeking promotion, as they can learn of wider implications, ideas, information, latest gossip, nuances of interpretation and fashions which others have come across on courses, through their networks, and so forth.

c If someone disagrees with a decision after it has been made, there is little scope for resistance to its implementation. *Collective decisions* are sometimes untidy, but they carry an unassailable argument: 'You had your opportunity to argue about it then, now let's get on with it.'

d Those who attend have opportunities for *improved understanding* of other aspects of the school's needs, as the mysteries of such activities as timetabling and finance are openly discussed. It is especially useful in developing among staff a sophisticated understanding of the increasing complexity of curriculum issues.

e *Debate* becomes an ongoing feature of school life, generally improving the quality of proposed changes and increasing the ease with which innovation can be handled.

f *Political power* is spread among members of the staff by their attendance at the meetings, which become the focus of influence and decision making in the school. The possession of that power by a larger number of people makes it more likely that it will be responsibly deployed.

g Senior members of the school are kept genuinely *in touch* with day-to-day events and opinions, just as junior members of staff are kept in touch with strategic developments. This, together with 'walking the floor', is much more effective than the open door, 'anybody can walk into my office', approach – an attitude held by those in authority which rarely produces the benefits claimed.

h There is an invaluable *escape valve* for tensions and grievances. Although most staff grievances require thorough analysis and treatment, an important minority are actually resolved by being expressed. Having 'made their point', the members of Department X will go ahead and implement the change in the curriculum that they have fought so strongly to prevent. The feelings of mutual suspicion that have been building up between Departments Y and Z will begin to evaporate once the matter is aired.

i There will be greater *staff cohesion*. Where the curriculum demands the crossing of discipline boundaries and team teaching by people from differing academic backgrounds with varying teaching conventions, then team building is aided by this cohesion.

Drawbacks

a The most obvious problem is the very great deal of *time* that is taken up. 20 people may spend an hour discussing something that could have been decided by one person in five minutes. As participative structures mature, participants discuss at length only those matters which need to reconcile important differences, while matters best decided by individuals will be left for individuals to deal with. But the early stages of participation are notorious for producing a great deal of 'inefficient' discussion. Also the substance of discussion needs constant repetition due to the varying membership of groups.

b There is a tendency to *re-invent the wheel*. Everything gets back to fundamentals unless the discussion is carefully chaired. An interesting example is the time spent on multicultural education; debating what 'multicultural' means.

c In practice participation *does not involve all*. Those who attend become highly involved, but they have no particular constituency to report back to. Those who do not attend and do not have a representative, or someone else, to ask afterwards would be less well informed than through traditional Heads of Department/Heads of Year meetings.

d It is often difficult to establish *monitoring* of a decision's after-effects. There is a danger that everyone is the father of success, while failure remains an orphan.

e A few *dominant individuals* can have a profound influence on meetings and decisions without bearing any responsibility for the consequences. Undesirable changes can be railroaded by a vociferous minority, but this minority is needed if all contributions are to be obtained.

f Many teachers seek the *security* of knowing what is expected of them and where they stand. They feel threatened by the participative process.

g Participation can become *the end rather than the means*. The process of participating can become more important in some people's minds than the objectives that the process is intended to produce. Internal wrangling and lobbying can preoccupy teachers and deflect them from the main task of teaching.
h The process of change can be *slow*, as support has to be solicited from most colleagues rather than only the Head.
i Poor decisions are *legitimated* by majority support.
j Unworkable decisions are more likely if reached by those who do not have a *responsibility for implementation*.

Conclusion

The fact that we collected material about participation reflects at least two things. First, we felt it was an important issue – several of the teachers attached to the project felt passionately about it. Second, this passion was often demonstrated in the schools we visited and particularly in individual interviews. Why should this be?

a The ideal of a democratic, collegiate profession is a vision held dear by many teachers, especially when so many feel that the profession has lost the social esteem that it used to enjoy.
b The enormous number of changes being imposed on schools require the expertise of all to be fully deployed in the integrated processes of the school. It is increasingly impracticable for management to be undertaken only by senior staff.
c To get initiatives working in practice as well as on paper needs to have people involved in making the decisions, because they are then committed to trying to make them work; 'people will support that which they have helped to create.'
d There is a need to co-ordinate expertise across the school for some of the new whole-school initiatives such as TVEI, Multicultural Education and Special Needs.
e Staff mobility is generally reduced when compared with the situation up to 1980, so teachers are staying in one school for longer periods and enjoying fewer opportunities for promotion. They therefore look for a more diversified involvement in their school and would like to influence decisions at a lower level in the hierarchy than was usual in the past.

For participation to be effective and not just a show piece, the staff need to have the confidence and trust to participate. This comes through the school culture, through appreciating and valuing each other, and through learning to trust. The best training for participation is to participate.

Participation brings with it its own difficulties; part of the new trend to school-focussed INSET will be the need to educate staff about the dynamics of working in groups, and to train them to get the most out of meetings. As Hargreaves (1982) pointed out:

> Most secondary school teachers lack the skills needed to work together . . . They have a defective sense of classroom co-operation. They can co-ordinate with one another, certainly, but in matters of collaboration, the strong form of co-operation, they must be judged remedial.

And as Southworth (1987) wrote:

> A collaborative, collegial staff requires certain pre-conditions (trust, acceptance of each other, stability) and will demand of all staff greater skills in handling group and interpersonal dynamics.

Not all staff want full participation, and some teachers have patterns of dependence on the Head which have become deeply ingrained.

There is also the risk of the process of participation being badly handled, accidentally or deliberately, and thus becoming discredited. Sham consultation is even worse than no consultation at all, and teachers are very good at seeing through it (Nias, 1980). A further problem is that, for most schools, a change to a participative system would in itself constitute yet another innovation to be coped with!

Nevertheless, we are convinced by our interviews and observations that participation is a necessary and realistic way forward in the management of schools, and it would in any event be a change 'cutting with the grain' of the majority of staff. The alternative would be a teaching body which is increasingly instrumental and alienated.

Simple steps towards increased participation may be to reconstitute the staff meeting as a decision-making body or open up the Heads of Department meeting to any staff who want to attend.

Do It Yourself

1 While we were working in William Barnes a new *curriculum statement* was prepared and the following groups were consulted:

- whole-staff meeting addressed by Headteacher for one hour;
- whole staff in 20-minute (maximum) House meetings;
- non-teaching staff in meeting with Headteacher;
- some parents.

After these discussions staff comments were reported in the Staff Bulletin.

In your own school:

a Who would decide that a new curriculum statement was needed?
b Who would write the first draft?
c Who would be consulted?
d How would the final version of the statement be made public?
e How would the proposals be implemented?
f How could any of the steps *a* to *e* above be done more effectively?
g i Would the methods of consultation used at William Barnes be appropriate in your school?
ii If 'no', why not? Be as precise as you can about the points in the curriculum statements where the methods would fail.
iii If 'yes', are there, nevertheless, methods which would work better in your school? What strengths are you playing to?

2 Take the list of disadvantages of increased participation earlier, and think how you would counteract these arguments.

References

Hargreaves, D., *The Challenge of the Comprehensive School*, Routledge and Kegan Paul, London, 1982.

Nias, J., 'Leadership Styles and Job-satisfaction in Primary Schools', in Bush, T. *et al.*, *Approaches to School Management*, Harper and Row, London. 1980.

Southworth, G.W., 'Changing Management in Primary Schools', in Reid, K. *et al.*, *Towards the Effective School*, Basil Blackwell, Oxford, 1987.

Chapter 8
Change

Change is one of the catchwords of the 1980s and an ability to manage change is a prime requirement of management success in the commercial world. This is largely due to competition and the need to innovate in the product market if one is to survive. The new design, or next year's model, or the new range are all the staging posts of keeping the business in business. The situation in schools is clearly different and makes it important that industrial comparisons are made with care. Between schools there is rivalry rather than competition, and that stimulus to change is relatively unimportant. If the curriculum is the product, then schools all produce the same thing. If children and their parents are the customers, then they are looking for similarity of product wherever they go, so that they can move from St Albans to St Asaph and pick up where they left off, knowing that *their* customers – employers and higher education – can only comprehend and respond to a standard product. Innovation in schools is centred on presentation of the product, not on the product itself; that is imposed by others.

Schools are faced, more than ever before, with a bewildering amount of change to absorb. Many of the demands for change come from external sources such as the DES, the LEA, HMI, advisors and governing bodies, and many initiatives are imposed hurriedly in a 'top – down' maner. In trying to cope with all these external demands, schools are in danger of losing their ability to identify their own problems and generate their own self-directed change. The management of change means not only responding to what is imposed, it also means creating opportunities for those within to develop their school, their department, their curriculum and themselves.

To some people change means excitement and the thrill of keeping up with the Joneses. For others change is a threatening dismantling of a stable order of things, bringing with it a great deal of frightening uncertainty. Four broad types of change experience can be identified.

1 *Imposition* is where the initiative comes from someone else and we have to alter our ways to comply with this new requirement. We lose our sense of security in being able to handle what we know. We can only respond and our response will be cautious because someone else has already made the rules. GCSE and the new curriculum are the obvious examples in this category.
2 *Adaptation* is where we have to modify our behaviour or learn new attitudes at someone else's instigation. This is very difficult, as the persistence of racial prejudice demonstrates, and we lack confidence in our ability to become the new type of person that is needed. The main reason why people retire early is because they lack the confidence to change the values and behaviours on which they have come to rely. Changes in school organisation or attempts to change school culture all pose problems of individual adaptation.
3 *Growth* is much more attractive, as the benefits to the individual are of greater competence, poise and achievement. We may be responding to the demands of others, but the scope for individual betterment is at the centre of our response. Promotion, transfer to a new school or change of duties within a school all offer this type of opportunity.
4 *Creativity* is where we personally instigate and control the process of innovation, bringing into being that which we have envisaged. Being creative is one of the most fundamental of human drives and most teachers in general conversation will refer with greatest pride to those aspects of their career where they did something that was their very own in this sense.

Most people are probably resistant to the first, uncertain about the second, delighted with the third and excited by the fourth. A familiar strategy of dealing with the problems of 1 and 2 is to offer someone the third – more money or status for the person who will take on the problems of TVEI or integrated curriculum. A part of the art of management, however, is to appreciate and offer a range of growth opportunities to as many people as possible: promotion is not the only means of growth. A further aspect of the art of management is to open up opportunities for creativity, as those who become creative become even more creative and a creative approach not only generates its own excitement, it also makes the bogeys of imposition and adaptation less frightening.

If we may be permitted a short homily: never write people off. No-one is too old to grow; no-one is too staid or ossified to lack *all* creative potential – well, hardly anyone.

Current practice

One of the most powerful 'tensions' that came to the surface was that between the need to adapt to changing demands and avoid stagnation, and the need for consolidation, stability and respite from change. Somehow, schools need to strive to attain an optimum balance of novelty and comfort for both pupils and staff, and to be aware that this is a legitimate goal. Scitovsky (1976) discusses how a number of psychologists believe that the novelty/comfort balance in human beings is always in a state of flux and that we are all constantly trying to maintain an equilibrium. Too much comfort can lead to stagnation and torpor, while too much novelty can produce neurosis. The young can generally cope with novelty better than those who are older, and this causes the tendency for many job advertisements to put in an upper age limit of 40 or 45.

The following is an example of mutual incomprehension regarding this process.

At Montgomery High, what staff described as stability, top management referred to as stagnation. Staff, who appeared to be confident and cohesive, attributed improvements in the school to the fact that many of the staff had been there for over ten years. Senior management, however, perceived the staff to be blinkered by the walls of their classrooms, entrenched and out-of-date, attributing improvements in the school to management's own strenuous efforts. There was little comprehension that the stability and cohesion of the staff constituted one of the strengths of the school.

There was a danger that attempts by senior management to 'shake up' the staff not only risked being ineffective but might also endanger the balance that currently existed for the staff between novelty and comfort. On the other hand, there was no recognition by the staff that the existence of a large body of long-serving members of staff could lead to a lack of innovation. Accordingly, unless the perception that comfort was unreservedly good could be modified, outright rejection by staff of senior management's attempts to get rid of certain elements of stagnation would continue to exist.

Tension between the 'old guard' and the 'young Turks' exists in schools, as in most organisations. At Pennine End school, the 'old guard's' perceptions of their Head of Department role had limited the Headteacher's scope for curriculum and other changes within the school. Unlike their younger colleagues who acquired new ideas from courses and study, Heads of Department were finding it hard to come to terms with new demands, such as mixed-ability teaching, courses for less academic pupils and fresh approaches to learning. Initiatives from senior management, as in many other schools we researched, were dismissed as publicity stunts or jumping on bandwagons.

Where a large body of staff have been at one school for a long period, there often exists a 'golden age' myth. Staff at Central High looked back on the successful seventies with a simplistic nostalgia, and lack of excitement with the present may have hampered the ability of the school to adapt to changed circumstances. We discovered that things which existed in the past were often perceived by current members of staff to be better in some way. The previous Head of Department or Head Caretaker had done a better job, the House system which was abolished two years ago had apparently solved a lot of pastoral problems in its time, or the Year system introduced three years ago had created additional problems which did not previously exist. The difficulties associated with the previous regime are not retained in the mind, and the circumstances in which the school was then operating may well have been different.

All change is motivated by one person or a group of people, but many changes do not go in the direction wanted by the motivated person. At Pennine End school, a curriculum review was instituted by the Headteacher and carefully planned. However, while being highly successful in achieving a sense of purpose for its duration, it failed to have any long-lasting result. The Headteacher said: 'Whilst we were doing it there was a sense of coherence – but afterwards, nothing. There was no apparent long-term effect.' This seemed to be because the review was introduced in a vacuum, with the school having had no previous experience of teamwork activities of this kind.

Many schools were able to show us that there is a world of difference between a well intentioned declaration on paper and a real commitment to bring about a change in practice or curriculum. At St Elmo's, a proposal for a new curriculum structure and new consultative methods was nearly shelved when the school failed in its TVEI replication funding bid, since the 'pressure was now off' – in other words, the commitment to those changes was not very deep. At Park school, which had a local reputation as being highly involved with curriculum change, we found that much of the involvement was purely cosmetic and resulted in little change in practice, with little contribution to the growth or direction of the school.

Westcliffe school, which had successfully established a good reputation against all odds upon comprehensivisation 11 years previously, had not recently taken on board any initiatives such as TVEI, integrated curriculum, or alternative curriculum strategies, but staff seemed to comment continually about how well thought of and how advanced the school was. In contrast, at Barnes school, where many new initiatives were now taking place after a long period of stagnation under a previous Headteacher, staff felt they were having an uphill struggle to keep abreast of all the changes demanded of them. These two schools had altered their position on the cycle of change without really being conscious of it.

Examples of good practice

We found that where high-quality human relationships exist, members of staff have the confidence to question themselves and each other, and are able to distinguish between useful change, and change for change's sake.

At Valley High, members of one department created an environment open to change by constantly interacting with each other, sharing new materials, seeing each other teach; they looked to themselves for salvation, not to outside agencies. The pressures to change came from their peers, not from their superiors. At Hillside school, staff were encouraged to be involved in outside bodies and meetings, and there was accordingly an openness to individuals and ideas from outside.

Whilst politicking does exist in schools, and can be a very effective initiator of change, our research shows that change can be and often is planned in schools in a less self-centred and more rational manner. The Heads of Department at Summerfield High who were discussing the adoption of a formula system for the allocation of capitation did not seem to be unduly disturbed by whether their own departments would come out better or worse under a new system, but concentrated on what seemed to be the most 'felt-fair' method of allocation.

Both Finance and Timetabling Committees at Jackson school operated on a system of departmental representation by a member of a different department, so that self-interest was tempered. The environment which encourages change via this latter method seems to be an environment of trust. Senior management can give staff confidence if it is seen to believe that groups of staff can bring about change. For this not to lead to a haphazard collection of unco-ordinated change, it helps if, as we came across at Hillside and Churchbrook schools, there is a shared view of the priorities of the school, and hence of the direction of change.

Conclusion

We discuss elsewhere the importance of understanding culture. Some cultures are more accepting of change and these will tend to coincide with non-hierarchical structures, simply because any change will test the structures themselves if approvals have to be sought and granted. But it is not enough to say that 'flatter' structures are more innovative; first, because schools are saddled with hierarchical structures of salaries and responsibility; second, because the most important impact of a change is not on a structure but on the people it contains.

A major problem for secondary schools is that so much change is being sought so quickly. Psychologically, we rely on several firm features of our lives and we can cope with, even welcome, change if some of these features remain untouched at any one time. Toffler (1970) called these features *stability zones* and sensitive management would recognise when its workforce felt these to be threatened. Many important stability zones lie outside the school (the family, the church and so on) but committed teachers as employees are unusual for the degree to which their work provides stability zones such as cameraderie, professional pride, the annual play and the long summer break. That work takes place within the culture of a school and, therefore, one aspect of introducing change must include an assessment of its 'cultural fit'; the less good the fit, the greater the skill needed for a successful outcome.

The process of developing a feeling of ownership for a new idea needs to be mastered by management. Again, 'flatter structures' work better because ownership is more readily and genuinely passed between relative equals. The remote Head imposing an idea seems likely to be less successful than the one who talks it through openly beforehand. The very talking through serves to answer two major concerns of the managed; these are 'What's in it for me?' (usually nothing material in teaching, but even this is better faced than not) and 'What does it really mean?' (many changes seem, at first sight, more drastic than they really are and it is the unknowns surrounding dry initial statements which cause most concern).

It is inevitable, given existing educational management structures, that much change to a school will be introduced by the Head at the behest of external bodies. The Head and the Senior Management Team need to identify appropriate members of their staff to assist change processes. Some of these will be the school's 'gatekeepers' (Allen and Cohen, 1969), those who keep themselves well informed of developments, naturally, in their subjects, in neighbouring schools and so on. These are important because they can help clarify the implications of a proposed change and because their technical expertise will lend authority to the proposals when wider discussions are held. Unfortunately, this same group is likely to include those who are best at generating their own ideas for change; management needs to avoid overloading this group. Other staff, perhaps union representatives or just the proverbial 'strong personalities', may need to be involved to reduce obstacles to change.

Advice on managing change comes from research in schools by Loucke-Horsley and Hergert (1985) quoted by Fullan (1986, p. 79). They base their guidelines on seven steps:

1 establishing the project;
2 assessment and goal setting;
3 identifying a solution;
4 preparing for implementation;
5 implementing the project;
6 reviewing progress and problems;
7 maintenance and institutionalisation.

They give the following wise advice:

1 *Acting* is better than *planning*. Protracted needs assessment can be worse than none at all.

2 The Head is not *the* key to school improvement. Although the Head is important, so are many other people.
3 Thinking you can truly create ownership at the beginning of a project is ridiculous. Like trust, ownership and commitment build and develop over time through the actual work of improving a school.
4 Help and support given to teachers *after* planning and initial traning is much more crucial for success than the best (pre-implementation) training money can buy.
5 Coercion is not always bad. A firm push, coupled with lots of help, can launch a project on a path to success.
6 New programmes and practices imported from somewhere else offer a viable, cost-effective . . . alternative to major development efforts.

While we recognise that some of this advice is at odds with several of our general findings, the challenging way it has been put should encourage faint-hearted managers to get on with the job of introducing those changes which have to come.

Do It Yourself

1 Idenfify a situation in your school whcih you would like to change and ask the following questions:

a What is the present situation and how has it arisen?
b Why is it problematic?
c How could it be different?
d What would stop us changing it, and what would help us do that?
e What problem are we really trying to solve?
f If we made a change, who would be affected?
g What would their reaction be, and why might they have these reactions?
h Therefore, how will we proceed?

2 Richards (1985, pp. 49–50) identifies these 'killer' responses to ideas and arguments. Can you identify occasions on which these have occurred?
What would more positive response have been? Can you honestly say you have never used these negative responses yourself?

- 'It will cost too much.'
- 'We've never done things that way.'
- 'If it's that good, why hasn't someone here done it already?'
- 'It's been done before.'

- 'Yes, but . . .'
- 'It can't be done that way.'
- 'It's impossible.'

References

Allen, Thomas J. and Cohen, Stephen I., 'Information Flow in Research and Development Laboratories', in *Administrative Science Quarterly*, 14 (1), pp. 12–19, 1969.

Fullan, M.G., 'The Management of Change', in *The Management of Schools*, Hoyle, E. and McMahon, A. (Eds), Kogan Page, London, 1986.

Loucke-Horsley, S. and Hergert, L.F., *An Action Guide to School Improvement*, Association for Supervision and Curriculum Development, Andover, Mass, 1985.

Rickards, T. *Creative Problem-solving for Managers*, Gower, Aldershot, 1985.

Scitovsky, T., *The Joyless Economy*, Oxford University Press, Oxford, 1976.

Toffler, A., *Future Shock*, Pan, London, 1970.

Further reading

Fullan *M.G. op. cit.,* (1986).

Stewart, V., *Change: the Challenge for Management*, McGraw Hill, London, 1983.

Part Two: Management Work

Chapter 9
Personal Credibility and Effectiveness

We use *credibility* to mean such things as being worthy of belief, trustworthy, convincing or being respected. It is closely related to authority as it is a source of influence and, consequently, legitimate power. It is not a right conferred upon people by office or by delegation; it has to be earned and sustained. People with high credibility are listened to and can get things done willingly by colleagues, where those lacking credibility meet resistance, misunderstanding or prevarication. Those without credibility have to rely on formal mechanisms to get things done and tend to reduce the morale of those working closely with them.

By *privilege* in schools we mean some or all of: larger salaries, less contact time, smaller classes, less marking, easier classes, non-teaching assistance, own room, telephone (particularly with an outside line). Additionally, privilege might mean jobs where success, and consequently failure, is hard to measure.

Some management writers make the point that the whole of management theory has been constructed to justify, support and maintain managers as quasi-owners and so sustain their privileged position in the organisation and society generally (see Bendix, 1956). Child (1969, p. 219) argues that British management thinking creates the idea of management as a profession possessing distinct managerial skills resting on knowlege, and so encourages the notion of management prerogatives. In schools the idea of senior staff as managers is relatively recent, dating from the 1960s. All too many of those holding senior posts in schools are seen by their colleagues as construing management as enjoying the privilege of being apart, with an emphasis on clean, gentlemanly work, being part of an ordered elite, and away from the hurly-burly of the real essence of schools, which is contact with the children. Our observations show there are a number of people holding senior posts who fit this sceptical stereotype. They enjoy, and sometimes flaunt, their privileges, but always then have a problem of credibility with those denied the same privileges.

Those with privilege have to work hard and consistently to maintain the credibility they need if they are to be effective.

Current practice

We found that in the eyes of the ordinary staff in secondary schools the following groups were particulary prone to suffer credibilty problems:

a Deputies. They were sometimes seen as doing low-grade clerical work and having little contact with the children. It was very rare for Heads to suffer this problem, because of the conspiracy to maintain the prestige of the figurehead.
b Senior Teachers. A similar problem to the Deputies when Senior Teacher posts were used as 'pure' management posts rather than as Heads of Subject or Pastoral Teams.
c ESL staff, Section 11 staff and Special Needs support staff. These were often seen as working with only one child, with no marking or examination classes.
d Teachers on secondment. Particularly 'old style' personal growth secondments that are sometimes seen as self-indulgent.
e Individuals with reduced timetables for cross-school responsibilty or championing new initiatives. Again, these are sometimes seen as individuals getting on bandwagons of fashion for personal gain.

These problems of credibility can be overcome, and frequently are, by individuals who ensure that both the quality and quantity of their work is appropriate to their constituency. For example, many Deputies and Senior Teachers were praised for the systematic approach to difficult children, Special Needs staff who had trained staff to deal with mixed-ability classes were often highly regarded, as were those who had made the new records of achievement appropriate to the particular needs of the children in their location.

Problems of credibility for senior staff in Park School

There is a distinct difference in what the Senior Management Team regard as important and that which is most valued and prestigious to the staff as a whole. In simple terms the staff value work in and around the classroom and the pupils, whilst the SMT espouse the supreme importance of management work. The fact that the structure grows larger and larger gives them increasing opportunity to busy themselves and, in their own eyes, appear more and more hardworking to the staff; but this is counter-productive because they are just re-emphasising the unimportant and so widening the gulf between themselves and the rest of the staff. Nearly all staff commented on Executive members always being too busy with something far more important to turn up on time to teach.

Supply teachers who found themselves with time to be filled were often used to take the classes of senior staff to allow them to be involved with management work, much of which could have been done at another time, if it needed to be done at all.

The Head rarely taught the four periods a week to which he was committed, causing regular public annoyance due to need for cover. An illustration of this point is the Executive teacher who posts a small notice, each morning, giving details of visitors in school, meetings, working parties, course involvement, etc. If there is nothing the Executive sees as important, he simply puts as the only item –'1. Seems like a quiet day!' The joke is lost and is a constant source of annoyance for the bulk of the staff, who are leaving the staffroom to face a strenuous day's teaching often made more exacting by the demands for cover.

Almost all change comes from the top and is disseminated through the SMT. Because the Head is so keen to follow all trends and to keep the school reputation for being first in almost every field, those charged with the responsibility for the implementation are kept busy. However, commitment to change decreases as it descends the pyramid and those who seem most enthusiastic for the particular flavour of the month are often mainly concerned to enhance their curriculum vitae. An example of this is the last Deputy who recently gained a Headship. One of his many curricular reforms was the total transformation of the tutor period as part of the introduction of a Personal and Social Education course. In reality, as one experienced Year Head pointed out, 'He bought a set of books for each year but they were never used after the first week. Form time is much as it always has been. The good teachers who get on with the kids well put it to any number of good uses.'

Many major changes exist almost entirely on paper. The staff development programme is the best example. The booklet details the various processes through which every member of staff has progressed and is packed with detailed information. Many staff could not even remember the booklet; some have vague memories of appointments being made with the Head but not being kept as he was then too busy with something else.

Over-commitment brings with it further involvement of the SMT away from the school. Less and less attention is paid to seeing if change really occurs in practice. The increasing remoteness of the decsion makers from those that are charged with the responsibility for action is a major obstacle in the way of meaningful progress.

Because the school is 'involved' in so many initiatives it is an ideal place for furthering a career. This strengthens the power of the Head and further alienates those that have served and maintained the reality of collective classroom life over a number of years. This factor is not helped by the Head regularly being interviewed for posts for which applications have been made successively after only two years at the school. When he is successful, the problem of re-establishing trust will be the major challenge for the new Head.

The Ridgeway

The three Deputies at The Ridgeway school are not responsible for the situation in which they find themselves: the apparent gap between themselves and many of the staff. That responsibility lies primarily with the Head.

The Head monopolises all those managerial responsibilities which might lend credibility to a Deputy Head. She has delegated little of any substance to them, retaining, for example, curriculum organisation and development, timetabling, and the co-ordination of the work of the Heads of Department. The Heads of Year are widely recognised for their competence in the guidance and control of pupils, and seldom need to involve the Deputies, who therefore are rarely involved directly in pastoral matters.

These two areas of school life, curriculum and pastoral, are the areas which impinge most on teachers' working lives. Since the Deputies are not perceived as having any direct involvement in either, they must inevitably lose credibility in the eyes of the staff.

The quandary of the Deputies is exacerbated by the fact that the jobs left to them are not 'rated' by teachers because they are administrative rather than managerial. By their very nature these jobs tend to be less visible and therefore engender the 'what do they do?' reaction.

The Deputies' professional unpopularity is thus related to the type of jobs they are required to do, decisions about which are outside their control.

Example of Section 11 and Special Needs staff at Oakhill School

There were three Section 11 staff selected internally. None of them were clear what their role should be as this school had a high Afro-Caribbean population so the language needs were not so pronounced as schools with a high Asian population. All three were keen and spent a lot of time talking to staff, but were uncertain what to do next and therefore spent a lot of time sitting in the staffroom. As one said to us, 'It's completely different from before. Now we are managing our own time and each week is different. I always carry some reading because staff can't always make it.' The Special Needs staff in the same school was an assorted collection of individuals with spare capacity on their timetable – sometimes with as much as three quarters of their timetable in Special Needs – except the Head of Department who was an expert. Many teachers resisted having these Special Needs teachers supporting in their classes as they were felt to be useless.

Examples of individuals from various schools with potential credibility problem.

a A Scale 4 English teacher seconded for a year on profiling, returned to set up a system for the school and dropped his role as Head of English as well as some teaching.
b A Scale 4 teacher who had developed PSE, Special Needs support and profiling in the last three years who was virutally off timetable.
c A senior teacher who had been acting Head of Lower School for two years, was not appointed to the post when it was advertised, but then given a permanent Senior Teacher post with no particular role. She fills in for other senior staff.
d A Scale 4 teacher who had been in charge of community liaison but the local policy was to drop this. He currently was part of the Section 11 team mentioned above.
e A Scale 3 Humanities teacher, who had developed a serious hearing loss, being used as an administrative assistant for the pastoral staff and all tutors.

Many of these were well respected by the staff in their schools, others were not. Why?

The people who are seen to have a problem of credibility within schools are usually those with several constituencies. For example, school managements have increasing demands from the DES, LEA, governors and parents as well as the staff within the school. Section 11 and Special Needs staff are charged with implementing legislation changing the way particular children are grouped in schools. They may then have difficulty balancing their credibility in the various networks to which they belong. The pressure for promotion often tempts people to nurture their credibility outside the school. Although this may enhance their career prospects, for them to be effective they need to enhance their credibility within the school. With privilege comes responsibility and this needs to be a real responsibility that is worth carrying out. How can this best be done?

There are two types of authority: to be *in* authority or to be *an* authority. In authority is the position or title which permits the owner to have power over others. Carter (1979) discusses how this authority is dependent on other sources of power, for example control of resources, to maintain itself. Being an authority is having the skill, knowledge and expertise that others consult willingly. It is surprising that senior staff and others with special responsibility so casually drop their expertise in the main task of schools, dealing with the children. For within school we found that contact with the children, reliability, resources and reducing others' problems were most frequently mentioned by teachers as features lending credibility to a colleague. It is this 'down to earth' quality that ensures that new ideas are based in reality and that there is a ready-made network to put changes into practice. It is in everyone's interest that those with privilege maintain their credibility within the school – not just to reduce the envy of those who do not have privilege.

Good practice

William Barnes School

Two of the three Deputy Head Teachers were recent appointments in a well established school. Derek arrived in September replacing a long-serving predecessor. Despite many people's initial wariness of a new person, he had established a lot of respect by the time we arrived in December. He was 33, which was very young for this staff.

The basis of Derek's acceptance was:

a He was reliable – if he said he would do something he did.
b He was consistent.
c He set up order – he set up systems for reports, discipline, exams, meetings, etc.
d He was visible – he patrolled the building, dining room, playground.
e He acted as go-between between staff and Headteacher, reporting each to the other.
f He took up individual problems but referred them to the system first.

Do It Yourself

1 What is the basis of your credibility within your school?
2 How much of your credibility is based on things you did before this academic year?
3 How many hours have you spent with children at school in the last week? Were other adults present?
4 What is your expertise within the school? How do you ensure this is still relevant?

References

Bendix, R., *Work and Authority in Industry*, Harper and Row, New York 1956.

Child, J., *British Management Thought*, Allen and Unwin, London 1969.

Carter, A., *Authority and Democracy*, Routledge and Kegan Paul, London 1979.

Further reading

Mant, A., *The Rise and Fall of the British Manager*, Pan, London 1979.

Chapter 10
Technical, Administrative and Managerial Work

One Deputy said to us: 'What this school needs is fewer Deputies and more clerks. Any literate sixteen-year-old could do this.'

One way of analysing the work of individual managers is to distinguish between their technical, administrative and managerial work. *Technical* work is that work that managers do because of their profession, experience or qualification. In schools this means teaching, preparing and marking the children's work, and anything involving the children directly; and discussing curriculum with colleagues. *Administrative* work is concerned with organisational maintenance. It is carrying out official, often regular, duties authorised by others; it is usually clerical work. In schools this includes filling in returns, making lists, putting out chairs in the hall, trying to get through on the telephone, using the photocopier and sorting papers out. *Managerial* work is that work a manager does which entails setting precedents. It often involves influencing others to assent to some non-obvious decision or behaviour. It is getting something done that would not have been done otherwise. In schools this involves such things as discussing with teachers how the timetable can be better next year, regrouping the children in the third year, walking round the school to pick up on what is happening, deciding the agenda for a meeting. Managers also have time spent on *social* activities which are the everyday social interchanges of organisational life and an essential part of anyone's work to create and sustain a sufficient network to get the job done. Some time has to be spent on purely *personal* matters, such as telephone calls with a spouse or fixing an appointment for the car to be serviced. Someone doing administration will also do managerial work. All managers' jobs contain all of these, no manager would have a zero for any category.

Current practice

Table 4 gives the results of our observations of 70 people who were observed for either a half day or a whole day, depending on their

Table 4: Percentage of time spent by 70 senior staff on different activities

	% of Time				
	Social	Technical	Administrative	Managerial	Personal
6 Headteachers and Acting Headteachers					
Mean	2.8	23	11	60.7	1.3
Range	0–6	3–64	4–18	27–82	0–4
33 Deputy Headteachers and Acting Deputy Headteachers					
Mean	5	21.2	31.27	39.3	2.6
Range	1–14	0–50	12–77	4–76	0–24
7 Senior Teachers					
Mean	5.4	33.3	27	30.9	2.4
Range	0–10	11–54	9–48	10–50	0–14
12 Heads of House/Year/Parts of School					
Mean	4.4	37.6	29.2	22.9	3.4
Range	0–23	9–62	2–58	5–65	0–12
10 Heads of Department, Faculty, Curriculum Area					
Mean	6.4	33.8	24	28.1	4.2
Range	3–14	0–67	7–53	15–56	0–16
2 Joint Heads of Subject and Pastoral Team					
Mean	9	48	18	24	1.5
Range	2–16	44–52	15–21	9–38	0–3

commitments. We categorised the activities as we observed them on the day they did least teaching.

To give more of the flavour of these observations, Table 5 gives three examples of one hour each. After typing these, the project secretary said, 'Is that what they do? I could do that!'

Perhaps the most stunning figure is the average amount of time Deputies (31%), Senior Teachers (27%), and Heads of pastoral (29%) and curriculum areas (24%) spend on low-grade clerical duties, that is, administrative work. Headteachers (11%) and those with both a pastoral and a curriculum responsibility (18%) are less likely to have such a high proportion of their time spent this way. Why is this so?

We have argued elsewhere (Torrington and Weightman, 1982, 1985, 1988) that managers need to examine the balance of their work. Table 6 summarises the advantages and disadvantages of the different sorts of work. It is important for several reasons that those with senior posts maintain their technical work. First, it is important for themselves, as often it is a source of pride in being able to do something well; it is the only way of really keeping in touch with the school's work; and it is the basis of being an authority through expertise. Second, maintaining technical work is important for the school so that experienced, able teachers continue to work with the pupils. Third, maintaining technical work is important for other members of staff. They can seek advice from someone who is seen to know what the problems are. All of these suggest that maintaining technical work is important for credibility.

The administrative work that senior staff do can create serious problems for both them and the school. When senior staff are seen doing a lot of low-grade clerical work their authority and credibility with the staff are seriously undermined. This is particularly true where non-teaching staff, who have been trained in this type of work, could do it more effectively. There are various reasons why many senior staff do more administrative work than they should. First, there is the attraction of actually being able to complete something. Getting to the bottom of a pile or completing a list can be very comforting in an otherwise hectic day in which everything else seems to have gone wrong. Secondly, when staff are promoted they look round for the new tasks that come with the job and frequently the obvious ones – and those often listed on the job description – are administrative tasks. This often leads to managers creating more administrative tasks in the mistaken belief that this is what management is about; they miss the essence, which is intangible, through focussing on the tangible trivia. Perhaps with increasing financial devolvement schools will be able to employ the non-teaching staff they clearly need and deploy the skilled senior staff in more fruitful ways.

The managerial work of senior staff is always the more uncertain, difficult, challenging and important. Precisely because it is about making things happen that would not otherwise happen all sorts of different skills are involved. Where policy making, decision taking, communications, personnel issues and procedures are all concentrated in the hands of the Headteacher it can be very difficult indeed for other senior staff to see what their managerial work might be. Clarifying this work is an important task for each school staff and those with management posts to undertake. We hope our research might help this process.

The research material we have described here deals with the quantity of work in each category that a teacher has done. It is, of course, a truism that the quality of the work is paramount. We have assumed that the quality within one person's work is equal across the categories and argue that despite the quality argument, the less administrative work done by senior staff and teachers, the better for all. It is ridiculous to see well paid professionals doing work that a properly trained administrator or clerk could do better.

Table 5: Time spent by three Deputy Heads

A: Example of a Deputy Head I

He is large, blue-suited, bearded, open-faced, sincere, caring, likes children. He looks a bit long-suffering.

	% of Time				
	s	T	A	M	p
Day	2	3	19	76	0
Hour	2	2	36	57	0

Time	Activity	Who with	Initiated by self/other	sTAMp
8.40	Conversation with Head re problem pupil	Head	Other	M
8.50	Informing members of staff re problem pupil	Self so far	Self	M
8.54	Spoke to pupil about a problem	Pupil	Other	T/M
8.55	Spoke to caretaker about workmen	Caretaker	Other	A
8.58	Gave pupil a piece of paper	Pupil	Other	A
8.59	Went off to find and inform some members of staff	Teachers	Self	A
9.00	Came back to room to answer telephone	Parent/Secretary	Other	M
9.01	Joan brought in a cup of coffee for him	Joan	Other	S
9.02	Alice came in with slip for him re pupil	Alice	Other	A
9.04	Pat came in with a query	Pat	Other	A
9.04	Tried to get Ray on internal tannoy	Self – no answer	Self	A
9.06	Discussed 3rd Year options brochure	Jean	Other	M
9.10	Answered telephone, Ray	Ray	Other	M
9.10	Discussed brochure with Head and Jean	Head, Jean	Other	M
9.11	Discussed TRIST cover problems with Jean	Jean	Other	M

9.12	Phoned the office re register	Secretary	Self	A
9.13	Left office to go to office	Secretary	Self	A
9.15	Started work on options brochure	Self	Self	M
9.19	Pupil question at door	Pupil	Other	T
9.20	Answered phone, secretary announcing arrival of parent	Secretary	Other	A
9.24	Parent arrived for confidential interview re child, I left	Parent	Other	

B: Example of a Deputy Head II

She is a small, neat woman, ex-PE. She is modest and polite, and makes no pretence at dominating staff.

	% of Time				
	s	T	A	M	p
Day	0.5	23	47	29	0
Hour	1.0	0	75	24	0

8.20	Fed available data into computer in secretary's office for cover	Self	Self	A
8.30	Returns to her own room to sort out messages for announcements	Self	Self	A/M
8.32	Went out to speak to Ian re appointment with a parent	Ian	Self	A
8.34	Returned to room to write out timetable for supply teachers	Self	Self	A
8.35	Peter (DH1) popped head round to remark upon some aspect of the previous night's meeting	Peter	Other	M/S
8.36	Continued, then went on to prepare notices for announcements	Self	Self	A/M
8.37	Back to secretary's office to print out first 'go' of cover by computer	Self	Self	A/M
8.38	Was asked to go to the phone – refused	Secretary 4 (YTS)	Other	A

Time	Activity	Who with	Initiated by self/other	sTAMp
8.38 +	School Secretary 1 informed her of another staff absence message	Secretary 1	Other	A
8.39	School Secretary 4 (YTS) came in with another staff absence message	Secretary 4 (YTS)	Other	A
8.40	Went back to her office to consult her notes	Self	Self	A
8.41	Returned to re-type the information into the computer for second go	Self	Self	A
8.44	Returned to her office to finalise messages	Self	Self	A/M
8.45	Gave messages to Year Heads on phone (internal)	Self	Self	A
8.46	Secretary 1 brought in list of staff not yet signed in	Secretary	Other	A
8.46	John came in with more information on staff arrivals	John	Other	A
8.46 +	All this time Mary was relaying messages to all year staff	Self, all Year Heads through internal phones	Self	A/M
8.49	Back to secretary's room to print out cover slips	Self	Self	A
8.51	Back to own office to cut up cover slips	Self	Self	A
8.53	Back to secretary's office to alter and update cover totals in programme	Self	Self	A
8.55	Finished in office (secs). Wrote up cover list in full for Peter and Joan's information	Self	Self	A
8.58	Took a printed copy of the cover up to pin on the board in the staffroom	Self	Self	A
8.59	Back to office to phone back Education Offices – the call she refused earlier	Official in LEA office	Self?	A
9.02	Pupil called to discuss a Christmas activity. Pupil called to pick up a cover slip	Pupil	Other	A
9.03	Paul came in, query re orals (French)	Paul	Other	A

9.04	Supply teacher called to pick up timetable	Supply	Other	A
9.05	Secretary came in to approve draft letter	Secretary 1	Other	A/M
9.10	Alan came in to query whether getting too many cover periods	Alan	Other	M
9.12	Ian came in to discuss pastoral matters	Ian	Other	M
9.14	We left to allow her to interview a parent			

C: Example of a Deputy Head I in same school as B

He is a tall, thin man, neat, efficient in his own terms, intelligent, hard-working.

	% of Time				
	s	T	A	M	p
Day	7	0	42	49	0
Hour	0	0	30	70	0

9.00	Resumed preparation for Presentation Evening	Alone	Self	A/M
9.07	Returned cups to office	Alone	Self	A
9.08	Spoke to Susie	Susie	Self	A
9.09	Ran to Special Needs Dept. Spoke to Philip	Philip	Self	A
9.10	Spoke to Jane re theft	Jane	Self	M
9.14	Walked through rain back to his room	Alone	Self	A
9.15	Dealing with admin. for Physics Scale 3 post	Self	Self	A
9.18	Checked return slips for Presentation Evening	Self	Self	A
9.19	Took application details to clerk for posting off	Joan	Self	A
9.20	Checked off a return slip for Presentation Evening	Self	Self	A
9.21	Pupil arrived with a Presentation Evening return slip	Pupil	Other	A
9.21	Checked off the pupil's return slip	Self	Self	A
9.22	Off to see how many tables in Arthur's room	Self	Self	A
9.25	Spoke to Arthur re tables for mock exams	Arthur	Self	A

Time	Activity	Who with	Initiated by self / other	sTAMp
9.25	Spoke to Mrs S. re Jane investigation of theft		Self	M
9.27	Interviewed pupil in his office (Asian)	Pupil	Self	M
9.31	Dismissed the pupil, spoke to the interpreter, dismissed him	Asian pupil interpreting	Self	M
9.35	Jane arrived with another pupil and another interpreter re theft	Jane	Other	M
9.36	Began to interview second Asian pupil re theft	Pupil	Self	M
9.41	Dismissed the pupil	Pupil	Self	M
9.41	Spoke to Jane in his room re theft	Jane	Self	M
9.47	Went to speak to Head, who had popped head in door	Head	Other	M
9.48	Went to clerk to ask her to type memo	Joan	Self	A
9.50	Jane arrived with another pupil to interview	Jane	Other	M
9.51	Began to interview pupil through interpreter re theft	Asian pupil	Self	M
9.58	Dismissed this pupil, began to interview another pupil	Another Asian pupil	Self	M
10.05	Dismissed this pupil	Pupil	Self	M

Table 6: The advantages and disadvantages of doing different sorts of work

	Technical	Administrative	Managerial
Advantages	Authority of expertise	Easy to do	Deals with differences between plan and reality
		Even pace	
	Keep in touch with schools' work	Keeps things running smoothly	Make choices and decisions
	Pride in work		Get things done that would not be done otherwise
	School keeps experienced teachers		
	Task-oriented		
	Credibility		
Disadvantages	Lose sight of overall aims of organisation	Subordinates irked by demands	Erratic demands
	'Generalist' skills not developed	Comfort of doing something certain creates more administrative work, particularly when other work is difficult or uncertain	Lot of time spent building networks, which can become more important than getting the job done
	Time it takes	Administrative work can become an end in itself	Beware 'being a manager' compared to doing managerial work
		Takes more time if inappropriate person does it	Difficult to know what should do

Example of good practice

The details given in Table 5, Example A of a Deputy I's morning shows someone doing a large amount of managerial work with a minimum of low-grade clerical work.

Do It Yourself

1 Record how you spend your day at work for at least one day on the form below. Try to do it during the day and not later, so you do not forget the small details. Every time you change activity start a new line. A change of activity is either moving to a new topic or a new person. Meetings count as one activity. Use the classification described above for s, T, A, M, p.

Even if you think you are too busy, it can be done and it is worth doing. If you work in a team it can be very profitable to do it for each other or in pairs, or do it intermittently for an hour at a time.

Time	**Who with**	**Whose initiative**	**sTAMP**	**Notes**

2 What percentage of your time was spent on:

- Technical work?
- Administrative work?
- Managerial work?

a Does this seem reasonable?
b How could you reduce your A work?
c How could you increase your T work?
d How would the teachers in your school view this record of how your day is spent?

e What about the M work that you do – does it fit the culture of your school?

3 This record can also be used to start thinking about how you manage your time.

a Are the interruptions reasonable?
b How much of your day is at your own initiative?
c Can you divide what you are doing into things you *must* do, *should* do and *hope* to do?
d What can be ignored?

A fuller explanation of the application of this method is to be found in Torrington and Weightman, 1987.

References

Torrington, D. and Weightman, J., 'Technical Atrophy in Middle Management', in *Journal of General Management*, Vol. 8. No. 4, 1982.

Torrington, D. and Weightman. J., 'Teachers and the Management Trap', in *Journal of Curriculum Studies*, Vol. 17, No. 21, pp. 197–205, 1985.

Torrington, D. and Weightman, J., 'The Analysis of Management Work', in *Training and Management Development Methods*, Vol. 1, Autumn, 1987.

Torrington, D. and Weightman, J., 'Middle Management Work', *Journal of General Management*, 1988.

Further reading

Stewart, R., *Choices for the Manager*, McGraw-Hill, Maidenhead 1982.

Pedler, M., Burgoyne, J. and Boydell, T., *A Manager's Guide to Self Development*, second edition, McGraw-Hill, Maidenhead 1987.

Chapter 11
Agendas and Networks

Kotter (1982) examined the role of general managers and defined their core behaviour as first setting agendas for action and then establishing and maintaining networks to implement these agendas. Agendas are lists of things to be done, written or not, thought out or not, short-term and long-term. They come about by generating possibilities, questioning plans and proposals, gathering information and calculating ways and means of implementing policies, plans, strategies and agreements. Networks are sets of contacts built up with those working inside and outside the organisation: current and previous colleagues, the bosses' boss and the subordinates' subordinates and many other people within the company and in other companies, customers, suppliers, members of professional bodies and so forth. They are co-operative relationships with people who can help to get things done. The networks Kotter's managers developed included hundreds or thousands of people, and every relationship was different. The network is for sharing ideas, information and resources. It is not the same as the old-boy system, which protects self-interest.

This attractively simple, analytical device seems appropriate to us to help examine the work of those with management work to do in schools, as it emphasises the reality of how things get done rather than the popular view of managers as calmly sitting in offices creating formal plans, control systems and structures, with action following effortlessly on decision.

Current practice

The actual content of agendas and networks will vary from individual to individual and with the role they play in a particular school. It seems, therefore, most useful to discuss the difference between those who have a clear agenda and network and those who do not.

1 Oakhill School: An example where agendas and networks are not well established for the senior staff

The Head has been in post for two and a half years and is still considered new by both himself and the staff. He sees himself as an innovator and has introduced integrated curriculum, a mixed-ability and a year system. He has a closed-door policy, staff can only see him by appointment or outside the school day. He does not go round school. The only time staff see him is during the daily briefing. He is seen by many as a nice man but not a very good Head. He seems to trust only those members of staff who are his own appointments; he makes little attempt to bring others along with him. Suggesting a lack of understanding about how organisations work, he assumes the personal touch will work although he makes no effort to go about the school. He has many agendas but a poor network.

The two Senior Teachers are well established members of the staff, with a pastoral role. They are the stable rock for the staff, but cut off from the Head. He did not see them as senior staff, because they participated in industrial action and thus did not attend meetings after school. They were not used as a bridge between senior staff and school and were not included in timetabled senior staff meetings. They had networks but a restricted agenda.

The Deputies all felt they were running round in circles, busy and frenetic. Brief job descriptions for them were being distributed for the first time whilst we were there. They were so brief as to be quite unclear about what issues each was to handle. There was an inadequate staff handbook so there was little specification of how things should be done. Consequently, there was no certainty about who would do what and action was spontaneous, unpredictable and inconsistent. The Deputies had limited agendas and poor networks.

Consequences

There was a serious split and suspicion between the Head and Deputies on the one hand and the Senior Teachers on the other. This was exacerbated by the Senior Teachers' exclusion from policy meetings. Consequently, their networks of contacts with staff through everyone being a tutor/co-tutor were not used. This contributed to the isolation of the Head, who saw only those who came to see him.

The lack of clarity of roles and responsibility for decisions meant a lot of 'crisis management', an example being a Deputy taking all day to arrange cover because there was so little co-operation. Several meetings whilst we were there took decisions that were then reversed by the Head. Many staff were feeling frustrated, unco-operative and alienated. The management work was often felt to be hectic and appeared chaotic because of a lack of individuals having both agendas and networks. They did not tie down decisions firmly, nor establish contacts to implement them.

2 Summerfield High: An example where both agendas and networks are nurtured by the senior staff

Whilst we were in the school the Headteacher was away for a term's secondment. Alan was acting Headteacher and his Deputy Headteacher role was taken by one of the Senior Teachers. Their basic roles were:

- Acting HT: Headteacher figurehead, main meetings, liaison with outside agencies.
- DHT: Day-to-day administration. Third Year options and pastoral issues.
- DHT: Careers, Fourth and Fifth pastoral.
- Acting DHT: Curriculum/timetable/primary liaison and First and Second Year pastoral.

As a group they theoretically met once per week. In the four weeks of our attachment to the school they only met twice, due to visitors and Alan being out of the school for a spell. This term was obviously different from normal, but felt by most to be not as different as was expected. The Acting Deputy Headteacher was an interesting addition to the senior team as he is far more part of the staff and sought their involvement, for example, he set up a meeting with Heads of Department to decide the timetable. This helped to overcome a problem observed in some other schools of the senior management team being quite separate from the rest of the school and a close-knit self-sufficient group.

This senior management team has a strong *sense of purpose*, constantly emphasising getting things going. In the year we visited they had started pre-vocational visits for Fourth and Fifth Years, industry visits where staff went into industry for two weeks at a time and four people from industry came in for four days, Primary links, and a Special Unit. The Acting Head used words such as 'a first for Summerfield High', 'we are a good school.'

The senior management team also *monitors* things and deals with problems. One Deputy walks round school to ensure that duties are being done. Headteacher and Deputy Headteacher Curriculum see each Head of Department or Head of Subject individually for one hour between curriculum planning meetings, that is, once per half term. They discuss items from the last meeting and the agenda for the next. Whilst we were there this involved next year's timetable, staffing and options. But other subjects are discussed.

This has led to the senior management team *dealing with problems*, particularly personnel problems. In the last two years they have dismissed one Head of Department who was seen to be incompetent, redeployed a teacher who was clearly very difficult, and arranged for a deaf teacher to work half a timetable and complete the contract with administrative work. These three solutions seem to be fully supported by the staff most closely involved. However, they did not always get it right; the disciplining of a member of staff over a jokey bulletin at Christmas was seen as a mistake by both staff and members of the senior management team.

As we discussed in the previous chapter, managerial work is setting precedents. What most members of an organisation want from their managers is an ability to pick up on what is going on, decide what is relevant and then do something about it. It is seeing ahead rather than constantly reacting to crises. For example, realising that numbers of staff will fall and then planning for it; reading HMI's report and thinking we must do so and so; hearing what the LEA is saying and doing something about it; picking up on the daily variations between plans and reality by being available for staff as school starts. To do this effectively, senior staff in schools need to have agendas of both large and small things they want to champion, get information about, influence or do. What these are will be influenced by a particular school's attitude to resources control, co-ordination, participation and change. To put them into effect each person has to develop an appropriate network of relationships which will vary with the person and with the culture of the particular school. Where the agenda or network is poor or inappropriate the work of getting things done becomes more difficult, as it can lead to irritation, frustration and, ultimately, chaos. The trick is having agendas and a network of relationships appropriate to your particular school.

Example of good practice

Terry's day (Deputy at Valley High School)

As with all our examples of good practice, this is not perfect practice. In the context of a real working day, what we particularly admired was the sheer number of different issues and people dealt with in a pleasant way after a frustrating start to the day.

The Head had gone into hospital the previous day and Terry was, therefore, acting Head. At that point he had no idea whether it would be for three weeks or thirteen weeks.

He came in at 9.27am because he had had great difficulty getting his Landrover up some hills near his home. He appeared to be in a foul mood, which made the prospect of tagging along behind him for the day somewhat unnerving. He soon regained his composure and began his day, which included:

- Discussions with the other two Deputies about a parents' meeting which was to take place that evening on the teaching about AIDS.
- Discussions, with one Deputy, on a possible option pattern for an Alternative Curriculum.

- Briefing a new supply teacher who was to take over his Fourth Year classes.
- Trying to sort out the problems created by a strike on the buses which promised to maroon a number of village children in the school at the end of the day.
- Extensive discussions with a range of people (including a Head of House who was on secondment and the teacher doing his job for the year) about a politically sensitive 'exclusion' meeting which was to take place four days later.
- An interview with a mother and her daughter concerning another girl in the school with whom the first girl was in dispute. Terry dealt with this himself because:

a the two girls were in different Houses and he did not have time, or could not be bothered, to write notes to, or find, the two Heads of House who should be involved;
b he was 'in credit' with one of the girls because she had done some good work for him in a lesson;
c both girls were in the Fourth Year and he was the Deputy responsible for the Fourth Year.

- Talking to the Head of Computers, on her initiative, about the morality of forming ability groups in the Fourth Year in a school with a mixed-ability policy. We assumed at the time that she was talking to him as 'Head' but it may have been with his Fourth Year hat on.
- Many attempts to telephone the Chairman of the Governors about the exclusion meeting.
- A meeting at lunchtime in the English Department about how they were going to teach about AIDS in the Third Year.
- Playing the diplomat in the school office in an effort to get one of their number who doubled as a dinner time supervisor off on a training course. Her colleagues were not being particularly co-operative.
- Talking to some children about playing musical instruments.
- Talking to a Head of Department about a problem probationary teacher in their department who was on the verge of failing.
- A long telephone conversation with the Head of another school about the possibility of TVEI extension.
- Attempting to make sense of some of the Head's dictated letters that had not recorded properly.
- A Curriculum Committee meeting which he chaired which went on until 5.15 pm.
- A poorly attended parents' meeting at 7.30pm. on the school's approach to teaching about AIDS.

Terry continued to work in the shared Deputies' room even though the Head's room was available. Most of the telephone calls and some of the interviews were conducted in the Head's room. This meant that he was constantly flitting from one to the other. The benefits of working in a shared office were more apparent than the costs, in that Terry was able to share his problems and bounce ideas off his colleagues whenever he wanted.

Terry's agenda for the day included long-term items such as TVEI extension, Alternative Curriculum; medium-term such as ability groups in computing, the exclusion meeting; and short-term such as the AIDS meeting, children in dispute. The network of contacts involved teachers, non-teaching staff, parents, governor, children and another school. All in one day.

Do It Yourself

1 What is currently on your personal agenda at work?
How does this fit in with the expressed plans for your department, the school, the LEA?
How much of this agenda is there because you want it? How much because you think it will help someone else out?
2 List all the individuals or groups who can affect how effective you are in your job, with whom you have a formal or an informal relationship. Give both names and positions. The drawing, which may look something like Figure 7, will describe your network.

a Rank order the contacts, formal and informal, in their importance to you in getting your job done effectively.
b Rate each contact on a scale between −3 and +3, according to how helpful the person is to you.
c What can be done to improve relationships with those you have rated between −1 and −3?

Rank	Contact	−3 −2 −1 0 1 2 3	Improved by
1			
2			
3			
4			
5			
6			
7			
8			
9			

Figure 7: Network of relationships

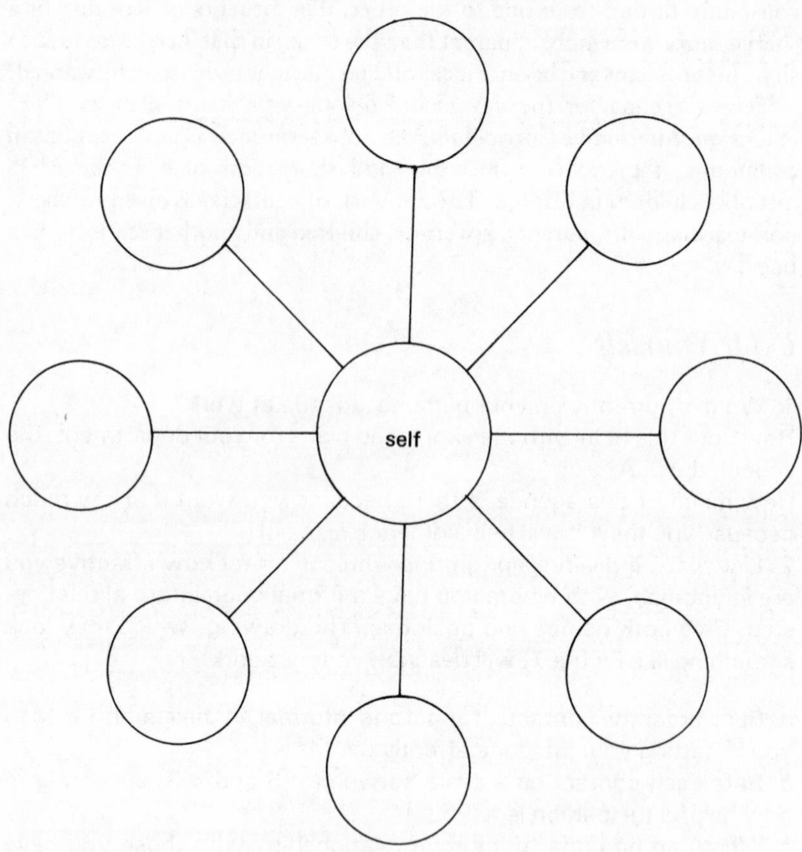

d **Is there anyone who should be in your network but is not yet?**

References

Kotter, J., *The General Manager*, The Free Press, New York 1982.

Chapter 12
Senior Management Meetings

The schools we visited talked frequently about their senior management teams. Murgatroyd (1986) avers that collective management in schools is likely to facilitate more change than charismatic leadership. He defines senior management's task as to review the effectiveness of the school in delivering programmes, managing resource distribution and proposing and managing change. Schools' varying levels of participation by staff may change who manages issues in this list but, in most schools, the senior management would expect to be involved in these tasks. Although there are other management groups in schools, most obviously Pastoral Heads of Year or House and Academic Heads of Department or Faculty, we confine ourselves here to the senior management.

An important part of how the senior management work together is the various meetings they have with each other. We found that in our 24 schools, 19 had scheduled meetings of senior management: two had daily, two twice weekly, fourteen had weekly and one monthly meetings of senior staff.

Current practice

The schools varied in who they included in senior management meetings. We found various forms:

a Conventional. In this form there were the Head and three Deputies, each of whom had one of the standard responsibilities: administration, curriculum and pastoral. In our 24 schools seven had this composition.

The advantages of this arrangement were that the group was small and easy to get together. The staff were clear about whom to see, and senior staff were each clear about their own position. The main problems with this arrangement were that the discrete duties of the three Deputies often isolated them from each other and made team working less likely. There was also likely to be a severe credibility problem for the Deputy with responsibility for administration.

b Modified conventional. This was similar to the first form, except that Senior Teachers were included who often had pastoral responsibilities, such as Head of Sixth Form, Head of Upper or Lower School, or were Heads of main departments. Out of our 24 schools, 14 had this composition.

With this arrangement a wider spectrum of opinion was included in any collective discussion and there was less likelihood of the group becoming a clique. There was the risk, however, that the diversity of background and specialised interest was such that group meetings achieved no more than an exchange of information.

c Idiosyncratic. Some schools had very individual groupings of senior staff. For example, Jackson School included two 'elder statesmen' on Scale 4, and Ridley, a religious school, included the Scale 4 Head of RE.

These arrangements reflected the particular culture and interests of the school. In both examples it helped to tie in the senior management to the rest of the school.

These different groupings of senior management were reflected in who attended the senior management meetings. Some schools had very centralised senior management meetings of Headteacher and Deputy Headteachers. Others were more devolved, to include Senior Teachers, some Scale 4s and appropriate individuals when particular topics were being discussed (see also chapters 14, 15 and 20).

The schools also varied dramatically in *what* was discussed in these senior management meetings. At one extreme the meetings can only be described as 'tea and tattle'. For example, at Westcliffe the content of a one-hour meeting of the Headteacher, three Deputy Headteachers and three Senior Teachers was:

4.09	Discuss	INSET funds
4.12		Whether legwarmers can be worn
15		Fun Run
18		Head of PE
20		Water supply
21		Accident
24		Expedition of Sixth Form
26		Presents for staff leaving
28		Dinner list
29		Outings
31		Next year's tutor list
52		Minibus
54		Letters about exams
55		Duty rota

5.00	Exam results
02	Calendar of events
04	Christmas Fair
05	Reports
06	Timetable
09	Modular curriculum
10	Brochure
5.12	Finish meeting

This school had other meetings, for example, Heads of Faculty and a board of all staff who took decisions. The Headteacher argued that senior management meetings were for team building and cohesion. So the content of the meeting was determined by what the Headteacher allowed.

We certainly found examples of this triviality in other schools and suspect some of this is agenda filling, for a timetabled meeting where the purpose of the meeting is not entirely clear. Most schools held senior management meetings where the agenda, often unwritten, jumped from items of information to major policy decisions. For example, at Francis Bacon School one meeting went from discussing the photographer's visit the next week to detailing the aims of the school.

Other schools had carefully considered what should be discussed at senior management meetings. For example, at Hall End they had different kinds of senior management meetings. Every morning, before school, there was an information swapping meeting about the day's events, forthcoming events, problems. For example:

8.33	Discuss Halloween Disco on 23rd
	Exam dates
	Probationers' meetings in next two weeks
	Study-skill packs available
	First Year assembly
	Teacher governor nominations by Friday
	Supply teacher, Mrs. S, in school
	Bilingual assistant
	Jackie (secretary) overloaded so can we decide priorities for her
8.45	Finish

On Monday evenings, after school, there were meetings to discuss issues. For example:

3.56	Discuss	Minutes – Duty Rota
57		Fire practice – PE and wheelchair problem
4.00		Exams
05		TVEI and Section 11 children

10	Option dates
20	Lunchtime supervision
36	Observation of a TP student about the school
50	Future agenda
5.15	Finish

Then, occasionally, there would be a single-item meeting on a Monday evening, identified several weeks in advance, to discuss something important. For example:

4.04–7.13	Curriculum Planning for next year

There was a difference in the *way* schools related the senior management meetings to the rest of the school. In some they were detached and floating free from the rest of the school. For example, at one school the Senior Teachers were involved in one senior management meeting per week but did not know that there was another meeting of the Headteacher and Deputy Headteachers each week. At Westcliffe the staff were very curious to know what was talked about at senior management meetings as there was no feedback from them or formal mechanism for getting an item discussed.

In several other schools the senior management meeting became the receptacle for all the unclear and uncertain issues concerning members of the school. For example, at Pennine End one meeting included talk about the bus timetable, individual children and break duties, all of which other members of staff were concerned about. The effectiveness of senior management meetings can only be examined as part of the whole structure of meetings within the school. It is an important part of the organisation and needs organising.

How senior management meetings work varied widely. The process by which meetings organise who talks, what is talked about and how ranges from the organic and random to the formal and mechanistic. We found several of the organic meetings that relied on trust and mutual esteem to get things done. We found other organic meetings where very little got done because everyone was lost. Equally, the formal meetings with agendas, minutes and controlling chair, ranged from the efficient decision-making body to the cold robotic meeting where everyone was afraid to make a contribution. As one Senior Teacher said to us, 'We sit with our diaries in one hand and knives in the other.'

The process of these senior management meetings often exemplified the culture of the school. Some senior management meetings suggested the senior staff were a group where there was a division of labour which came together at these meetings to be co-ordinated. Other schools had meetings suggesting the senior staff were a team coming together to get a contribution greater than the sum of the individuals. The work of Bales

(1950) and Belbin (1981) is useful for looking at these process aspects of meetings.

Conclusion

We asked ourselves several questions after observing senior management meetings. Why should this be discussed by the senior staff? Why not by another group, for example a general duties group? What is being discussed here that cannot be dealt with elsewhere, for example, by individuals? Quite frequently items discussed in senior management meetings are trivial and could be discussed elsewhere or dealt with by individuals.

The real stuff for senior management meetings seems to us to be where items cannot be dealt with elsewhere. This includes different sorts of issues:

1 Co-ordinating and dealing with uncertainties that individual senior staff feel they cannot deal with.
2 Where a 'helicopter' view is needed, for example, with cross-curricular co-ordination.
3 Where the experience represented in the group is important, for example, in deciding the tactics, strategy or procedures for implementing some outside initiative that needs a response.

We see the main role for senior management meetings as this kind of issue. With increasingly less autonomy within schools it is even more important to have a management and organising structure where ownership of ideas is accepted. Not least because the follow up by LEAs often includes whether the initiative has reached the ground floor and been adopted. This gives the senior staff the important task of translating the initiatives from the DES, LEA, MSC, exam boards, governors and others. This includes deciding a plan of action on how to get things done. For example, whether to present the initiative to the Heads of Departments to discuss, or get a working party to decide the details, or lobby individual staff, or write a discussion paper, or earmark funds for the new resources needed. All of these decisions seem to us more appropriate items for senior management meetings than discussing the children who were caught smoking. Undoubtedly, senior management meeting for a cup of tea and general gossip as part of their social activities at work is appropriate. What seems to us inappropriate is to call this a meeting and to give it such a priority on the timetable as we sometimes found.

Like any group of people with related working interests, members of the senior management team are able to do things together which none of them can do individually. One of their important functions is acting as a clearing house for information and the shaping of school actions by their collective decisions.

The clearing house function is directing information to where it is needed, when the direction is not obvious, and adding more information when appropriate. For example, information from a local employer might be directed to the Head of Careers and to the Head of Fifth Year, with the additional information that the personnel officer is a parent who has offered to come and talk to children in the school at any time.

The shaping of school actions stems from the discussions about how to react to developments or how to stimulate initiatives. How, for instance, should the school respond to an invitation from the LEA to participate in introductory training for performance appraisal? This is not just a question of passing information on, it is a need to discuss and shape a policy response, covering the degree of consultation with all staff that should take place, whether the invitation should be accepted or ignored, tentative ideas of how appraisal will be handled within the school, and so on. There is also a host of incidents during the school day which people are handling and mostly these incidents are handled by individuals without involving anyone else. Some will be passed on to other members of staff who are regarded as more appropriate, but some will raise novel issues on which a broad spectrum of wise opinion is needed. The senior management team is an appropriate forum for shaping the thinking that will produce the response.

To be effective the senior management team must represent and express within its membership the difficulties of implementation, so that their thinking shapes actions which can be taken rather than expressing vague ideas of principle that cannot be put into practice. The team is not just passing a job on, they are passing on – or passing back – a job with practical suggestions and ideas that other people can develop.

Do It Yourself

We spent a lot of time observing senior management meetings. Initially we tried using variations of Bales (1950) and Belbin (1981), but found that we lost information about the decisions reached and actions agreed. To understand the operation of teams we felt this information was necessary for follow-up conversations and actions to be put into context. We offer our own research form as a suggestion for observing senior management teams in their meetings as a start to understanding how they work.

Questions to be asked are:

- Who contributes most?
- What order do they contribute in?
- Does the Headteacher dominate?
- What contributions do each of them make?

- What real things were discussed?
- How much time was spent on items that an individual could have dealt with?
- what was the relative contribution of the members in terms of quality and in terms of influence?

This form can be filled in by a participant, but is very much easier for a non-participant to concentrate on.

Time	Person speaking	Summary of content of verbal contribution	Process comments along Bales/Belbin lines with non-verbal behaviour recorded

References

Bales, R.F., *Interaction Process Analysis*, Addison-Wesley, Massachussetts 1950.

Belbin, R.M., *Management Teams: Why they Succeed or Fail*, Heinemann, London 1981.

Murgatroyd, S., 'Management Teams and the Promotion of Staff Well-being', in *School Organization*, Vol. 6, No. 1, pp. 115–21, 1986.

Chapter 13
The Management Work of Individuals

We argue that all adults working in a school have management work to do. Everyone has to organise resources, influence other people and get people to do things that they would not have done otherwise. Most obviously this is taking place within the classroom with the pupils, but it is also part of the interaction of the adults within the school. It is this adult management work of each individual that we discuss in this chapter.

If we look at our central issues, discussed in Part I of this book, it is clear that for these to work everyone has a contribution to make. For example, all members of a school staff can express how much they value the efforts, expertise or experience of a colleague. Anyone can help ensure that the system for using the video or computers is the most effective use of the resource. Members of the school who have particular knowledge, experience or interest in a proposed change can participate in discussions and planning for the change. All of these are possible in a culture and organisation that encourages individuals to contribute their abilities.

The word 'management' tends to imply elite or superior in the hierarchy. No doubt many of those in senior posts will do more management than those in junior posts. However, the distinction between those in managerial posts and others is not an 'either/or'.

In the last 20 years there have been many studies of what managers actually do. Mintzberg (1975) concluded that there were various myths about the work of managers contrary to the reality of their work.

- Folklore – Managers are reflective, systematic planners.
  Evidence – Their work is characterised by brevity, variety and discontinuity.

- Folklore – Effective managers have no regular duties.
  Evidence – Rituals and links are necessary.

- Folklore – Senior managers need aggregated information (reports).
  Evidence – They prefer oral communication.

- Folklore – Management is a science or profession.
  Evidence – We are ignorant of what it is.

Mintzberg's book mainly looked at how managers spent their time, as did the study of British Headteachers by Hall, MacKay & Morgan (1986).

Stewart (1982), also basing her understanding on empirical evidence, analysed the more qualitative aspects of managers' jobs to try to understand why things were done in particular ways. One classification tool she uses is to examine how jobs vary in:

- The *demands* that are made: what has to be done and cannot be avoided or delegated;
- the *constraints* that are put on the job by such things as lack of resources, the attitudes and expectations of others and the buildings;
- the *choices* available to particular managers both in what they do and how they choose to do it.

Different jobs will have different configurations, but Stewart contends that managers always have more choices open to them than they think they have. We would argue that simply believing you have choice probably produces more appropriate and proactive managing, rather than being passive and reactive to what is handed out.

This is the case for both those in senior posts and those in junior posts.

Current practice

We found many examples of main-grade (Scale 1 and 2) teachers doing managing work. Amongst many instances, here are a few examples.

1 The teachers at Hall End School were closely involved in helping supply teachers with the details of what to teach, whom and where. It was these main-grade teachers who answered queries over difficult pupils, lack of resources and which methods worked best. This was because they were the ones who knew the classes as they did most teaching.

2 In the English Department at Oakhill School all the teachers contributed examples of poems, stories, books and videos to a resource book about space. Their contributions were based on enthusiasm, not salary scale.

3 At Summerfield High teachers of English, PE, Commerce, Computing, Music and Home Economics helped the Drama teacher to get an evening of drama for the parents going. At William Barnes the school play was organised and managed by the school nurse.

4 We came across several examples of supply teachers, who had regular contact with a school, who contributed a great deal by showing a genuine

interest in the work of their permanent colleagues. This valuing made many isolated teachers feel they were making a decent contribution.
5 The school office in many schools is in the front line in managing the day-to-day differences between plans and reality. We saw examples of pupils, parents, staff and visitors being given advice about how to make something happen as well as the information sought.

We also observed more extensive management work by individual main-grade teachers when they wished to change something. For example, Nigel, a young, new teacher in a Business Studies Department had organised the school's participation in a joint project with a large car manufacturing plant. He had then set up a school enterprise company making and selling various stationery products. The school, the pupils and Nigel were all enjoying this successful enterprise.

Those with senior posts are likely to have more management work than their colleagues. For example, Tom, a Deputy Head who tries to make things happen.

Tom: Deputy Head

Job Description

1 Taking charge in the absence of the Head.
2 Day-to-day modifications of the timetable.
3 Substitution to cover staff absences and special functions.
4 Co-ordination of all functions and units.
5 In close consultation with the Headmaster, responsibility for the construction of the general school and invigilation timetables.
6 The maintenance of a good standard of boys' appearance.
7 Drawing up staff duty roster from timetable.

The reality
He has assumed responsibility for the day-to-day running of the school and it is to him that both staff and pupils relate.

Tom's voice is the dominant one where options and timetable are concerned and it is with him that Heads of Department will negotiate. He publishes the main timetable in June and it is still possible, at this stage, for Heads of Department to suggest amendments. He also publishes a list of the constraints he is working under and draws the staff's attention to any aspects of the timetable with which he is not satisfied himself. Thus, he is trusted by the staff to be fair and we heard no criticism of his construction of the timetable.

Staff at the school lose very few free periods, largely due to Tom's skilful use of supply staff. Practically every absence seems to qualify!

He is in charge of internal and external examination arrangements.

He is actively involved with the School Association and has, amongst other things, organised many car boot sales on Sunday mornings.

He is the channel of communication between the cleaners and the Bursar, largely because he is the only member of staff around when they are working, particularly in the morning, when he starts at 7 am.

Other responsibilities he has taken on include the issue of cycle permits, the gathering of agendas for meetings and the organisation of the weekly programme of events.

Nobody has overall responsibility for discipline, so a lot of the problems end up with him. Often pupils are sent to Year Heads when they are teaching, so they go to Tom.

He has a teaching load of 19 out of 35 periods; that means most of his planning and timetabling has to be done at home or at school in the evenings.

It is important that senior staff ensure that all staff can contribute to management to get commitment. By this we mean allowing people to influence things and make things happen. Not just allowing them to take on trivial tasks.

Dave: Head of Mathematics and Computers, Scale 4 (aged 34)

Dave is an example of getting important things done without creating work for others or taking over their work.

Dave 'runs Maths'. His job, as he sees it, is to ensure that everything is right: right curriculum, books, stock, sets and groups. He monitors the work of his department, supports his staff and oversees the work of the Computer Department. He takes his disciplinary responsibilities very seriously but complains that these take an increasing amount of his time. He is also one of the GCSE Phase 4 Co-ordinators, chairs the School Fund Committee, co-ordinates a Primary/Secondary Maths Liaison Group and is seconded to the County 'Software Centre' every Friday.

Dave derives enormous pleasure from organising things and 'seeing a job rounded off properly'. He hates messy rooms. Most of all he says, 'I enjoy being with kids and getting feedback from them.' One result of this child orientation is that his departmental meetings are concerned as much with pastoral matters as they are with the academic. He says he finds it very difficult to make value judgements about the relative importance of pastoral and academic work.

Dave's penchant for organising things also runs to creating and running working groups, ensuring a high degree of collaboration and mutual support. He used the word 'ensure' a good deal in the interviews but, despite this apparent directiveness, Dave insists that as a Head of

Department he is, first and foremost, a facilitator. 'I work from within people and try not to be too directive. I must admit, though, I do put pressure on the team to reach decisions.' Observations suggest that Dave is directive but there is also evidence that he does run his department along collegial lines. 'I like to think.' he says, 'that in my absence the department would be able to carry on without me.' Which it does every Friday!

Whether one is a main-grade teacher, a member of the non-teaching staff or someone with a post of responsibility, management is part of the work.

There are vast numbers of courses, books, models and people giving those with management jobs in schools advice about what they should and should not be doing. The easiest topic on which to write or run a course is something systematic, preferably with a neat diagram. The reality of most jobs is a constant stream of minutiae piling up on the desk and at the door and a rather harassed individual wondering why they never quite get round to having coffee in the staffroom to keep in touch. How can the two be describing the same jobs?

Several of the people we observed and interviewed said they wished they knew more about time management or managed their time better so they could get round to planning or be more involved with the longer-term issues. We suggest that the felt problem with time is really a presenting symptom. Most jobs attract more demands than can be met so some strategy for prioritising the work has to be used and some possible activities not done. Analyses that are more helpful than just structuring one's time better are suggested in Chapter 11, 'Agendas and Networks', and Chapter 10, 'Technical, Administrative and Managerial Work', but the important thing is to analyse what the job is really for. Our research was aimed at trying to clarify this issue. Too many of those we observed seemed to be uncertain about what their work really was and ended up darting all over the place at the beck and call of anyone. A clear sense of what is, and what is not, important to do could make more sense of the job for the individual and, possibly, increase their credibility within the school. For example, Simon, a Head of House, spent his day chasing people, equipment and paper at other people's request rather than deciding what was important for him to do.

The management work of individuals is not simply being systematic nor is it just being nice to people; it has to focus on getting things done. To do this you have to know what things you want to get done.

Good practice

Any of the examples above.

Do It Yourself

Demands

What are the demands of your job? That is, the things that *have* to be done by you. They cannot be ignored, delegated or passed on. What are the penalities for not doing them? It might help to think of the following areas:

1 subordinates;
2 from above;
3 peers;
4 people outside the organisation;
5 administration – procedures and meetings;
6 others.

Constraints

What are the constraints that stop you developing your job in absolutely the way you would like? For example:

1 the resources, eg buildings;
2 legal;
3 technical limitations of equipment;
4 physical location;
5 organisation policies and procedures;
6 attitude of others;
7 other.

Choices

What are the choices available to you about *what* you do, *how* you do it and *when* you do it?

1 within your unit;
2 with your peers;
3 to protect the unit from disturbance;
4 upwards;
5 elsewhere in the organisation;
6 outside the organisation;
7 other.

References

Mintzberg, H., 'The Manager's Job: Folklore and Fact', *Harvard Business Review*, July/August, pp. 49–61, 1975.

Stewart, R., *Choices for Managers*, McGraw Hill, Maidenhead, 1982.
Hall, V., MacKay, H. and Morgan, C., *Headteachers at Work*, Open University, Milton Keynes, 1986.

Further reading

Stewart, R., *The Reality of Management*, second edition, Pan Books, London. 1979.

Part Three: Taken-for-Granted Roles: A Reappraisal for Management

Chapter 14
Headteachers and Deputy Headteachers

We have found it necessary to discuss the role of Headteachers and Deputy Headteachers together. This is because one cannot understand the role and position of Deputies in isolation from their particular Head, on whom they are dependent to a much greater degree than any other member of the school, with the possible exception of the Head's secretary. Also one cannot envisage Headship being a coherent 'do-able' job without Deputies sharing that unique responsibility in a more sensible way than is common at present. Our research shows that the difficulties faced by Headteachers of being the centre of attention, demand and accountability create an overload for them and at the same time this centralisation can diminish the contribution of Deputy Headteachers.

We did not set out to study the job of Headteacher any more than any other in the school. This clearly struck people in education as odd. For example, when we were first negotiating for secondees with LEAs they said such things as, 'We can't possibly release Heads at such short notice.' As the work of Heads has been extensively studied, we replied that we would prefer Deputies, Heads of Department and main-grade teachers. There was surprise that we should regard such people as suitable to study management. This was yet another manifestation of the extraordinary centrality of the Headteacher in British schools. There is an almost universal focus on this job as being the pivot of all management and organisation within schools. This is found not only in the work of academics such as, for example, Rutter (1979) and Mortimore (1988), but also in the continuing statements of politicians.

This centrality of the Headteacher has puzzled us for some time:

> When comparing the organization of secondary schools with the organization of most other employing organizations, the position of the head is almost unique in the power vested in it. The head teacher is the leading figure in an organization employing somewhere between 50 and 125 people. Those people, plus the parents of the children in the school, plus the children themselves, the school governors

and the local authority administrators all seem anxious that the head teacher should be kept remote and should exercise considerable power. Very rarely will any member of the staff address him by his first name. Although there may be consultation, it is expected that the head will personally resolve major aspects of school policy. When subject heads decide who shall teach their subject at different levels, these decisions only have the status of recommendations that the head may well change as he, and he alone, has effective authority in relation to members of staff.

(Torrington & Weightman, 1985, p. 199)

And two pages later:

Effective delegation is essential, but the power assumptions about the role of the head teacher are so deep-rooted that the delegation is difficult to contrive.

(p. 210)

We cannot think of any other established organisation where this is the case, except perhaps the position of a British Prime Minister in relation to the Cabinet – which may explain the confirmation of universal power that politicians offer. The nearest more ordinary comparison is with the founder–owner of a small business.

Our research since the above words were written has not reduced our puzzlement about the centrality of Heads, but has confirmed our belief that it is one of the main impediments to improving school organisation. It has become clear, however, that we shall not convince many people within education of our argument! The research associates who worked so closely with us for so long continue to offer condescending smiles when we advance this point of view. We do not understand, but we do accept the phenomenon.

The most recent empirical study of headteachers is by Hall, Mackay and Morgan (1986), who studied the working lives of 15 headteachers and found them to differ widely; but all could be characterised by fragmentation, a wide variety of tasks and a strong emphasis on talking to people. In many ways this coincides closely with studies of general managers in commercial organisations, but also demonstrates that there is no consensus on what the job of Headteacher consists of. The authors decry the lack of 'the baseline of a formal description'. Since the Hall, Mackay and Morgan research, there has been the development of the new contracts for members of the teaching profession, but these are very broad guidelines and Headteachers remain free to organise their jobs in almost any way they choose. It is sad that the Hall study shows many Heads to be at the mercy of events, responding to every problem as important and involved in mainly trivial matters. That type of reactive, rudderless approach has inescapable implications for everyone else, for example:

> . . . each head's style of working with staff was significantly tied to the kind of relationship they had with senior staff; and the extent to which they had consciously instituted systems into the school management structure for ensuring tasks were carried out.
>
> (Hall, Mackay and Morgan, 1986, p. 206)

Two of the Heads in the Hall study seemed to have developed a meaningful role for Deputies, despite contrasted approaches to the job of Headship. First Mr Dowe:

> He preferred a collegial rather than hierarchical approach to staff relations. The extent of his availability to staff, to whom he was always considerate and respectful, was curtailed by his extensive teaching and examining commitments . . . He sought to demonstrate through his own professional competence as a teacher the ways in which he wanted staff to see their own teaching roles . . . he delegated running the school extensively. As a result he was required to spend relatively little time in dealing with matters requiring immediate attention; his teaching commitments dominated the space available.
>
> (p. 210)

Mr Shaw interpreted his job differently by emphasising his leading professional role more generally in school affairs, but there was still a significant enablement of Deputies:

> The main features . . . were his systematic involvement in the whole range of the school's activity, in spite of extensive commitments to activities outside the school; his strategic view of school matters, ensuring continuing attention to longer-term planning; and his proactive stance towards innovation and change . . . he approached systematically the task of building and maintaining interpersonal relations with staff, pupils and parents; as well as creating mechanisms for providing staff with the knowledge and skills to do their job effectively. He did this by involving staff consistently in the school's decision-making processes, making extensive use of his close working relationship with his senior management team to secure the staff's support.
>
> (p. 211)

We now move on to consider the outcomes of our own empirical work. The examples and discussion that follows examine the effect of the Headteacher's role on others working within the school – we did not look at the important work that Headteachers, and others, have to do outside the school. This chapter is not intended as a complete examination of the role of the Headteacher. We are trying to demonstrate the need to reappraise the taken-for-granted view that Headteachers need to be strong leaders and that all good schools need a strong Head.

Deputy Headteachers, by contrast, seemed to have the least clearly defined jobs in schools. The work that Deputies did varied enormously both within schools and between schools, but many were essentially personal assistants to the Headteacher rather than senior staff with clear and significant responsibilities justifying the status and salary. We found many Deputies who had been in post a long time. With most schools having three such posts, it is clear that not all will become Headteachers. Being a Deputy is the opportunity for some to be a 'Head-in-waiting', but it is the final post for many others. If these people do not have whole and coherent jobs to do they will become fed up, with their enthusiasm blunted. The Head loses an opportunity to shed some of the workload of Headship and other staff resent the privileged position of people whose extra contribution they cannot see.

Current practice

An example of Headteacher power

The Headteacher, Peter Ford, was universally respected and admired by the staff in the school. Such words as 'fantastic', 'exceptional', 'outstanding' were frequently used. He was also seen as powerful and influential with the phrase 'The Peter Ford Show' occurring time and again.

What were the sources of his power?

First, the traditional *position* of Headteachers. The received view that Headteachers should be strong leaders that is demonstrated, for example, in *Ten Good Schools* (HMI, 1977).

Second, *historical* factors. The Headteacher had set up the present school 12 years ago following reorganisation. He had been there from the beginning. During the initial years, policy decisions were required on everything from mixed ability to school uniform. His model of 'Board and Working Party' meant most staff had been involved somewhere in deciding school policy. 1974 was also the heyday of teachers' pay following Houghton ie new grades, large salary increases, etc. Also plenty of money for development and equipment. This was clearly a period of great excitement in the school, following the amalgamation of an apparently depressed boys' secondary modern and a girls' secondary modern. This time was frequently referred to in interviews, perhaps summed up by a shared memory of a golden weekend in St Annes-on-Sea. The Headteacher was seen as the person who had made this happen.

Third, *individual loyalty*. The Headteacher was given loyalty by many individual members of staff for various acts of personal consideration. Many thought that they had been promoted further than they would have thought possible for themselves because of his encouragement and persuasion – this was a comment only heard from women teachers. Many gave examples of personal consideration shown by the Headteacher over domestic problems and crises; one summed it up by saying. 'He makes it clear that our personal lives are important and should come first.' This was valued and appeared not to be abused. The Head was seen as approachable on matters both large and small. The Head had a clearly stated policy of playing to people's strengths. This was seen to be in effect through the staff development procedures and by encouraging individuals to seek responsibility.

Fourth, *information*. The Headteacher was involved in various national bodies, eg NAHT, CSCS, NDC, as well as various local organisations. This ensured he always had the latest information and ideas. He used this information to good effect by making powerful presentations to meetings, eg. Heads of Faculty, Senior Management Group, and sharing the information quickly with colleagues, ie he was a source of new information and was seen as someone who shared it.

Fifth, *Senior Management Group (SMG)*. The SMG was charged with seeing to all the administrative, individual, day-to-day variations. Great efforts were made by the Headteacher to ensure the SMG was a cohesive group, eg SMG meetings every Wednesday after school where each member described or discussed little items that had come up in the week. He describes these meetings as ensuring a corporate, Medusa-like body who could act as one whoever a member of school saw. It would also be quite difficult for any member of SMG to build their own empire within the school when there is such a strong emphasis on SMG as a single entity; for example, they all had rooms on one corridor, a member of SMG was assigned to various tasks but individuals were not specified, and tasks were rotated around SMG over the years. This enabled the Headteacher to be powerful in two ways. He was not involved in the daily detail which is so often a source of irritation to those lower in the hierarchy and, on his own repeated admission, was protected from the loneliness of being a sole Headteacher by having a cohesive group to support him.

Drawbacks of Headteacher power

Powerful Headteachers can create several problems within the school. First, if all decisions and systems depend on the Head there is a real vacuum when they are absent. For example, in Peter Ford's school the senior staff were reluctant to take decisions when he was absent as they were frequently undermined or the decision was reversed when he returned, as we witnessed on several occasions.

Second, staff cannot develop beyond a mediocre level without being a serious challenge to a powerful Head. They are restricted by needing to behave in acceptable ways and have congruent ideas and approaches.

Third, in two schools we visited that had very powerful Headteachers, the staff had organised themselves in formal unions to represent their views to the senior management within the school. Both these Heads were national figures.

Fourth, the school tends to reflect the weaknesses as well as the strengths of the Head.

Fifth, it is becoming increasingly impracticable for one person to encompass the diversity and work necessary to manage and organise a secondary school.

These five aspects suggest that a powerful Head can only take their school so far in development, that is, there is a limit on the capacity for commitment and self-renewing. There is no doubt that strong leaders can recover difficult situations, as Peter Ford had done in coping with the aftermath of two schools being amalgamated, but they need to change as time passes. Also there is a shortage of powerful Heads who are competent. Peter Ford was very successful in many ways and attracted the enthusiastic support of his staff. Other heads operate in a similar centralised way without having the personal qualities 'to get away with it', so that the whole school is disabled by a power structure without effective power.

An example of Deputy Headteachers' lack of power

Job description of one Deputy Headteacher, Jim

1 To deputise for the Headteacher as required.
2 To have general responsibility for all aspects of safety, progress, discipline and pastoral care towards all pupils in the school.
3 As Head of Upper School to have particular responsibility for the Fourth and Fifth Year pupils. This responsibility will include:

a Supporting Form Tutors and Year Heads in their pastoral work.
b Contact with parents in matters concerning welfare, progress and discipline of pupils.
c Liaison with external support services.
d Oversight of the preparation of homework, timetables, pupil reports and records.
e Assisting Heads of Year in the organisation of Parents' Evenings and Assemblies.
f Assisting with the conduct of external examinations.
g Providing general support to the work of the Heads of Year.

4 To liaise with Heads of Year and Head of Lower School regarding mid-year admissions.
5 To have a knowledge of the school-based and external careers guidance available to pupils.
6 To be responsible for the Vocational Links Curriculum as it affects the school.
7 To have oversight of the health and safety at work provisions and to liaise with the health and safety representatives at school.

8 To deal with all matters concerning repair and maintenance of the campus.
9 To have regular contact with the caretaking staff regarding matters affecting the school building and to interview/appoint caretakers/cleaners.
10 To contact police and travel companies as and when necessary.
11 Together with the Heads of Year, to deal with matters relating to the suspension or exclusion of pupils.
12 To take assemblies.
13 To carry a teaching load.
14 To undertake other duties as may be detailed by the Headteacher from time to time.

This job description is chacterised by imprecision and a lack of wholeness. It does not describe a job but is a rambling list of odds and ends. Furthermore only 8, 12 and 13 are specific duties that stand on their own; all the others are supporting, assisting, liaising or in some way dependent on someone else to share their work.

To show how impotent this renders a Deputy here is an extract from our observation.

90 minutes in Jim's day

9.58 Deputy Head in his office. Head of Boys' PE asks him to talk to two boys who he has caught leaving a French lesson early. Head of PE explains that he would have taken boys to Head of Fourth Year if he had been available.
9.59 Boys left outside room. Deputy Head continues telling the researcher about the school's problems with an external support agency.
10.05 Boys are brought into the room and told off by the Deputy Head.
10.09 Boys leave. Deputy Head talks to the researcher about the position of Modern Languages in his school.
10.14 To the staffroom where he chats to the washing-up lady and then to the researcher. He explains that he always has a cup of tea before break begins so that he can be on duty at break.
10.30 Returns to his office.
10.31 Tells a boy to see a teacher.
10.32 Tells some girls about new bus times.
10.34 Stands around outside room 'on duty'.
10.35 Passing comment to a teacher in the corridor.
10.35 One of the (10.05) boys tells him that he has apologised to the French teacher.
10.36 A boy returns 50p to him.
10.36 He asks a girl to move away from a painting.

10.37 Boy asks if he can fetch a bag.
10.38 Chats affably to a group of girls about their cookery lessons.
10.40 Picks up a plastic bag on floor. Asks a boy to fetch the girl who has dropped it.
10.41 Talks to girl who dropped the plastic bag.
10.42 Talks to two boys.
10.43 Talks to some other boys about bus times.
10.45 Returns to own office.
10.46 Talks to Head of Fourth Year about boys who skipped French.
10.55 Head of Fourth Year leaves. Deputy Head goes to the staffroom.
10.59 To the staffroom, then to Lower School building. Meets caretaker on the way. They talk in passing. Deputy Head's 'bleeper' goes off. He hurries to a Lower School office to telephone in to the main school office.
11.05 Lower School secretary tells him that a teacher would like him to check a window in a classroom that is being blown about by the high winds. Asks boy outside the secretary's room why he is waiting there.
11.06 Goes to check the window in the classroom.
11.08 Returns to his own office in the main building. He is 'bleeped' en route. He goes directly to the school office in response to the paging.
11.10 Talks briefly to the school secretary about some coaches. Returns to his own office. He meets the caretaker on his way.
11.13 Gives a form to the caretaker in his office. The caretaker leaves.
11.14 Telephones County Hall about bus timetables. There is a knock on the door whilst he is telephoning. It is the Second Caretaker. He is asked to wait outside. Deputy continues with his telephone call.
11.25 End of the call to County Hall. He invites the Second Caretaker into his office. They discuss caretaking arrangements after the retirement of the First Caretaker and before a replacement has been made.
11.33 A teacher knocks on the door. He is asked to wait outside.
11.38 Ends conversation with Second Caretaker. Goes to the door to look for the teacher who knocked. He has gone.

Other activities on the same day

1 Re-writing bus schedules for the pupils on the Link Vocational Courses.

2 Arranging a programme for a visit by the Educational Psychologist.

3 Sticking up a number of 'What to do in case of fire' notices in different parts of the building.

4 Talking to the Head of Fifth Year about the poor morale in the year group.

22 per cent of this Deputy's day was spent teaching or talking to children (mainly teaching them). 22 per cent was spent on administrative tasks, such as bus schedules and storm damage. 28 per cent on managerial activities, such as talking to the caretakers and Heads of Year. 24 per cent in activities of a personal nature.

Conclusion

Headteachers are clearly central figures in their schools, but this does not mean they should be dominant. Where all decisions, procedures, communications and systems are focussed on the Head, serious weaknesses of management and organisation emerge. Not least is the problem of what happens when the Headteacher is out of school Many Heads are not in school because of the increased work needed outside on such things as negotiating with the LEA over staffing, resources and policy; visiting primary schools to recruit children; public relations visits to local organisations. Our research did not look at this work of Heads, but it was apparent to us that many Heads are out of school two days a week, a figure also found by Hall, Mackay and Morgan. It became obvious that significant management decision making and implementation within the school must be undertaken independently by other members of staff as well as the Head, and without them feeling dependent on the Head for authorisation and confirmation of the decisions they make.

We are counter-cultural in arguing for less concentration on Headteachers. We may, of course, be wrong. An example of the established view is how HMI concentrate on Headteachers in their inspections and visits. This may be because they have to come to grips with a particular school quickly, but this concentration on the Head is neither universal nor helpful. In France and the USA, for example, they do not centralise things on the Headteacher.

We think that the two essential tasks for the Head are to be the mover of the mission and to manage the boundary. The first is a subtle, bridging activity and we give an example of good practice later in this chapter. The literature suggests a need for leaders in schools to fulfil a role which involves, in Hoyle's words:

> identifying, conceptualising, transmitting and gaining acceptance of a mission for the school, an idea or image of where it is heading.
>
> (Hoyle, 1986, p. 123)

Leaders of this type have been variously described as '*transformative leaders*' by Burns (1978), '*Symbolic Chief/High Priests*' by Sergiovanni (1984), '*Poets*' by Hodgkinson (1983), '*institutional leaders*' by Selznick (1957) and possessing '*Hands-On, Value-Driven*' attributes by Peters and Waterman (1982).

In moving the mission the Head makes use of the unique position that Headship confers of being the figurehead and principal representative of the school, the person to whom most information from the environment is first put, the recipient of the memoranda, the person in contact with the LEA, HMI and advisers, as well as being in touch with the school's clientele. That welter of data and ideas is then translated into plans:

> The head who would create a mission for the school would have the continuous task of selecting from these clusters of knowledge which, as modified by an awareness of forces within the head and within the teachers currently teaching in the school and such other organisational forces as structures and resources, would fashion a set of goals for the school which could be construed as a mission.
>
> (Hoyle, p. 125)

The nature of the mission is not likely to be brought down by the Head from a mountain top inscribed on tablets of stone, as it will involve extensive consultation to discover and clarify, but the Head will then *move* the mission by winning staff commitment to it, and will move it further by actually making it happen. Splendid dreams and ideas that are excellent in principle are not as good as less grand schemes if it is only those that can be made to work. The Head can become the personal embodiment of the mission, by living out whatever it may be.

The second essential task of the Head is representing and selling the school in all the necessary dealings with the outside bodies on which the school depends, from the LEA 'office' to local employers, other local bodies, national educational institutions, courses and conferences and the local press. The risk in all of this is of becoming a showman, a rather stagey figure who loses touch with the school and loses the confidence of the staff.

The first task requires Heads to be out and about the school and the second task requires Heads to be out of school a lot. Consequently, they cannot do the other management jobs: something has to be given up. It is not appropriate for a Headteacher to be involved in everything. For example, appointing junior staff could more sensibly be done by the Head of Department and some other senior staff such as the Staff Development teacher, but in every school we visited Heads in practice decided the appointment of *all* staff.

Although Deputy Heads have the word 'deputy' in their title, this can be no more than an incidental part of their role. To have value they must be in charge of something important. If they were called, for example, Curriculum Manager or Personnel Manager this would be describing a coherent job and not just bits of the Headteacher's job. A Deputy Prime Minister is seldom a person of great influence unless that function is added to a 'real' job, like Home Secretary or Chancellor of the Exchequer. By giving each Deputy a proper job to organise and develop, a senior team of self-confident, competent professionals comes into existence that can enrich the life of the school, provide an efficient and valued service to the staff and make the job of Deputy Head a job to relish rather than to die in. Deputies then take on the essential, discrete tasks of implementation that fall outside the responsibilities of Heads of Department, Heads of Year and similar office holders. This seems to us a more productive use of experienced, senior staff than their most frequent role at present – to be the butt of dissatisfaction within the school.

There is essential work to be done by both the Head and Deputies. For example, there is all the work we have outlined in the first part of this book. This work needs to be shared so each person has areas of responsibility to take decisions about, influence others and make things happen. This sharing not only helps the school to run well, it also enables other staff to develop their contributions, their careers and themselves. Even if they disagree with the Headteacher's view on an issue, when work is shared they do not run the risk of undermining the Headteacher's position.

Examples of good practice

Sam is our example of a Head who is committed to the school's mission and is always prepared to articulate this and make it explicit in his everyday behaviour. For example, in the School Year Book on the twentieth anniversary of its comprehensive reorganisation he says:

> The decisive decision was to organise the new school on a house system. Immediately our children 'belonged' and that special relationship, civilised, warm, trusting, between adults and young children was born . . . The staff see the way ahead clearly. We must value all our pupils equally, cherishing those with practical and creative skills, valuing the academic, building a community of mature, self-aware young people . . . Over twenty years those early values persisted and strengthened and our pupils and parents have responded.

It was readily apparent during the period of the attachment that a genuine attempt had been made to reify these values; they were not simply high-sounding but hollow platitudes. At no point during our seven weeks in the school did we hear a teacher shout at a pupil; the usual way of dealing with recalcitrant pupils was in a 'laid-back' manner, lots of talk, lots of patience and no verbal bullying whatsoever. The point was also made that whatever caring views new teachers (inexperienced or otherwise) might have professed at their interviews it was often difficult for them to come to terms with the 'non-violent' aspects of the school's ethos, although after a difficult induction year most seemed to do so.

Vicky's experiences are a case in point, particularly in the way they exemplify Sam's normative but practical approach to communicating his vision about how children ought to be handled. Vicky, now the Head of Music, admits that she found it difficult to adapt to the school, since her own schooling and teaching practice were in more authoritarian establishments. In one of her interviews she professed:

> It took me two and a half years to work it out . . . there's no point in shouting at them. I've changed my style because people kept telling me, in a roundabout sort of way, that shouting was not the way. I didn't realise it at the time but I do now. Unfortunately a lot of people argue that we're simply too soft.

Sam's ongoing role in encouraging her to change her style emerged during his main interview. He recognised during this interview that 'non-shouting' strategies were part of the school's ethos, that you ask children to do things rather than tell them. He went on:

> There was a fascinating example today. I came across Vicky in the Hall having a confrontation with Steven S. There was lots of hostile body language – arms folded, head pushed forward – as she argued with the boy. I didn't say anything at the time but I thought I must tell Vicky about not physically confronting children. I know her well enough to go into her music lessons. I can wander in there and see some excellent teaching and learning. I know she can handle this sort of informal approach.

Here is a Head attending, in Peters and Waterman's terms, to both detail and ideas, 'value-shaping' through 'daily events', recognising the importance of 'walking about' as a managerial strategy. His awareness of the importance of 'MBWA' (managing by walk about) was evidenced by the occasion when, mid-way through an interview with the researcher, he suddenly stood up and suggested that the interview might continue whilst they wandered around the school. He explained that he had been out of school on business a good deal recently and needed to increase his visibility. It became apparent during the walk about that followed that Sam was not simply 'showing the flag', as it were, but interacting purposefully en route with many individual teachers and pupils. There was a marked contrast with the observation of Ronald, described earlier, who merely hovered aimlessly (although amiably), waiting for things to happen.

The events described above relating to Vicky and Sam would also appear to be a good example of a leader retailing a 'story' in support of his basic beliefs, a technique employed by the 'excellent' companies in Peters and Waterman's study.

> The excellent companies are unashamed collectors and tellers of stories, of legends and myths in support of their basic beliefs. Frito-Lay tells service stories, J&J tells quality stories, 3M tells innovation stories.
>
> (Peters and Waterman, p. 282)

And Sam tells stories which demonstrate his extensive knowledge of the pupils in his school and their families, stories which lend credence to his belief that you achieve more through patience and kindness than hard-line tactics. There was ample evidence in meeting after meeting, formal and informal interactions with his staff, that he knew the children in his school as well as those staff, like the Heads of House, who were 'paid' to be informed about them. Like Peters and Waterman's 'excellent' companies, Sam gave the impression to the outside observer that he was indeed 'really close to the customer'. Judging by the number of times interviews were interrupted by children knocking on his door, it was clear that direct access to the Head was not discouraged, although it needs to be said that a number of these contacts involved Sam in providing some sort of 'disciplinary' support for staff.

Maureen: An example of a Deputy Headteacher with a real job to do

Maureen's title is Deputy Head Administration and Staff Support. This gives her a role very much like that of a personnel manager. Her role is listed in the staff handbook as responsible for:

Pupil standards – jointly with all senior staff
School functions
Physical environment
School Brochure
Newsletter
Transition to FE
Liaison with community
Schemes of work jointly with curriculum Deputy
External exams
INSET – internal
Staff resources
Printer resources
Admin Handbook
Staff Handbook
School calendar
Home–away diary
Option system
Supervision of supply, temporary, probationers and students
Section 11 staff
Staff development
Staff welfare
Anti-racism and equal opportunities
Special Needs

She sees her main tasks as staff development and anti-racism – that includes links with the community. The administration side of her role she sees as a necessary task to be done efficiently and she delegates as much of the clerical work as possible to non-teaching and teaching colleagues.

She explains her relationship with the Head:

> I have links – if I pick up signals I take them to him (the Head). It may irritate him because I'm telling him things he doesn't like. I like working with him. I will see him about areas of concern and tell him what I think. We're opposed and we're trying to evolve our difference of views but it's not power games. We are the buffer between two pressures on the school – the community and the LEA.

Examples of good practice by Deputy Headteachers are found in several other chapters. For example, Derek in Chapter 9, Personal Credibility and Effectiveness.

Do It Yourself

If you are Head, answer the following about yourself. Everyone else, ask your Head, or ask yourself about your Head.

1 Which of the following need your approval?
Timetable
Syllabus
Grouping of children
Time out of school
Rooming
Petty cash
Letters to parents
Use of minibus
(please add)

2 Who would you delegate them to?

3 Next time you are out of school for a whole day or more, list the requests for decisions made on your return. Could someone else have taken the decision about any of these in your absence? How are you going to ensure a similar list is not there next time?

4 What real responsibility do you allow your Deputies? Are you sure these are not low-grade tasks and jobs?

References

Burns, M., *Leadership*, Harper and Row, London, 1978.

Hall, V., Mackay, H. and Morgan, C., *Headteachers at Work*, Open University Press, Milton Keynes, 1986.

HMI, *Ten Good Schools*, HMSO, London, 1977.

Hodgkinson, C., *The Philosophy of Leadership*, Blackwell, Oxford, 1983.

Hoyle, E., *The Politics of School Management*, Hodder and Stoughton, London, 1986.

Peters, T.J. and Waterman, R.H., *In Search of Excellence*, Harper and Row, New York, 1982.

Mortimore, P., Sammons, P., Stoll, L., Lewis, D. and Ecob, R., *School Matters: The Junior Years*, Open Books, Harmondsworth, 1988.

Rutter, M., *1500 Hours*, Penguin, London, 1979.

Selznick, P., *Leadership in Administration*, Harper and Row, New York, 1957.

Sergiovanni, T.J., 'Cultural and Competing Perspectives in Administrative Theory and Practice', in Sergiovanni, T.J. and Corbally, J.E., *Leadership and Organizational Culture*, University of Illinois Press, Urbana, 1984.

Torrington, D.P. and Weightman, J., 'Teachers and the Management Trap', *Journal of Curriculum Studies*, Vol. 17, No. 21, pp. 197–205, 1985.

Chapter 15
Deputy Headteachers: A Case Study

As we saw in Chapter 14, 'Headteachers and Deputy Headteachers', the work of Deputy Headteachers seems to vary considerably and seems the least clear-cut of any job in secondary schools. This can be partly explained by the fact that they are Deputy to the Headteacher both in job title and in the way the job is interpreted within the school. This dependence on the Head creates difficulty for Deputies in establishing real work of their own. Deputies can only be as useful as their Headteacher lets them be. Relevant to this problem is our discussion of the balance of management work in Part II.

Current practice

Below, we give a detailed description and analysis of the work of the three Deputy Heads in one of the schools we studied. The situation was typical of many of the other schools as well.

Jim

Jim spent most of his teaching career working in the earlier grammar school. He went there as Head of Physics but eventually became Second Deputy and then First Deputy.

Jim became Deputy Head on amalgamation. He was then 47 years old. His present duties involve:

1 The pastoral oversight of all Upper School pupils and support of the Heads of Fourth and Fifth Years and Form Tutors.
2 Oversight of caretaking and cleaning staff and health and safety.
3 Preparation and monitoring of the Upper School homework timetable and oversight of pupils' reports and records.
4 Liaison with the Local Consortium Curriculum.
5 Oversight of P + SE / Careers Education.

6 Safety, repair and maintenance of the site and care and presentation of the Upper School buildings.
7 Liaison with the Works Department.
8 Liaison with parents.
9 Liaison with external support agencies.
10 Taking assemblies.
11 Contributing to the formulation of school policy and its implementation.

Until October 1986 Jim was responsible for cover arrangements. This has now been transferred to Les, and been replaced with point 4 on the above list. Jim has been granted another four non-contact periods to enable him to undertake this task, bringing his teaching load down to 12/40.

Jim on his job

When asked what he does on a day-to-day basis, Jim focuses on his 'firefighting' role; dealing with problem children sent by the Heads of Year; stepping in and supporting staff when the Heads of Year are not available; helping staff in lessons, and 'doing jobs for the Head'. 'Many people might not find what I do creative', he said, 'but I find it satisfying'.

This satisfaction is derived partly from an autonomy which he never had when he worked in the grammar school, and from the trust which he believes the Head has in him. He mentioned, with some pride, that he had been Acting Head during her term-long secondment.

Jim also prides himself on his ability to get on with people but admits that he avoids confrontation with them. He sees himself as the 'oil in the machine, not the grit'. He says it is nice to be around teachers, so that they can 'sound off, get things off their chests'. He says he has tried hard not to isolate himself from the staff and makes a point of going into the staffroom; 'That's why I have no tea making facility in my office.'

Some of Jim's comments suggest that he finds it difficult to fulfil point 7 above because the Works Department is not always co-operative. 'There's real hassle with them.' He has come to rely on the Senior Clerical Assistant to make the contacts for him. She used to be employed in the Works Department and knows how to get around the men who work there.

A typical day with Jim

Jim's typical day was characterised by the following features:

a The organisation of amended bus times for the pupils who travelled on Consortium buses. This involved re-writing schedules, pinning them up on a noticeboard and informing the pupils as and when he saw them.
b Arranging a programme for the proposed visit of the Educational Psychologist. This involved close liaison with the Head of Special Needs.

c Supervisory patrols at the beginning of the school day, at breaks and at assemblies.
d Discussion with the Deputy Caretaker about his duties following the retirement of the Head Caretaker.
e Providing support for a French teacher from whose lesson two boys had absented themselves. He informed the Head of Year verbally later in the day.
f Checking on damage to the building which was being buffeted by some very high winds. He asked the clerical assistant to notify the Works Department about the damage.
g Drinking coffee in the staffroom either before or after break.
h Sticking a number of 'What to do in case of fire' notices up in different parts of the building.
i Talking informally to the Head of Fifth Year about the poor morale of the Year Group.
j Interacting on 22 different occasions with children. Most of these were of a very short duration and consisted of giving them information about the new bus schedules. Whilst on break duty he chatted to a group of girls in a pleasant, affable manner. Their reaction suggested that they were relaxed in his presence and used to speaking to him.

22 per cent of Jim's day was spent on Technical activities, mainly teaching and talking to children; 22 per cent on Administrative activities, such as the bus schedules, storm damage and fire notices; 28 per cent on Managerial work, as when talking to caretakers and Heads of Year; and 24 per cent on activities of a Personal nature, including fetching his wife to work in the school for the afternoon, talking to the researcher and sitting in the almost empty staffroom.

Comment
Although Jim was 'busy', the day was far from hectic. He engaged the researcher in conversation to an extent which suggested that he was not working under pressure. This is reflected in the fact that nearly a quarter of his activities were classified as personal.

Les

Les became a Deputy in one of the previous schools when he was 31. He is now 40. He was made Deputy/Head of Lower School when the schools amalgamated. He became Deputy/Head of Administration shortly before our period of research. At the moment he is based in the same office in Lower School although a good deal of his work involves close liaison with a clerical assistant who is based in the main school. His present duties include:

1 Responsibility for statistics; including numbers on roll, attendance analysis, Forms 7 and S96 etc.

2 Organisation of duty rotas.
3 Organisation of cover for absent teachers.
4 Timetabling and rooming of internal and external examinations.
5 Oversight of entries made in the school log book.
6 Liaison with the Senior Clerical Assistant with regard to staff absences.
7 Participation in the work of the PSE Working Party.
8 Exam statistics.
9 Responsibility for the School Fund and School Travel Accounts.
10 Responsibility for the minibus and tuckshop monies.
11 Liaison with County auditors and other officers.
12 Responsibility for organising visiting speakers for various special assemblies.
13 Contributing to the formulation of school policy and its implementation.

Les on his job

Les says that his main day-to-day task is arranging for cover for absent teachers. Although money is available to pay for supply teachers who are covering for teachers on various types of INSET, they are not always so easy to obtain. The responsibility for contacting supply teachers rests with Les, although people in the office do the bulk of the telephoning. Nevertheless, Les has at times spent 'all morning on the 'phone'. He doubts whether the staff appreciate the difficulties of finding suitable supply teachers.

Les has completely reorganised the administrative aspects of cover in a way which, he believes, is more obviously fair. This has taken up an enormous amount of time since he took up his new responsibilities. Les enjoys administration and believes that the Head is exploiting his strengths. He likes to think that he is personalising administration by taking every opportunity to talk directly to teachers when he is giving or soliciting information. 'I'm always thinking about the effects of my work on the staff. It's a matter of being sensitive to their needs.'

At the moment he finds his job creative and says he has a lot to do, particularly by putting a lot of the administrative data onto a computer system. County policy on this is, he says, holding him back.

A day with Les

Les's day was characterised by the following features:

a Cover arrangement, which took, in all, 85 minutes, or nearly 70 per cent of his administrative work for that day (administration taking up nearly 30 per cent of his total day).
b Seeking out and then trawling through class registers to collect data relating to pupil attendance. This task should be carried out each week

but Les had not done it for three weeks and was, therefore, catching up on the day he was shadowed. The task was being carried out on the explicit instructions of the Head. Altogether he spent 73 minutes on the task, including time spent moving round the school whilst hunting for missing registers.

c Les's friendliness towards the Lunchtime Supervisors, but lack of meaningful contact with anybody on the staff. All but six of his interactions with staff were very short. He spent only nine minutes in either of the staffrooms. At no time did he sit down 'at his ease'.

d A marked lack of interactions with pupils outside lessons. He only spoke to six pupils in such circumstances, although his relationships were obviously relaxed and friendly.

e A large number of internal telephone calls. Most of these involved communications with the office about supply teachers.

f A good deal of time spent telephoning around trying to arrange speakers for the assemblies in the last week of term.

33 per cent of Les's day was spent on Technical activities – mainly teaching; 28 per cent on Administrative activities – mainly cover arrangement and attendance records; 19 per cent on Management activities; 3 per cent on Social activities; and 17 per cent on Personal activities – including talking to the researchers.

Comment

Les, like Jim, was busy, but he too had more than enough time to involve the researcher in conversation. He seemed very defensive when he was asked why he was compiling the statistics from the registers. There was an implicit recognition that such a job could be carried out by somebody else. His dependence on the office with regard to supply teachers was marked.

Les's defensiveness was also evident in the number of comments he made about how atypical that particular day was and how stressful the job could be. There was also many ironic comments about the difficulty of convincing non-administrative teachers that people like himself were putting in an honest day's work.

Meg

Meg was the Senior Mistress at the grammar school and continued in the same role after reorganisation. She had recently been promoted to Third Deputy (Staff Development) in the re-shuffle of deputies' responsibilities. Meg is 59. She teaches Home Economics and has an office directly across the corridor from the Head and adjacent to the main school office. Her present duties include:

1 Sharing in general oversight and assisting in the work of the First Deputy and Senior Teachers.

2 Responsibility for Staff Development: probationary teachers, students and the INSET library. Liaison with outside training agencies.
3 Being responsible for routine communications between the Head and members of staff.
4 Appointing temporary lunchtime supervisors and clerical staff.
5 Liaison with the LEA's GCSE adviser.
6 Being the school's 'named teacher' with respect to the statementing of Special Needs children.
7 Collection and distribution of papers for internal exams.
8 Liaison with the School Medical Service, ensuring that medical and hygiene supplies are available.
9 Reception and comfort of visitors to the school.
10 Maintaining regular contact with the catering officer and school meals adviser.
11 Maintaining contact with the school uniform suppliers.
12 Sharing the conducting (*sic*) of school assemblies.

Meg on her job

Meg has a 50 per cent teaching load; 'the rest of the time I'm racing about looking after . . .' (mentioning some of the duties listed above). Meg appears to be very staff oriented, commenting that, 'I've kind of had the feeling that the adults in a school are neglected. Unless they feel that someone cares for them they won't work. They need someone they can go to if they feel an injustice has been done . . .' Meg believes that many staff might say that she provides this support role.

Meg makes it her business to contact staff if they are ill or have other problems and says that she is always available. She believes the non-teaching staff 'lean on me'. She sees herself as one of the means by which staff tensions are resolved and a link between the staff and the Senior Management Team. She did not know if she was used more or less than other Deputies in this way. She pointed out that the Head tended to ask her what people in the staffroom were thinking. 'I think I've got quite a useful sort of role.'

In her Staff Development role, Meg says she talks to people about going on courses and provides them with the information they might need. She keeps a record of course attendance and has a Staff Development Committee. When asked about follow-up activities to off-site INSET, she said she had no time to do anything like that; 'I'm always too pressured with regard to time. I had to fly down here this morning from the Home Economics room to make a 'phone call'.

Questions about her involvement with the Heads of Year indicated that although she got on with them they tended not to refer children to her unless the 'offence was sex specific'. She admits that she is not used as much as she could be by the Heads of Year, who 'like dealing with things themselves. They feel a sense of failure if they can't cope.' Anyway, 'I don't want to be involved on the pastoral side. I'd have to change considerably if Heads of Year saw me as somebody they could use.' Meg fears being seen as a dragon by the children. To become more pastorally oriented, 'I would have to change my priorities. I'm 110 per cent occupied now.'

We did not observe Meg.

What the teachers say

Comments made by many teachers indicate that they have a view of the work and role of the Deputies which is not, to say the least, always consistent with that of the Deputies. In fact, the strength of the hostility towards them could, at times, be intense. There was a general feeling that:

1 They did not have very much to do with children; they had no time for children; the only time they came into contact with children was when Heads of Year involved them, they never took the initiative; nobody ever sent children directly to them.
2 They did not do very much; their work hardly impinged on the day-to-day activities of the teachers; teachers did not know what they did, how they earned their money.
3 The jobs on the job description were concerned with 'overseeing' or 'assisting' or liaising' or with tasks which were carried out infrequently or which involved only nominal responsibility; they were not real jobs.
4 They had too much non-contact time; often appeared to be bored, underemployed; did not understand the pressures under which classroom teachers worked because they were not under pressure themselves.
5 They were rarely seen in the staffroom or at social events; they hid away in their rooms or behind their desks; were rarely seen about the school, invisible; had not got their finger on the pulse of the school.
6 They were incompetent, inexperienced; were where they were because they happened to be in the right place at the right time; if you wanted a decision you went to the top, by-passing the Deputies.
7 They could not cope with people and their problems; ran away from confrontations and conflict; were administrators not managers, highly paid clerks.
8 They turned a blind eye to situations which the staff had been told to tighten up on, for example, snowballing; adopted a 'do-as-I-say-not-what-I-do' attitude, for example, sending children off early.
9 Les was difficult to relate to; hypersensitive himself; insensitive to others; self-serving; transmitted the 'wrong' signals; insincere.

Comment

There was no doubt that there was a gap, if not a gulf, between many members of staff and the Deputies. Although the Head was regarded by many staff as fairly remote and difficult to relate to, the staff did not talk about her in the same terms. The criticisms were directed at the Deputies. In the minds of the staff they were somehow responsible for their own professional unpopularity, for being seen as ineffectual and lacking in credibility. The matter was complicated by the fact that Les, unlike Meg and Jim, was also the subject of some personal abuse. Did the explanation of the problem lie in the personalities of the Deputies or was there something about the organisation structure of the school which caused the three Deputies to be criticised by so many of their colleagues so vociferously?

We believe that the problem was mainly because the Deputies were doing a lot of trivial clerical and administrative work, and very little managerial work. This was largely because the Headteacher had not provided them with opportunities for developing important roles. The timetable and curriculum, for example, were very firmly in the Head's control.

Response to our analysis

The staff response

The version of the above hypothesis was put to a number of teachers towards the end of the period of attachment, in an attempt to understand the problem without recourse to an explanation based on personalities!

The general drift of the analysis was regarded as valid, and the teachers welcomed the opportunity which it presented to stand back and view the situation in their school from another perspective. It was pointed out that Meg was the weak link in the argument since her main job, staff development, was primarily managerial. There was a measure of agreement that her lack of credibility was due largely to her lack of managerial *skills* – although she was doing managerial *work* – and the fact that she did not seem to have much to do with children in the normal course of her work.

There was also agreement with the idea that the Head had, in effect, neutralised her Deputies by not providing them with the opportunities to become involved with key management responsibilities, such as the timetable or curriculum development.

The teachers offered a number of possible explanations for this. First, the Head enjoyed the intellectual and organisational challenge of timetabling and curriculum development so much that she could not relinquish it to anybody else. It also brought her into direct contact with her Heads of Department. Second, she had no confidence in the ability of her Deputies to cope with timetabling and curriculum. Third it had never occurred to her to devolve responsibilities of this sort onto Deputies because she had never done so before. Most of the teachers opted for the first explanation.

The response of the Deputies

Follow-up interviews were conducted with Jim and Les when, in the context of discussing the shadowing exercise, the above hypothesis was introduced and their response invited.

Jim was initially unhappy about accepting the existence of the perceived gap between Deputies and staff, maintaining that he and his colleagues were close to the staff. If there was a problem in this area it might have something to do with the fact that, 'we have to make decisions for them and sometimes they can't do what they want to do.'

He was, though, prepared to admit that he probably was not as visible as he would like to be and agreed that there was a need for a more management-oriented style of leadership from the Deputies; 'getting out and about, mucking in, that sort of thing'.

After further thought Jim went on to admit that, 'in a sense the Head is lumbered with two elderly Deputies and two whom she inherited on reorganisation. Perhaps if she'd had different Deputies she'd have used them differently.'

He noted (not complained) that the Head had never asked anybody to get involved in the design of the timetable, although she had mentioned recently that she would like somebody else to do the rooming. What she had done, he said, is to 'offload the mundane, day-to-day stuff, like buildings and cover, and then let us get on with it with the minimum of interference.' He said he enjoyed his autonomy but recognised that it might have been bought at the expense of his credibility. Jim thought that the Head probably did not realise the effect she might have had on her Deputies.

Les, on the other hand, was fully prepared to accept the validity of the hypothesis and went on to make the following observations:

1 The Head was aware of the problem but did little to change things because she enjoyed working with her Heads of Department, many of whom she had appointed. He believed that many of the Heads of Department were more secure in their relationship with her than were the Deputies. He was, he said, frustrated that she had done so little to extend the professional development of the Deputies by not giving them more substantial jobs. He implied that this might be understandable in the case of Meg or even Jim, but 'I'm only forty.'

2 Les accepted that he is probably seen as being fairly remote from the staff but maintained that this was as much a function of his personality as the management structure of the school. He explained that when he first became a Deputy at 31 he was extremely ambitious, arrogant and self-serving. He admits that he was very insensitive in his dealings with staff, but a few years ago underwent a religious renewal which, he believes, has changed his attitude to his job and the staff with whom he works. He

recognised that although he has spoken to staff about the new direction of his life, 'some of them still see me like I used to be. They haven't forgotten what I was like.'

3 He recognised that at the moment he is less involved with children than he was when he was Head of Lower School because of 'the pressure of other things'. 'I can see why they feel like this – I've given up an appalling amount of time to setting up the cover system.'

4 He accepts that he has less face-to-face contact with staff than he used to have, but sees no reason why he should have to raise his profile by visiting the staffroom more often. 'Sitting in the staffroom is not at all important to me. The worst thing you can do is sit around in the staffroom, because people assume you have nothing to do and it could be inhibiting.'

5 Time prevented him from 'putting himself about more'. He maintained that he could not do 'more of the admin stuff' at home because he 'needed information which I can only get from the office'.

6 Although he is not seen to be involved in Curriculum Development at the moment, he will become more so in the future by participating in the school Working Parties on Gender and Multi-Cultural Education. He says he is already involved in the Working Party on PSE (although the researcher reports Les has not attended either of the first two meetings of this group).

7 Generally speaking he is pessimistic about whether it is possible for him to increase his credibility. This is partly because of the sort of person he is, but also because staff take efficient administration for granted. 'If you attempt to justify your job overtly then that comes across as defensive and counter-productive. Anyway, I haven't got the skills to convince staff that an admin job is credible.'

The Head's response

The Head regarded the hypothesis as a 'valid perspective, but it's difficult to do anything about it. Much of what I would have liked to delegate is not delegable because of the career pattern and lack of experience of my Deputies. I don't see either of them as effective Curriculum Deputies. Also I'm simply interested in it. It's an area where I can work fruitfully with staff.'

She recalled that when the school had been set up, she had offered the timetabling task to her Deputies (including one who has since left) but they all refused the offer. 'The timetable is better not done by a Head. It's tremendously and unjustifiably time-consuming.' Les had not been interested then 'but has become so – a good thing'. Nevertheless, she foresaw the possibility of some personality conflicts with staff if he did the timetable. In the short term she would ask him to do the rooming for the timetable which she was preparing for

September. She had no intention, even in the long term, of giving up her responsibility for curriculum development, which she saw as a Head's job.

She talked about how important it was that a Deputy should have a 'high profile', commenting that when she had had a similar job to Jim, as Head of Upper School, she had a 'much higher profile. Although I offended many Heads of Year by being like that.'

There were clear indications in many of her comments that she was disappointed that many of her attempts at devolving responsibilities had not 'come off. It's a pity they're not seen to be into things more. Perhaps it's because of the people they worked with previously. My predecessors did not require them to have a high profile.'

Conclusion

This extended description and analysis of the situation in one school shows three people holding highly paid positions all being under-utilised and manifesting varying degrees of dissatisfaction and sense of failure. It also shows the school staff generally disparaging the role-holders and under-valuing the position of Deputy Head. The Head is seen as someone who apparently does not need or welcome Deputies that make a significant contribution to the school, and who sees no prospect of making better use of the Deputies currently in post.

Although a fairly extreme example of the 'credibility' problem, it was not uncommon. Seldom did we find a situation in which Deputies had full jobs and never did we find a situation in which three Deputies were actually needed.

In this particular case, to what extent has the Head's hegemony in so many areas of school life stultified the professional growth of her Deputies, whatever their personal or professional limitations? Should a Head devolve major responsibilities onto Deputies if that Head knows that he could do a far better job himself? The answer must be that the school needs the skills, talents and commitment of all the adults in the school to maximise its achievement and that the relative ineffectiveness of these three is an element of under-achievement and vulnerability that no school can afford. It is a management axiom that managers manage with the people they have rather than with those they would like to have:

> The manager selects a few members of his team . . . but tolerates the vagaries of many others. One could almost say that picking one's own people is an abdication of management, a part of the art being to organise and co-ordinate the contribution of different types of people, including those one does not get on with. This involves the manager adapting his style and approach to the varied expectations

and needs of others, rather than being able to work only with kindred spirits, hand picked for their compatibility.

(Torrington and Weightman, 1985, p. 169)

References

Torrington, D. and Weightman, J.B. *The Business of Management* Prentice-Hall, Hemel Hempstead, 1985.

Chapter 16
The Head of Faculty or Department

An established view of the obvious importance of departments is neatly expressed by the Welsh Inspectorate:

> Whether a pupil achieves or underachieves is largely dependent on the quality of planning, execution and evaluation that takes place within individual departments.
>
> (Welsh Office, 1984)

A subject department seems such a natural division of labour (although some schools have adopted broader faculty groupings) within a large secondary school, and one that has existed for so long, that by now one might expect to encounter a large degree of similarity and consensus in the way departments operate. Nothing could be further from the truth; not only are there considerable differences between departments within the same school, there can also be striking differences between the way the same subject grouping operates from school to school. However, in all our schools it was the fundamental working group, with the shared technical expertise of its members bringing about the necessary cohesion and team working.

In our 24 comprehensive schools, we encountered a wide variety of subject departments. Some of the factors determining the way departments functioned were 'givens' of their situations, such as subject, size, staff, and whole-school procedures (the rules of the game which all departments have to obey, such as how to requisition stock). Other factors, while fairly stable, were presumably not immutable. Examples were the location of departments' facilities, the type of rooms at their disposal, the resources available, and the opportunities and constraints of the timetable. A third group of factors were more fluid, and open to the influence of the Head of Department and (to a lesser extent) the departmental staff. These were such matters as departmental procedures and practices, the degree of cohesion and understanding between members, departmental ethos and culture, and morale, which varied markedly between departments in the same school.

The job of Head of Department or Faculty is not just the administrative tasks that job specifications tend to enumerate. Heads of Department influence how the adults in the school work together and it is they who actually deliver all the issues we have outlined in Part I. Whether the Heads of Department are conscious of doing so or not, teachers in departments will experience the culture, resources, control, co-ordination, valuing, participation and change of the school most directly and immediately through the way Heads of Department manage and organise departmental affairs.

In our investigations we found in the most effective departments that all members, not just the Heads, demonstrated responsibility for managing their departments. Achieving effective sharing of responsibility – not just giving people jobs to do – can be a stark challenge for departmental heads used to a more limited role. Consider the following example of Heads of Department at Pennine End.

Their lives under the previous Head had been very much easier. They were responsible, in the main, for determining curriculum content, ordering text books and setting exams. They had few meetings to attend and did so mainly to 'receive instructions' from the head. They also had many more non-contact periods, with pastoral responsibilities limited to taking the register. They were not expected to be interested in matters outside their immediate subject areas nor to do anything without first 'clearing it with the Head'. When discipline problems arose, these too were handled by the Head. The main task of Departmental Heads was to maintain or improve the school's success in external examinations. Times have changed. The new Head has been trying to open the minds of his Heads of Department to the need to manage staff as well as organise and administer departmental resources. He has also encouraged them to take initiatives rather than orders and plan in terms of collaborating teams rather than individuals alone in their classrooms.

Current practice

Our schools provided evidence of the importance of departmental groupings and of the Head of Department role. But we also found that, despite glaring disparities between departments, it was most unusual to hear open discussion of either a department's effectiveness or the work of a particular Head of Department. It may be that they were simply taken for granted. Another view would be that open discussion of these issues within the school itself is taboo, since discussing differences between departments will inescapably involve consideration of the different ways those in positions of responsibility within departments interpret their roles and 'earn their money'; this runs counter to the cultural norms of the profession of teaching. Why should differences between departments and Heads of Department matter anyway? Surely we do not want uniformity from department to department, from school to school? One answer to this is that, despite contextual difference, there is a range of ways of running departments that can be loosely classified as satisfactory or good practice and another range that can be seen to be unsatisfactory or dysfunctional.

Here are four case studies to illustrate the variety of Heads of Department both within schools and between schools. Dick and Edward are at the Ridgeway School. Tom and Alan are at the Valley High School.

The Mathematics Department – Dick (Age 38), Scale 4

Dick took over the Maths Department in 1982 one year after reorganisation. He was able to appoint a like-minded second in the department in 1984. Between them they have 'imposed' on the Maths Department a new individualised resource-based Maths scheme. Dick recognises that he has been able to accomplish this only because the department accepted his right to do so. This is one of the benefits of working in a hierarchical school. He says there have been many problems along the way including: the original second in the department who 'ran out of his Fourth-Year class and resigned on the spot'; Dave, the ex-Head of Department, who had a raw deal when the schools were reorganised, but who is now co-operative and helpful; a lack of meetings exacerbated by the industrial action but stemming from the disinclination of staff to attend them in the first place.

Dick chairs his own meetings, when he has them, about once every half term ('too many' according to Dave). He uses the meetings to present the department with a 'lot of stuff from the outside'. Whilst he tries to ensure that the agenda comes 'from the floor', he admits that, 'you've got to have a certain amount of direction in a department which isn't used to open discussion'. Dick believes that people are more prepared to share ideas and materials now than they were, as a result of being exposed to a range of INSET activities. Most of his contact with people in his department is on an *ad hoc* basis, mainly in the staffroom, since his department does not have a common base, as such. A home-produced teacher's guide to the new course helps to supplement the lack of formal departmental contact.

The English Department – Edward (Age 33), Scale 4

Appointed Easter 1985, at the height of industrial action, he took over from John who was, according to individuals in the department, a difficult act to follow. He sees his job primarily as management, which he defines as 'growing people'. He believes that many of the people in his department see him as the Chief Administrator, not as the manager of a team, but believes that things might have been different if industrial action had not stopped him having meetings when he first started in his job.

English Department meetings provide some interesting insights into the attitudes and relationships of the teachers in the department and the problems with which Edward is confronted. The following features characterise the meetings: Edward fulfils his Head of Department role by introducing the teachers in the department to new ideas; he pressurises them to reconsider their existing practices; he displays enthusiasm and excitement for the teaching of English; but he struggles against the resistance of many teachers to his ideas, including a different approach to examining English in the Lower School and many other developments. There is a formality reminiscent of staff meetings. Formal votes are taken and minutes kept. The meetings are concerned with either administrative matters or with responding to a 'request' from the Head to discuss particular issues. For the most part discussion of these issues is perfunctory, although the minutes (which have to be sent to the Head) suggest that proper discussion has taken place.

Perhaps Edward will have to leave 'his' desk in the staffroom quiet area and come and sit in the main part of the staffroom where the alternative (or is it the authentic?) English Department meets. There is definite evidence that *ad hoc* decisions are made at these informal gatherings which threaten Edward's position and put pressure on him. At one meeting Graham lets slip, 'we have decided that Edward should ask the Head to . . .' Although they do not seem to have much use for Edward's ideas, they do seem keen to use him as their 'front-man' in dealings with the Head on their behalf.

The Science Department – Tom (Age 39), Scale 4

His commitment to the children and the school is shown by his attendance at meetings and extra-curricular activities. In the week beginning the 26th January, for example, he attended a Parents' Evening (two and a half hours), a basketball practice and match (three hours), the Staff/-Governors Consultative Committee (one and a half hours), a Curriculum Committee Meeting (one and a half hours) and a departmental meeting (three/four hours), a total of nine and a quarter hours. Tom would have no trouble whatsoever in achieving 'Baker's 1265' hours per year. He might even be able to begin his summer holidays in June.

For all his commitment and energy, Tom is a frustrated man. He complains that what he calls 'low-grade clerical' work prevents him from doing his job properly. When he should be 'providing leadership' he is often sorting materials or doing all manner of paperwork. 'There's no time in my week, no space, for really talking to staff, extending ideas, developing teaching strategies, or preparing my lessons properly. I'm living off my fat, on the experience I've built up over the years.'

Tom talks quietly but deliberately, contrasting the job of the man who was his first Head of Department with his own. He would not want such an easy life, but he does want the time to be able to do his job properly. Having a Head of Department allowance is all very well but it does not stop him feeling frustrated. Tom's situation is exacerbated by the fact that he cannot delegate any of his administrative work to other teachers in the department because they are 'heavily tied up in their own subject areas' or are still in their probationary years. One of these probationers has been experiencing considerable difficulties, so creating a situation where 'virtually every one of my non-teaching periods has been taken up providing her with some sort of support.' Although Tom prefers talking to such teachers quietly after a difficult lesson, he has been asked by the Head to intervene directly. Apparently there have been parental complaints and the Head feels that he cannot afford to be complacent about them. So Tom 'went in shouting', whilst believing that such a tactic would have only short-term effectiveness and, in his view, undermine the teacher's confidence rather than restore it. Although he does not like compromising his beliefs in this way, Tom was prepared to do so on this occasion out of respect for the Head and an understanding of his predicament.

The Humanities Department – Alan (Age 45), Scale 4

Alan wonders where his enthusiasm went. He talks about teaching being a 'young man's game', how tired he has become and 'living off his fat'. What he would like, he says, is either 'a new start in a Junior School' or a department of new teachers, 'who I would have to invigorate'. He has not been in a position to appoint any new teachers for many years now and suffers, if that is the right word, from the tendency of the staff to stay put and work with commitment and energy. Alan wants to fulfil a leadership role within his department but the people with whom he works do not need leadership, just a secretary to the committee who will do all the 'low-grade clerical stuff'. 'They do the leading. They're younger and more energetic and, in many ways, more competent than I am.'

Although he is over-dramatising his situation, there is an element of ironic truth in it, because he is, in effect, being forced to revert to a more 'traditional' Head of Department role: the orderer of books and tidier of shelves! At one point in the interview Alan even suggested that the logical outcome of his situation was that the role of Head of Department should 'revolve' and the extra points be shared. 'Financial realities,' he went on, 'make this impossible.'

Looking outward from his department, Alan notes that there is no longer a clear role for Heads of Department because of the full involvement of the staff in the school's participative arrangements. He does not speak for his department any more, they all turn up and speak for themselves. Alan is not unhappy about these moves towards more democratic structures; far from it. But he does wonder what is left! Alan would appear to be one of the first victims of collegiality and will be one of the first to feel guilty about his Incentive D.

The four examples given illustrate how each has to manage the particular culture of his department. Dick accepts a formal hierarchy, although in the same school Edward does not. Tom has to be an authority to a probationer but also a clerk. Alan sees little need for a manager as his department has developed away from this. We emphasise this aspect of Heads of Department's work as a contrast to the more common interpretation of Heads of Department's duties as administrative tasks.

Contrasted approaches to the Head of Department role

The prescriptive approach

A concrete approach to the role is to start with a list of the duties of the Head of Department. We find that there is, in fact, a body of writing that is basically an extended commentary on just such a prescriptive list, as in Marland (1981, p. 2):

1 Structure a departmental team . . .
2 Take a major part in appointing teachers.
3 Deploy teachers . . .
4 Monitor teachers' work.
5 Assist the development of teachers' professional skills.
6 Contribute to the initial training of student teachers.
7 Take a part in the planning of the school's overall curriculum and lead the planning of the curriculum within the department.
8 Oversee the work of pupils.
9 Manage the finances, physical resources and learning methods efficiently.
10 Assist the overall leadership of the school.

This sort of approach was echoed in the influential Cockcroft Report on the teaching of Mathematics, in which the duties of the Head of Mathematics were specified as follows:

'the production and up-dating of suitable schemes of work;
the organisation of the department and its teaching resources;
the monitoring of the teaching within the department and of the work and assessment of pupils;
playing a full part in the professional development and in-service training of those who teach mathematics;

liaison with other departments in the school and with other schools and colleges in the area.' (Cockcroft, 1982. p. 154)

The prescriptive approach seems to have become the current orthodoxy amongst Headteachers and Advisers and on courses and it is now common to find such lists in school or departmental handbooks. Ribbins (1985), in an extensive and useful review of the literature and theories of school middle management, shows that this orthodoxy has not gone unchallenged. He indicates various criticisms of this approach, including the lack of research to underpin the prescriptions; the utopianism of such prescriptions, which require a veritable paragon to carry them all out thoroughly; the reported increase in role conflict and stress ('manifesting itself in tiredness, physical ailments, psychosomatic illness and sickness among Heads of Department', p. 361) in trying to carry out all these prescriptions while still being required to carry a heavy teaching load. The Welsh Inspectorate concur:

> The status of Heads of Department . . . has diminished in recent years at the same time as their responsibilities have increased.
>
> (Quoted in Lodge, 1984)

Ribbins indicates that one of the major sources of criticism of Heads of Department lies in the performance of their supervisory function.

> Many commentators emphasise the importance of control, supervision and the monitoring of the work of departmental staff as a key, even *the* key, function of the middle manager . . . This may well be correct, but it is almost equally widely recognised that this is an aspect of their work which causes many Heads of Department great role-strain.
>
> (p. 361)

Ribbins quotes HMI in explanation:

> There are wide variations in the extent to which department heads are exercising their responsibilities. In some cases inadequate action is the result of failure to appreciate the extent to which responsibilities have multiplied and increased in importance but this is often accompanied by a traditional reluctance to interfere with the professional work of one's colleagues.
>
> (p. 361)

There is undoubted truth in this diagnosis; such monitoring runs counter to the culture of the teaching profession, and culture is one of the aspects of an organisation which is least responsive to prescription. There was also evidence from our research that even conscientious Heads of Department felt that formal monitoring by classroom observation was a very sensitive issue. Even where they felt they had a right or duty to do it, there was a feeling that such obvious flexing of status muscles as observing colleagues teach and inspecting mark-books and exercise books might well undermine good departmental relationships and other aspects of team building. Another factor is that classroom observation and feedback takes time, which is the scarcest commodity in a large secondary school; when we asked, 'What is the greatest constraint on your effectiveness?', the commonest response from the staff that we interviewed was 'time'. Nevertheless, it is probably the counter-cultural aspects of monitoring that carry the most weight; time can always be re-scheduled if the will is there.

It seems, therefore, that despite increased pressures in the name of accountability, the kind of management thinking embodied in such statements as:

> Within a school or college superordinates have a right and an obligation to monitor and judge the performance of subordinates.
>
> (Lambert *et al.*, 1985)

is not easily or readily translated into action by practitioners at the level of the secondary school, at least not in the sense of the formal line-management paradigm expressed in the more prescriptive literature. Nevertheless, the intentions expressed in this approach (co-ordination, quality control) are worthy and cannot be discounted. Can they be realised through some other method?

Department culture and leadership style

Whilst the specifying of duties and expectations in an analytical way is useful, more important to the success of the departmental team are such synthesising aspects as departmental culture and such process factors as leadership style. These receive hardly any attention at all in the prescriptive literature for the Head of Department, possibly because they are 'softer' issues and do not lend themselves to the sort of comforting specificity favoured by such literature. Yet there is a considerable body of theory and research which can be drawn upon to inform our understanding of this issue.

A useful continuum of leadership styles is 'tells, sells, consults or joins' (see, for example, Sadler, 1970). It is undoubtedly possible to create some of the features of an effective department by a 'tells' or 'sells' style of leadership and it is likely that subordinates will always prefer these to a 'passive' style (cf Nias, 1980) that we can call 'abdicates'. Yet it seems that at the level of the department the 'consults' or even the 'joins' end of the leadership spectrum is likely to be the most effective as well as the preference of most subordinates. These involve a collaborative process of planning, choice and preparation of materials and a collegial atmosphere of mutual trust and support which will enable such collaboration to include the key element of being able to visit each other's classrooms and to observe and discuss each other's work in a positive, non-threatening way.

Research into school and business effectiveness has highlighted the importance of culture and ethos at the macro level of the organisation; it is likely that in the same way and for the same reasons, departmental culture is of importance at the micro level. In most secondary schools Heads of Department are not afforded the extensive and expensive time necessary for constant close supervision of their subordinates' work; and, as we have seen, many are apprehensive about even attempting this formally. Culture (shared basic assumptions and values) and the normative peer-pressure of collaborative work can provide a cheaper and potentially more effective substitute in creating departmental co-ordination, cohesion and quality control. We suggest that these issues are delivered within departments by developing along lines we have discussed in part I of this book.

Since our fieldwork was completed, performance appraisal for teachers has developed considerably as an issue and will be operating in all schools soon after this book is published. Indications from our current discussions with those preparing schemes for appraisal is that this will make the role of Heads of Department even more equivocal, as it seems unlikely that many of them will actually carry out the appraisal itself, even though they are likely to do classroom observations. Despite all the apprehension about appraisal and its 'sensitivity', the apparent unwillingness to entrust departmental heads with this key feature of managerial work will further weaken their effectiveness, despite their probable initial relief at being able to avoid an unenviable task.

Good practice

Mike – Head of English (Age 43), Scale 4

Observations suggest that Mike only sits down at meetings. It is a good thing then that he has between two and five department, school and 'other' meetings in a typical week. He may sit down in lessons but was not seen to do so. When he is not teaching or sitting down at meetings he is: 'contacting staff, making phone calls, duplicating materials, ordering books and equipment, checking facilities in the teaching bases, tidying and re-stocking shelves and writing letters to parents'.

He is also a GCSE Phase 4 Co-ordinator and a teaching representative on the English INSET Committee at the University. But, most of all, he is 'organising a collaborative democratic team of teachers'. Mike talks of having a team which is 'pupil-centred', that works with children using their 'own culture to develop their language skills'.

The team has its own purpose-built suite of rooms, including an office/meeting room. These are comfortable but constricting. The core of the team is rarely seen out of the English Block and certainly not in the staffroom, apart from a smoker who left at Christmas.

His team is less coherent than he would like it to be, partly because he has had to make do with temporary staff, but also because three-quarters of the Senior Management Team work in it. 'They are as committed as they can be.' This commitment includes teaching their (mixed-ability) classes, but they sometimes miss the meetings around which Mike works.

Observations suggest that Mike is a very effective leader of such meetings. He is meticulous in the way he elicits comments and ideas from everybody sitting around the table, and he draws these ideas together very sensitively. Even more impressive is his ability to do all this whilst making and pouring out a pot of tea for those in attendance. There is ample evidence that Mike enjoys the full support and loyalty of the team, partly because he is so hard working, but also because he is so patently competent in his work and believes in what he is doing. His influence in the department is certainly based on these qualities; whilst his influence in the school as a whole is derived from the fact that he 'leads a strong team of teachers who are at the heart of the school'.

Mike's problems would appear to be at two levels. On an instrumental level, he is concerned about the 'pressures which prevent you from teaching properly', which include a less than stable staff, a lack of time, resources, space and a timetable that does not allow him to work in one-and-a-half-day blocks. On a philosophical level he is concerned about what he calls the 'permanent crisis about what should be taught in English' and the increasing tension between a teacher's subject and caring responsibilities in schools which are increasingly sensitive to 'outside' pressures.

Do It Yourself

1 How are the following decided in your department?

- The timetable.
- Who teaches which groups.
- The content of particular lessons.
- The overall methodology in class.

2 How often does the Head of Department talk for more than five minutes to each member of the department?

3 Who decides what should be discussed at department meetings?

4 What is in the departmental handbook? Who decides this?

5 When did you last go into a colleague's lesson? When did someone come into yours?

6 Do you know what your colleagues were teaching to-day?

References

Cockcroft, W., *Mathematics Counts*, HMSO, London 1982.

Lodge, B., 'Department Heads Drop in Status', *Times Educational Supplement*, 11th May, 1984.

Lambert, K., Ribbins, P. and Thomas, H., 'The Practice of Evaluation', in Hughes, M. *et al.*, *Managing Education: The System and the Institution*, Holt, Reinhart and Winston, London, 1985.

Marland, M., *Head of Department*, Heinemann, London, 1981.

Nias, J., 'Leadership Style and Job Satisfaction in Primary Schools', in Bush, T. *et al.* (Eds), *Approaches to School Management*, Harper and Row/OUP, London, 1980.

Ribbins, P., 'The role of the Middle-Manager in the Secondary School', in *Managing Education: The System and the Institution*, Hughes, M. *et al.* (Eds), pp. 343–70, Holt, Reinhart and Winston, London, 1985.

Sadler, P.J., 'Leadership Style, Confidence in Management and Job Satisfaction, in *Journal of Applied Behavioural Science*, Vol. 6, No. 1, pp. 3–9, 1970.

Welsh Office, *Departmental Organisation in Secondary Schools*, HMSO, London, 1984.

Chapter 17
The Head of the Pastoral Team

Problems of pastoral leadership are well recognised, for example:

> Those holding key pastoral posts usually work hard and are honestly committed to the well-being of pupils, but because training is unavailable or based on limited conceptions of the task, the caring turns out to be a constraining form of tension reduction or unthinking tutelage for obedience.
>
> (Hamblin, 1986, p. 141)

There are also management and organisation problems affecting the whole school that are worth exploring. The problems associated with the pastoral structure seem to us to be related to several unresolved *ambiguities* in the work of the Head of Year/House.

First, who are their *clientele*? Is the job to work with pupils establishing and maintaining the ethos of the school? This is frequently done by being visible in the school, maintaining standards, and encouraging appropriate behaviours and activities. A major feature of this emphasis is dealing with individual children and groups who do not conform to school norms.

Or is the job to work with staff, so as to develop their skills in dealing with individual pupils, their knowledge of the various procedures and to ensure they can all cope with the newer participative methodologies associated with PSE?

Most readers will doubtless answer the questions of the last two paragraphs by saying that both aspects are essential, yet there is a conflict between them if both are attempted simultaneously and this can lead to role strain, especially as the role is one that implies a higher degree of skill in an activity with which every member of staff is concerned. The ordinary teacher of Chemistry is not likely to query the technical expertise of the Head of Modern Languages or begrudge the additional payments received for the discharge of that responsibility, but that same teacher of Chemistry might reasonably claim comparable expertise with the Head of Third Year and be very dismissive of the job holder's competence.

When someone gets paid extra to do something in which everyone has a stake, then other people's application to this task will be reduced. So, although the 1987 contract spells out that pastoral duties are the responsibility of everyone, this will not be carried out thoroughly when others are seen to have privileges for doing this work.

Second, what is the message for *form tutors*? Are form tutors asked to be autonomous in how they work with their forms? Is active tutorial work encouraged? Can the tutors decide what to do, how and when with their forms? Or are there so many administrative tasks decided by the Heads of Year/Heads of House that form time is completely taken up with such things as letters home, uniform checks, money collection, homework book checks, forms filled in? It is a very mixed message many form tutors receive – encouraged to do active tutorial work and yet receiving an avalanche of papers demanding completion by the pupils. There is a special quandary for Heads of Pastoral Teams when introducing PSE and active tutorial work. There is a tendency to spoonfeed rather than encourage active participation in developing the materials so teachers 'own' the materials. This may be due to a felt lack of time for consultation but it may be a shoring up of the authority of the Head of Year/Head of House by claiming an expertise. This is in contrast to many subject Heads who encourage a professional approach to work.

Third, what is the *power base* of the Head of Year/House? Frequently they have privileges, such as reduced timetables and their own rooms, and special meetings in school time with the Deputies or the Head, which suggest real position power. All of these separate them from the form tutor as they are not in the staffroom at breaks and dinner times. This is because they are frequently making staff dependent on them by dealing with, and taking away, the problem children. At the same time Heads of Year/House are telling staff that they must deal with problem children themselves or use the procedures which mean going to the Head of Department. Positions of power always need supporting with something else, such as resources or expertise. Until ambiguities surrounding the role of Head of Year are resolved, they are likely to use their expertise with children as the basis of their power, but this is not compatible with encouraging staff to deal with their own problems. The word 'Head' of Year or House is a signal that they are in charge of something. If the role needs changing, it might be differently construed if they were called something like 'consultant' or 'assistant'. The first suggests an expertise that can be consulted by staff; the second someone with time and resources to put at staff's disposal.

Current practice

We found several problems associated with the pastoral structure. Many Heads of Pastoral Teams were feeling stressed, subject teachers felt too much time was spent on pastoral matters, and all 24 schools felt they had not got this aspect of their school right.

We quote here a description, written by one Head of Year, that typifies the stress felt by many Heads of Pastoral Teams:

> This year I have one 'free' period less than last year and two less than the previous year. Other members of the English Department have a norm of six 'free' periods, without the pressure of examination work that I have, and I have eight 'free' periods – leaving two periods in which to deal with Head of Year work. Periods are freely taken from this allocation of two for supervision for absent colleagues, case conferences, meetings with EWO, parental and social worker visits and discussions, and so forth. Day after day I am forced to surrender my break and often spend the entire day without any respite at all, save for lunch, in which to catch up on other work. Even so, I have this term had virtually no time at all to deal with such matters as filing and record-keeping and a mountain of this work is steadily piling up. Toward the end of last summer term I worked unremittingly to try to catch up with this and other Year tasks with which (of necessity) I had fallen behind, often through lunchtimes, while I noticed that certain other members of staff, in some cases paid a higher salary than I, spent their lunchtimes and free periods playing tennis.
>
> I *never* enjoy the luxury of a 'free' period in school in which to chat with colleagues or sort out my office or stockroom or acquaint myself with the latest English Department acquisitions or simply to rest and recover. Preparation and marking must be taken home because an often unmanageable build-up of work means that I do not have time to even begin them in school. Form periods are for me 'rush hour'.
>
> Since last Easter I have been ill very frequently, apart from spells of illness during the last Christmas, Summer and Easter holidays. Partly, I believe, as does my doctor (who will verify this), because of lowered resistance stemming from exhaustion.

In all 24 schools there was *current dissatisfaction* with the pastoral system. The move to PSE and the time taken by form periods was felt excessive by those trying to get through GCSE syllabuses with the fourth and fifth years. Many form tutors complained about the amount of paper-work they were asked to monitor. For example, some handed out letters to parents and then checked that return slips, to confirm the letters' receipt, had all come in.

Form tutors often feel they are little more than register takers and the medium for the communication of information from Heads of Year to pupils. Every school was trying to insist that problems occurring in the classroom should be referred to the Head of Department. Most schools felt that discipline problems within the classroom should be referred by the class teacher to the Head of Department whereas the problems outside the classroom should go to the tutor and Head of Year/House. In fact, problems were usually going straight to the Head of Year. Consequently, many Heads of Year found themselves with a heavy disciplinary role and a lot of senior staff time and effort was expended exhorting people to use the proper procedure which, clearly, did not work. The distinction between 'in class' and 'out of class' is clearly less obvious than that between 'Academic' and 'Pastoral' issues.

An example is the following description of a day spent with Will, Head of Third Year, whose day was characterised by:

1 Regular patrols in the corridors and foyers of his 'territory'. He was very visible to both children and staff.
2 Frequent but gentle cajoling of the children. There were no actual conversations with children, although he interacted with 45 during the course of the day.
3 A good deal of 'travelling' between the Lower School and the Main School (four return journeys).
4 Apparently frequent interruptions when children knocked on his door and asked for jotters and dinner cards. (This was said to be atypical.)
5 Patience with children who knocked on his door and restraint when telling children off. Despite the restraint his interactions could not be categorised as counselling, more mild reproving.
6 Automatic phoning home to inform parents that their children have been reprimanded. Many of the attempts to reach parents fail because there is nobody in. During the course of the day Will made 14 external phone calls, only four of which were successful.
7 The fact that he spent 16 minutes in his room with apparently nothing to do, waiting for something to happen. The time he had to make phone calls would appear to be further evidence that Will was not constrained by time factors.
8 An almost complete lack of 'social' or 'personal' interactions. The nearest he came to this was a number of pleasantries to teachers and dinner supervisors. No time was spent in either staffroom.
9 A number of pleasant, helpful 'managerial' exchanges with other Year Heads in their shared room. It was obviously useful for all three that they shared a room, although there were bound to be many inconveniences.
10 A lack of contact with either Deputy, even though one has an office next door. He talked to the Head when he was 'on duty' first thing in the morning but seemed to ignore the Deputies when he saw them about the campus.
11 The completion of only one 'organising task' – arranging for a group of children to participate in a tree planting project. The arrangements, which took approximately 24 minutes spread through the day, involved rearranging some classes and writing out some lists. Will said that he should not have done that, which begs the question, what would he have done instead during the day of observation?
12 A complete lack of paperwork of any kind apart from writing out a list

of names of the children who were to be involved in the tree planting. No records were maintained of any of the multiple disciplinary sessions he had with children.

Will was a pleasant chap who recognised his own limitations. He was not particularly articulate nor forthcoming with original ideas. He did not have any ideas about how the pastoral system in the Lower School could be improved, nor did he appear to have given the matter any serious thought. 'At the moment I don't know if any major changes are necessary, unless they're part of a whole change of policy', by which he meant changes decided elsewhere, presumably by the Head.

What Will had done, perhaps intuitively, was to change '. . . the emphasis a bit by being around more . . . with the kids . . . than was the case previously with this post.' (This was the nearest he came to criticising Paul, his predecessor.) 'Regardless of what other responsibilities you have in school you've got to be seen with the children.'

Will's success in changing the emphasis was recognised by many of his colleagues who seemed to have great respect for him. The fact that he was seen with children and knew them and their problems gave him considerable credibility. They perceived him as working hard, with children, on their behalf. The evidence of our observation, on a day which Will recognised as typical, might suggest that the staff perception was false. Compared to other teachers in a similar role in other schools, Will appeared to have a relatively easy life. There was no pressure on Will on the day in question yet his credibility, quite rightly, remained intact. Why?

Firstly, teachers on the staff recalled that in their view he had been the *de facto* Head of Third Year before he was officially appointed to the job. They had had little or no confidence in his predecessor for reasons which had more to do with his personality and way of operating than his role. Secondly, Will was far more visible than his predecessor, happier reacting to teachers' needs, supporting them in their 'crises', being available without any complaints, than the predecessor was. Whether, objectively speaking, he worked under the same pressure and stress as, say, the Heads of House at the school is irrelevant; in the eyes of his colleagues he, and his fellow Heads of Year, worked so hard that, to quote one respondent, 'They meet themselves coming back.' This may not be true in absolute terms, but is certainly the perceived reality in this school.

This Head of Year was not constrained by time compared with our earlier example. We argue that each school needs to consider whether the use of resources such as time, salary, rooms, is appropriate for the task of Head of Pastoral Team.

Conclusion

What are possible solutions to the problem of widespread dissatisfaction with the pastoral head role? The ambiguities discussed above could be resolved if the nature of the Head of Year post was clarified. We believe that this job lacks respect and acceptance by other staff because it is seen as less central. Teachers come to teach their subject or to teach children, not to do pastoral work apart from that which is closely connected with their teaching. For example, they expect to mark work at home but not to mark homework notebooks. So a lot of pastoral work in form time seems to them to be 'administrative' rather than 'technical' work. If the Head of Year is charged with nurturing the school ethos, this will not be achieved through control mechanisms leading to administrative chores for others. Nor will it get the willing co-operation of staff as we discussed in Part I of this book. Uncertainty in any job tends to lead people into doing more administration.

One useful role for Heads of Year might be in staff development about methods of dealing with children. This would be a good use of the two extra non-contact periods of many Heads of Year; those that have half timetables could spend more time teaching, and the 'frees' could be more equitably distributed.

One approach we found which worked well was where the Head of a Pastoral Team was an older, established member of staff. These often were wise people who, with the minimum fuss, calmly established order and maintained the school ethos. They usually did the minimum of paperwork, were highly visible, spent as much time talking to adults as children and were well respected by their colleagues. These, often rather old-fashioned, Pastoral Heads established a secure environment that set standards of behaviour for the pupils that we found freed other staff to get on with new initiatives and exciting teaching.

A lot of work done by Heads of Pastoral Teams is administrative or clerical. For example, keeping records, checking registers, phoning home, contacting EWOs and social services. Much of this could be efficiently done by having more non-teaching staff permanently allocated to pupil support. In one school a disabled teacher was filling this role half-time for all the Heads of Year in the shared pastoral office. It was seen as very successful.

Examples of good practice

Duncan, Head of Upper School (Years 3, 4 and 5) and Joe, Head of Lower School, share an office. One obvious benefit of their smallish school is that the pastoral system which they organise can be kept simple. Duncan acts as a Head of Year 5, with two staff heading the other Upper School years;

Joe has an Assistant Head of Lower School whose newly established role is mostly concerned with induction.

Both men are long established in the school and, though they have firmly expressed differences, get on well with each other. They have substantial teaching loads but still meet the needs of staff for support on discipline. With the children, they are rigidly fair; during interviews of pupils, they are controlled, writing down answers not only for the record 'but to show seriousness of intent and to give time for considering action'. Both seem to have phenomenal memories for pupils' backgrounds (and earlier misdeeds) though, in part, that is because of their thorough note-taking and record-keeping.

They have had a consistent example of style to follow from the Headteacher, who admires their work and takes an encouraging interest in pastoral matters, both at the individual and school-wide levels. The interest does not extend to interference.

The strengths of this pastoral structure are:

- its simplicity;
- the operation of common standards arising from common location and experience;
- the rigour of the actions – nothing is swept under the carpet or allowed to go by default.

The potential weakness, which could develop into a major problem, was the workload Duncan and Joe put up with. Subject specialisms meant that neither could easily shed much teaching, so the school needed to lighten the pastoral work they did so well.

Do It Yourself

1 Consider the resources your school attaches to Heads of Pastoral Teams:

a extra non-contact time;
b extra allowances;
c rooms;
d non-teaching assistants.
Could these be better used?

2 Collect information about the felt effectiveness of the system. For example:

a Do people short-circuit the system?
b Do Heads of Pastoral Teams complain that folk do not use the system?

c Do Senior staff make public statements asking people to use the proper system?
d How is the work across the school co-ordinated?

References

Hamblin, D., 'The Failure of Pastoral Care?', in *School Organization* Vol. 6, No. 1, pp. 141–8, 1986.

Chapter 18
The Registrar

In the private sector of education, individuals called Bursars are employed to handle many of the non-academic aspects of the day-to-day running of the school. Such a person manages and controls the resources of the school, including finances, buildings, equipment and non-teaching staff. The state of the lavatories and the appointment of a new clerical assistant is left to these administrative managers, leaving the Head and senior teaching staff to get on with the job of managing teaching staff, the curriculum and all the other things to do with the direction and conduct of the school. There is much current feeling, especially with the issue of Local Financial Management and the consequent devolution of aspects such as maintenance and running costs, that Heads and senior staff should be appointed for their love of teaching, not for their skills as chief administrators.

Chapter 10, 'Technical, Administrative and Managerial Work', shows that we discovered individuals at Deputy Head level spending nearly one third of their time doing administrative work, often of the type that a member of clerical staff could perform with only a small amount of explanation – such as the allocation of bus duties to staff, taking into account their last teaching location in the split-site school. In one school, jobs being done by teaching staff that we considered should really reside in the general office under the general control of the Registrar, included: adding up and producing lists of charges for departmental photocopying bills; a similar task for the school stationery stock cupboard; form and subject listings and examination statistics; monitoring of registers for absence statistics and attendance prizes; liaison with county plumbers and decorators. These jobs are being done by five teachers with the Grades 3, 4 or ST. Many schools have a Deputy Head especially responsible for Administration. In another school, administrative jobs farmed out to members of teaching staff include external exams, transport, campus maintenance, school lunches, fire and safety, and litter; duties which all carry an extra point. One school has a Head of Administration at Deputy

Head level who is formally responsible for the 'smooth running of the school organisation on a day-to-day basis; duty teams, examinations and statistical returns'. 'Special events' include activities such as school photographs, distribution of bus passes and speech days. Whilst this individual is perceived to be doing a competent and necessary job, and some staff earning extra points for performing administrative duties appeared to be satisfied with the extra financial reward, how much more sense it would make if these jobs were included in the remit of a Registrar, not a senior teacher.

However, this appears only rarely to be the case in maintained secondary schools. Registrars – also called Bursars, School Clerks, School Secretaries or Administrative Officers, depending on the local authority – are employed on administrative grades 2 to 6. At the grade 2 and 3 level, they are little more than clerks and, therefore, cannot be expected to take on many of the responsibilities listed above (which is not to say that some of them would not be capable of it, since this position is often filled by mature, experienced and intelligent people, perhaps who have gone back to work after their children have reached school age). A grade 5 or 6 Registrar should, however, be sufficiently experienced and skillful to take on the management of these things, and devolve them to members of clerical staff. One local authority whose schools we were in had a deliberate policy of not employing Registrars below grade 5 and, indeed, had just made a decision on the basis of an in-depth job evaluation exercise to award grade 6 to all Registrars in schools with over 1,000 pupils. Unfortunately, it was not concurrently reviewing the people holding these posts, so it seemed likely to us that there would be grade 6 individuals in jobs who were not necessarily able to grow into the additional responsibilities now being placed on them. The authority was in the process of introducing a centralised computer database, with all schools having their own terminals and computer controls. In deciding where the control of the system should lie, they were recommending that a Deputy be assigned the role of systems manager, while the Registrar would be made responsible for the operation of the system.

Current practice

Job descriptions

Job descriptions for clerical staff in schools did exist, although they were by no means universal. In some cases, there existed a blanket local authority job description, but this was sometimes so brief as to be worthless. One such that we saw has seven brief items on it, one of which was to cover for other members of ancillary staff. Here are two examples of individualised school job descriptions that we discovered.

1 The Bursar of this Group 11 school has 'general responsibility for the school's physical resources, all school monies, the appointment and management of all non-teaching staff (with the Head) and the compilation of official orders and the inventory'.
2 The Registrar of this Group 12 school has the following job description, which is printed in the Annual Staff Brochure:

Function – to provide a comprehensive administrative service to the school.
To assume a degree of responsibility for the organisation and welfare of the non-teaching staff.
To collect and be responsible for monies connected with all school activities.
To complete staff registers and prepare time-sheets.
To deal with all administration connected with repairs to equipment and buildings.
To process all school requisitions and oversee stock books.
To organise the school minibus system.
To monitor school lettings.
To liaise with teachers, non-teaching staff, caretakers and canteen staff, on various matters.
To provide coffee system for the staff.
To be responsible for some official returns to the Authority.
To collect and return various goods to suppliers.
To carry out other duties as requested.

Some of these the post holder certainly does, not least supplying coffee packs to staff. Others we did not see any evidence of while we were there, including organisation of the school minibus system or liaison with kitchen staff. Indeed, the responsibility for the oversight of the minibus is also listed in the job description of one of the Deputies, as is responsibility for completion of official school returns. The Registrar knows that these jobs are being done by other people in the organisation and, as she is kept very busy on maintaining a splendid but time-consuming flexibility in the day-to-day finances of the school, it is understandable that she does not do them.

Observation of a School Clerk, Margaret

We carried out several observations of the work of the Registrar. This seemed to us to be typical of the activities undertaken by such individuals, although not all Registrars actually did typing themselves. Observation began at 8.35 and ended at 11.50, on a Friday in the Spring term. The school is Group 11.

During the period 81 changes of activity were recorded, 31 on Margaret's initiative and 50 as a result of an initiative or stimulus from elsewhere. The tasks were broken down into ongoing routine activities, expeditions and interruptions, as follows:

The principal *ongoing activities* of the morning observed seemed to be:

- preparing and giving out dinner tickets to monitors;
- opening and sorting post;
- preparing a bundle for the 'caretaker post';
- typing the school newsletter;
- sorting out money for the bank, and accounting.

Expeditions were trips out of the office for:

- delivering post to Head and to staff pigeonholes;
- going to reprographics/filing room to copy documents for use files.

Interruptions to ongoing activities were chiefly:

- operating the switchboard (incoming and outgoing calls);
- attending to visitors;
- dealing with teaching and non-teaching staff (invoices, requests for information, stationery, keys, expense forms, change, etc.).

In a large school, the sheer quantity of clerical and secretarial work generated will normally lead to the employment of further clerical staff under the School Clerk. Although the extra hands can obviously be put to good use, this also adds a further dimension to the job, in that it will now require some management skills on her or his part. There will need to be a measure of delegation, with its delicate balance of trust and supervision. Margaret has the assistance of two part-time office staff. During the morning of the observation, it appeared that the work of these had been successfully divided and routinised, so they got on with their own tasks without overt intervention or supervision by Margaret. She re-directed the work of one of them on one occasion during the morning. The atmosphere was pleasant but business-like.

We were struck by the large amount of paperwork dealt with by the school office and the vast system of files and records maintained by the School Clerk. Some of the paperwork involves standard forms, some devised by Margaret, which help to eliminate duplication of effort. Some paperwork is generated by the LEA, some by school routine and some of it simply constitutes Margaret's preferred method of working. The fact that two different banks of pupil records existed, one maintained by Margaret and one by the Heads of School, raises questions about the necessity of all this paperwork and the contribution that computerised records could make.

The most striking feature of Margaret's work on the morning observed was its fragmentation. She was busy for the entire period of the observation, but the characteristic pattern was one of activities begun on her own initiative being interrupted. It is likely that, without the presence of her two assistants for periods in the morning, the fragmentation would have been even greater; they were able to shield Margaret to some extent, for example, by staffing the reception window and the switchboard, while she got on with typing the school newsletter.

Description of the roles of two Registrars

1 *The efficient harridan*

The Bursar of this Group 11 school, Susan, is a middle-aged woman who identifies closely with the job. She is actively disliked by some staff and grudgingly respected by others for the apparently efficient manner with which she fulfils her responsibilities, particularly with respect to the school finances.

Comments made by teachers about her included:

> She is a harridan who bites, who is obstructive to staff and non-teaching staff alike.
>
> We can't sack her because she is marvellous with the money and keeps us on the straight and narrow. The auditors can never find fault with her.
>
> She can be abrupt and does put people's backs up, but you do need some tight control on the money.

There is some perception amongst some staff that the Head's lack of interest in regulations and procedures renders him dependent on Susan. He also, it was suggested, uses her as his 'hard face', referring financial decisions to her when he does not want to be associated with refusals for finance. In this way, she is given some of the Head's 'dirty work' to do, which she is not surprisingly not keen about. The Head claims she takes on such activities by choice.

Her knowledge and competence, built up over many years in local government and school administration, give her considerable power and autonomy. It appears that she relishes her key role in the administration of the school, whilst complaining that she has more freedom than the regulations state. It is clear that she wants the Head to fulfil a more authoritarian role in the school, especially with those teaching and non-teaching staff who do not follow what she regards as simple systems or who do not share her enthusiasm for administration.

There is some evidence of inter-personal antipathy between Susan and the other non-teaching staff. Some of this may be due to her insistence on rigidly adhering to regulations regarding, say, working hours during the holidays, and to a lack of warmth and sensitivity to the feelings of her non-teaching colleagues. Her personality seems to make others less efficient than they might otherwise be. Staff do not, for example, always keep her informed because of her unapproachability. Information about an extra-curricular activity might not be communicated to the caretaker because the teacher concerned has not told the Registrar, and she insists on being told first so that she can tell the caretaker. When the caretaker complained to the Head about this, the latter told him to go and see Susan.

Susan's understanding of her role, together with her personality, make it difficult for her to delegate responsibility. She does not trust other people to do things properly. The Head is not prepared to try and sort things out with the Registrar. His answer is to wait for her to retire.

2 Unsure, but competent

Amanda has been a Registrar in this Group 10 school for four years, having previously been employed as a part-time clerical assistant in the same school. She has received no formal training for the job and learns as she goes along. The Head is a great help to her, particularly in financial matters. They work well as a team, but he insulates her from pressures such as dealing with unco-operative staff. Her work appears to fall into three main areas:

a Acting as the Head's secretary. She opens his post and does his typing for example, confidential staff references. She finds it easier to type the Head's work herself than to delegate it to one of the other clerical staff and then have to check it. She does not type much for the staff except when the others are under pressure.

b Financial responsibilities. She sees finance as being the most important part of her job. The school has voluntary-aided status, and has a greater responsibility for paying its own bills in certain areas such as buildings and external maintenance. On the occasion she was observed, she spent most of her time checking departmental orders.

c Management of other non-teaching staff. She organises the work of the typists/receptionists, the reprographics clerk and the welfare assistant. In theory, the laboratory technicians, craft technician and librarian should be under her control, but she is content to allow the relevant Heads of Department to organise their work.

Amanda has a very good working relationship with her staff and there is a pleasant atmosphere in the office, with morale high. She is rather unsure of herself and her abilities, even after doing the job for several years, and is lacking in assertiveness. She would probably benefit from a formal job description and some formal training.

The job and skills of the Registrar

We have already discussed aspects of the job of the Registrar in the introduction. The preceding descriptions of Registrars in a variety of schools cannot really do justice to the variety of different ways in which individuals and schools expect this job to be performed. In some schools, the Registrar is no more than a glorified clerk (and paid accordingly), with the bulk of the job of administrative management falling largely on the shoulders of teaching staff. In others, Registrars are taking on tasks which usually fall to teachers, such as examination entries and collating examination statistics for governors, press and parents.

On occasions that were only too frequent, however, we discovered Registrars who, because they have been doing the same type of job for many years, often in the same school, are bogged down in procedures, paperwork and record keeping – and there is nobody in the school to stop or help them. Many such Registrars are well-intentioned and scrupulously honest. But it is not surprising that over-elaborate paperwork activities cause others to be neglected. Unfortunately, no one has seen fit to sit down with them, go through exactly how they spend their time, identify with them what benefits arise from, and what use is made of, these multiple procedures and bits of information, and generally help them to make more sense of their jobs. There are cases where a good and conscientious job is being done, but it could be done even better with a bit of standing back and looking at the ultimate purpose of the activities being undertaken. Many times, we came away from schools surprised by how little supervision and direction of her or his tasks the Registrar received.

The job of Registrar in a large school is a varied and responsible one, offering much potential job satisfaction, as well as high levels of stress. As well as the routine recording and other clerical functions of the job, the Registrar occupies what may be seen as a hub role, involving a vast network of actual and potential contacts, both within and outside the institution. See Figure 8 for a diagrammatic representation of this central position occupied by the Registrar. Contact can be face-to-face, by telephone or by letter and can be initiated by the job holder or by another person. In all these cases, the Registrar is likely to need to employ skills of communication, judgement, empathy, patience and tact.

The continual possibility of inputs from this vast network introduces into the job a considerable element of uncertainty and unpredictability, which will always threaten to play havoc with the efficient planning and implementation of administrative tasks which are otherwise fairly straightforward and routine (such as monitoring of capitation and invoices). When time becomes short, there is the difficulty for the Registrar of prioritising tasks which, in the absence of clear and agreed guidelines, can cause great frustration to those reliant on his or her services. Skills of personal organisation are required to cope with these multiple demands and to prevent the urgent driving out the important. Social skills are needed if the Registrar is to be able to deal sensitively with people of different ages, backgrounds, abilities, needs, jobs and status. Management of clerical subordinates calls for subtle skills of delegation, as mentioned previously, and working out ways of

Figure 8: The 'hub' role of the Registrar

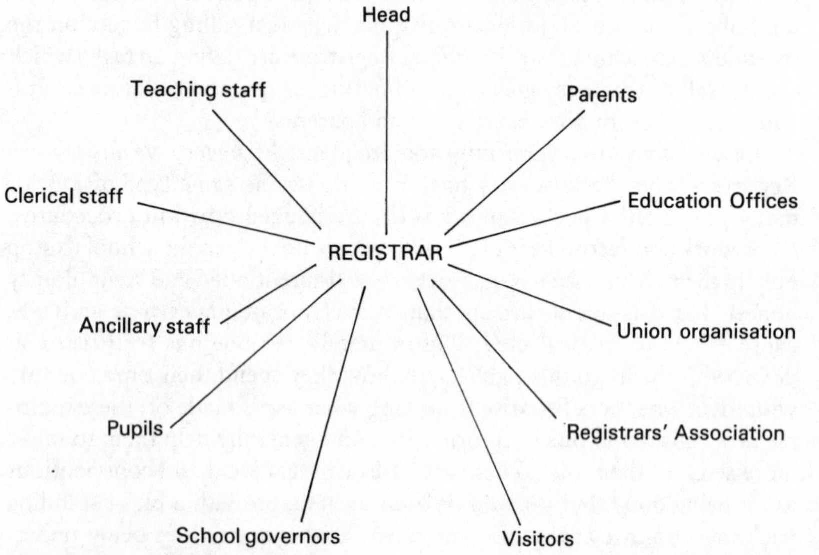

supervising the work of people who are often regarded as colleagues rather than subordinates.

Training opportunities

In one local authority, there had been training courses in interviewing skills and computing, and also a four-day management course for non-teaching public-sector staff, but this was unusual. In most cases, the opportunities for formal training for administrators at Registrar level are limited. In some of the less urban local authorities, the courses are often held in towns some distance away, or are not easily accessible by public transport for those who do not have the use of a car. There is always the problem, too, of work piling up in their absence.

Cross-school meetings

Registrars were one of the few groups of people we found in schools, teaching and non-teaching staff alike, who were members of a district or area professional body, although this was not universal and the degree of participation varied. In one school, the Registrar was adamant about the benefits to her and the school of being a member of the County Registrars' Association, which met four times a year. She said they discussed things such as county supply contracts, perhaps visiting the supplier concerned and talking over any particular problems, and the meeting participants were kept up-to-date by staffing personnel in County Hall of developments in staffing matters. Each district has a representative at the meeting, and each of those representatives also convenes meetings of Registrars within his or her own district, so that information is cascaded down. One such district representative expressed the opinion that 'Registrars who don't involve themselves in these meetings lose out.' In another metropolitan authority, a group of Registrars meets once a month in the Town Hall. Town Hall staff are also present, resulting in the useful spin-off of familiarisation with 'what makes them tick'. A participant said of these meetings, 'as a group, we stand some chance of getting things changed.'

Participation in school meetings

We would have liked to have discovered that, where whole-school staff meetings occur in school, the Registrar is an automatic participant. This, alas, is not the case. Registrars do not, on the whole, see themselves in the position of being the guardian of the non-teaching staff, with a responsibility to keep themselves informed of school business and issues under discussion. Whilst much discussion at such meetings invariably concerns specific pupil or curriculum problems, there will also be many matters discussed to do with the overall aims of the school, ways in which non-teaching staff can help the teaching process, events in the school calendar and general information about school life. By making themselves aware of the educational intentions of the school, Registrars can often help to implement them.

It seems rather a pity that the views of the non-teaching staff on policy issues are rarely sought. There is an assumption made that the interest and influence of Registrars is confined to how willing or otherwise they and their staff are to co-operate with the decisions taken by teaching staff, rather than being regarded as having a valid viewpoint and contribution from their own position. There is undoubtedly a reluctance on the part of many Registrars to get involved; they see their bulging in-trays, the constantly ringing telephone, their beleaguered office colleagues and decide that, this time, they will not attend the meeting.

On governing bodies, opportunities for non-teaching staff representatives, where they exist, are sometimes not taken up. They are seen as rather daunting occasions for someone who occupies a relatively subordinate position during normal school hours. We would suggest that a Registrar should have the ability and motivation to overcome these hurdles, or at least should be encouraged and helped to do so.

Relationship between the Head and the Registrar

There is little doubt that many Heads find the existence of a mature and competent Registrar indispensable. Comments we heard in schools included: 'Goodness knows what would happen if she left. She knows so much. The Head absolutely depends on her.' The individuals holding these two posts may work closely together. It is often not only the Head's secretary who acts as a barrier between the Head and others, or who exercises a role as a 'gatekeeper' of information, but also the Registrar. His or her views may sometimes be sought out by members of teaching staff as to whether the Head is likely to approve or disapprove a certain proposal. Sometimes, however, (as we have described previously) relationships are strained or at arm's length. A Registrar in one school expressed disapproval that the new Head involved himself in certain aspects of her job rather more than his predecessor had done. These included dealing with the caretaker and sorting through the Head's post, tasks which previously the Registrar was accustomed to doing, and the absence of which decreased her knowledge about what was going on in the school. One Registrar had the feeling that, although the Head was more than happy to support her in her battles and differences with the Education Authority, this was not the case when the two parties were the Registrar and a member of the teaching staff of the school. As with many boss – subordinate relationships, it would be useful if the opportunity could be created when concerns such as these could be mutually discussed, instead of being left to fester.

Registrar as Section Head

The Registrar often has a considerable number of clerical staff, with whom she or he has to work closely and who consume a large amount of school resources in the course of their duties. We found that, despite this, Registrars were not always actively involved in the interviewing and election of non-teaching staff. Often, if they did attend, it was to sit on the sidelines without contributing to the nature or flow of the interview. It seems strange that the person who knows the most about the work of the school office, and who has to work so closely with his or her colleagues in the office, should be so little involved in their selection.

Even less common, we found, was the concept of the Registrar being a budget holder in his or her own right. There was often a sum of money, variously called or buried within items known as the contingency fund, strategic reserve, administration or secretarial expenses, resources, office funds, etc, which included much of the expenditure which administrative activities incurred, such as whole-school photocopying, postage, office equipment and stationery. These could amount to as much as £4-5,000. In some cases, no one was really keeping an eye on how these resources were consumed, and they were regarded as unavoidable and necessary running expenses. This may change with the advent of devolved financial flexibility.

Good practice

These are two portraits of Registrars we met during our research whose jobs seemed to make sense, and who were considered made a real contribution to the running of the school. (We would not want to imply that everything in these descriptions should be emulated, for example, we would not advocate that it is always a good thing if a person does without a lunch break, or works excessively long hours.)

Kevin is the Bursar of a large, Group 11 school. He sees his task as being one of service to staff, to relieve them of day-to-day financial transactions and to provide them with proper financial information as necessary. His tasks include looking after finance, orders, deliveries, stationery, security and school funds. He has taken over a lot of administrative jobs from teaching staff, which they are happy about. He is very much a facilitator and often convenes meetings with members of staff to sort things out. There is a bookable meetings room nearby which he can use for this purpose. He provides departments with regular feedback on the amounts of capitation they have left. He is visibly well organised. His status amongst teaching staff is that of a respected member of management.

He works throughout the day without a proper coffee or lunch break. His office is situated close to both the staffroom and the other administrative offices and his door is open to any member of staff to go through at all times. Its location is a major contribution to his effectiveness. He does brief tours of the buildings, including a daily visit first thing to all the other administrative offices, and he maintains excellent relationships with non-teaching staff. He is seen as a 'father figure' to the technicians and caretaking staff and provides a respected 'court of appeal' in the case of any differences between teaching and non-teaching staff.

Janet has been the Registrar of her Group 11 school for about a year and a half. She cites the supervision of the ancillary staff in the school as being her principal responsibility. When she first arrived in the school, she got all her staff to write their own job descriptions and had discussions with them all on their jobs. There have been quite a few changes since then, including the relocation of people and offices. These changes were discussed by Janet at joint ancillary staff meetings. She runs all the interviews for non-teaching staff. Her staff are generally on low grades, but they seem reasonably happy to be there, and some of this is due to the feeling of being cared for by the Registrar. She talked to us about development opportunities for members of her staff and is taking active steps to widen the job experience and skills of the office and resources staff. She rarely finished work before 5 or 5.30 pm each day but, despite feeling that she is under-graded, she admits that other, more highly graded jobs might be a lot more boring.

She works closely with the Finance Committee on school financial matters. She is the school's Examination Officer, compiling entry lists and sorting out double entries and clashes. She is conscious that, due to the hectic nature of demands made upon her, it is very easy for quantity to become more important than quality. She welcomes the concept of local financial management, whilst recognising that it will create more work and require new skills. She thinks it will make school members more aware of costs and give a sense of economy, including with regard to administrative activities. She puts a lot of effort into maintaining relationships with both teaching and non-teaching staff and is popular with and respected by both groups.

Do It Yourself

Using the following checklist, examine the dimensions of the role of Registrar as it currently exists in your school.

1 Is there a job description for the Registrar? If so, is it school-specific or a general one drawn up by the local authority? Is it a true reflection of the dimensions of the job? If not, ask the Registrar to draft another one.
2 Who is the Registrar's boss? The Head? What supervisory and development activities does this person exercise with regard to the Registrar? When did he or she last receive any training?
3 Does the Registrar have formal responsibility for the work of non-teaching staff? What does this involve on a day-to-day basis? When did the non-teaching staff last have a joint meeting convened by the Registrar? Does the Registrar have responsibility for the selection and interviewing of non-teaching staff?
4 Does the Registrar come into contact with all the groups of people in Figure 8? What is her or his relationship with these people?
5 Does the Registrar have his or her own office, or does he or she sit in the general office? What are the advantages and disadvantages of either – to the Registrar, to the school?
6 Does the Registrar do the financial record keeping, or is this devolved to other members of clerical staff? When was the last time the school examined its production of records and information, and the value of these?
7 How much computerisation is there in the school office? Is the Registrar taking on the responsibility for this? What does he or she see as the advantages and disadvantages to the school of having pupil and financial records on computer files?
8 How much is the Registrar involved in school policy making? Does he or she attend staff meetings?
9 Does the Registrar participate in cross-school meetings with other Registrars? What does he or she see as the benefits of this?
10 What particular skills does the Registrar in your school require to do his or her job?

Here are two quotes from Joseph Heller's well-known book *Catch 22*. They may seem rather extreme, but how much do these reflect the feelings of the teaching staff about the work done by the Registrar and administrative staff? If they do, what could be changed? If not, how has this been achieved?

Without realising it, [they] discovered themselves dominated by the administrators appointed to serve them. They were bullied, insulted, harassed and shoved around all day long by one after the other.

Nothing we do in this large department of ours is really very important . . . on the other hand, it is important that we let people know we do a great deal of it.

References

Bush, T., Glatter, R., Goodey, J. and Riches, C. (Eds), *Approaches to School Management*, Harper and Row, London, 1980.

Paisey, A., *Organization and Management in Schools: Perspectives for Practising Teachers*, Longman, London, 1981.

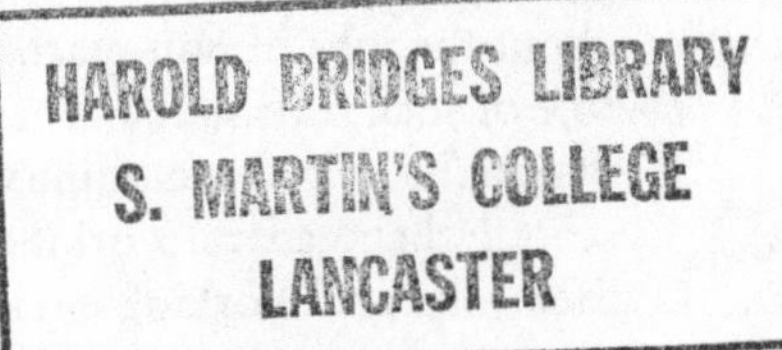

Chapter 19
The Non-Teaching Staff

In 1981 Marland suggested that 'one of the clearest certainties of the future is that a study must be made of the needs of the schools for a proper level of clerical and secretarial help.' We conducted interviews with over 170 non-teaching staff. It was not in our remit to investigate in detail local authority reasoning behind the level and quality of non-teaching staff provision in schools, but we did discover its effects. We sought evidence about the jobs of non-teaching staff and how these were carried out; the role of such staff in the general management of the school; their position within the school community; how their roles were viewed by others in the school; their general working conditions; whether they were satisfied with their jobs and working environment; and who was responsible for their work and supervision. In short, we were trying to meet Riches's (1984) criticism that the roles of non-teaching staff in schools have been largely ignored by previous writers and researchers in the field of education management.

We found a dedicated and reasonably satisfied group of staff, making a considerable contribution to the running of schools, working closely and profitably with each other and with their teaching colleagues. Many school workers are performing a vital function of oiling wheels; some are doing a lot more. Much of their work is routine and laborious, but it seems to be possible to have fun doing it.

Unfortunately, this was not the case in all schools. Sometimes we discovered a general feeling of distance from the fortunes of the school, staff with little understanding of their jobs, strained relationships not only with teaching staff but between non-teaching staff, unclear lines of responsibility and poor supervision, bad working conditions and inconsiderate treatment from teaching colleagues.

Local Education Authorities have widely differing policies on the non-teaching establishment of their schools. Some of the variety is reflected in Table 7.

In numbers, the non-teaching staff in a school may actually exceed the

Table 7: Numbers of Teaching and Non-Teaching Staff in Seven Schools

School	Group	Teaching Staff (including Part-Time)	Non-teaching Staff (including Part-Time)
Ridley	8	33 (5 PT)	40 (34 PT)
Abbey	9	33	30 (7 PT)
Churchbrook	10	41 (2 PT)	66 (59 PT)
Park	10	49	38 (18 PT)
William Barnes	11	63 (3 PT)	51 (39 PT)
Ferndown	11	74 (10 PT)	85 (72 PT)
Francis Drake	12	92 (5 PT)	72 (58 PT)

teaching staff. School management needs to be aware of this and recognise that the roles they fill put them in very different situations for supervision and give them very different working relationships with teaching staff and pupils. Typically, non-teaching staff live more locally to their school and are more a part of the catchment community than teachers; they, therefore, provide an important link between the school and its community. Whether that is used at all, or only to carry bad news, are issues management needs to consider. Good conditions and sensitive supervision will not be wasted on anybody.

Table 8 sets out the various non-teaching roles we found in schools. Several issues will be clear to readers from within schools.

a Few, if any, schools will have a tidy, one-for-one matching of personnel with roles. We know of schools where ink-stained Reprographic Technicians were also Health Assistants, where storekeeping duties fell to Deputy Heads or specially promoted teaching staff or Library Assistants.
b 'New' activities may not be easy to fit into existing structures. There have been increasing demands for reprographic services and increasingly ambitious 'in-house' arrangements have been made. 'A Roneo in the office and a Banda for the staff' are no longer sufficient. But schools have not been provided with additional staff assigned to this development and have had to reorganise within existing, or even decreasing, allowances. Information technology (particularly word-processing) presents peculiar problems; it is not always a matter of 'I don't see why I should change', but sometimes it is 'why did they get the chance when I didn't?' Lunchtime supervision of pupils by specially employed staff is potentially a most awkward area because there can be no guarantee that the schools' senior managers will be available throughout lunch periods.
c In caretaking and refectory work schools are constrained by often highly detailed management arrangements made by their LEAs. In our schools, surprisingly little difficulty was reported either by

Table 8: Management of Non-Teaching Staff

Roles	Whose Job?	Supervision
Maintaining the fabric	Caretakers and cleaners	By an LEA officer and the Head (or delegate)
Health	Health assistant (Matron or first aider)	By Head (or delegate)
Technical classroom assistance	Technicians	By appropriate HoD
Classroom assistance	Nursery nurses	Head of Special Needs
Secretarial/clerical/administrative	Bursars, school clerks, clerks, typists, telephonists	By Head (or delegate)
Library	Librarian or library assistant	Head (or member of teaching staff i/c Library)
Nutrition	*a* Refectory staff	By LEA officer and the Head (or delegate)
	b 'Tuck shop'	Various
	c Staffroom	Various
Reprographics	Reprographics technician (but see discussion)	Head (or delegate)
Breaktime supervision	*a* Teaching staff	Head (or delegate)
	b Ancillary staff	Various
Storekeeping (stationery, AV equipment)	Various	Head (or delegate) or teaching staff i/c activity

Heads or by Caretakers and Refectory Managers working for two supervisors.

d It is useful to be clear about the nature of the authority being exercised in a supervision role. A Deputy Head, whose job description includes the delegated task 'supervising the work of the Caretaker', has not got the same relationship with the Caretaker as, say, a Head of Science has with the Science Technician. The former relationship is based largely on positional authority, the latter relationship on expertise. A Librarian will have different needs for (and attitudes towards) supervision than either a teacher 'promoted' to be 'in charge of the Library' or the Library Assistant working for such a teacher.

e There are widely differing interpretations of some posts. As a particular example, within one LEA we found a school where the most senior non-teaching post, the Bursar's, had authority over *all* non-teaching staff, and another, smaller school, where the highest grading for the corresponding post gave its holder little authority over anybody.

Our research did not concern itself with the work of cleaners and refectory staff because so little of what they did involved contacts outside their own groups and so much of what they did was prescribed by LEAs. We did spend time in School Offices, libraries and subject 'prep rooms', the staff in which had frequent contact with teaching staff.

Current practice

The working conditions of non-teaching staff ranged from good to disgraceful. Apart from sheer physical discomfort, in unventilated, windowless offices or prep rooms with nothing more than lab stools for seating, there was frequent working discomfort.

An example of an afternoon in a general office

The researcher is tucked away in the corner of the School Office towards the end of an afternoon's observation. Already there have been 120 visits to the office by staff and pupils and 20 telephone calls have been received. Throughout this, the ladies have maintained an easy courtesy towards each other and all callers while getting on with several jobs; the prevalent sound has been of two typewriters being used simultaneously. A visitor to the school, with business to conduct with a teacher, is known socially to the office staff and 'just pops in'. This causes little break to the work, but then:

- the telephone rings and somebody not easily found needs to be called up;
- a pupil comes for the toilet key;
- a teacher who also knows the visitor spends ten minutes in the office talking with the visitor (there is ample, comfortable space outside the office, there is not inside).

It is this last lack of consideration which confirmed for the researcher the 'taken-for-granted' excellence of this office team. Although, from the Head to the most junior, teachers had had nothing but praise for the office staff, the same teachers often acted as if they had no appreciation of the office's work. After a day observing another school's office at work the researcher noted, 'It remains a mystery why two, or more, people can be expected to operate noisy machinery and do concentrated clerical work in the same small space all day, yet 'senior managers' need an office of their own to be out of much of the day and to work quietly in for most of the rest.'

Failure to provide good working conditions was not always matched by failure to establish good working relations. Indeed, the latter appeared to be the more important, but difficult for different reasons. As senior managers in schools are drawn from the ranks of teachers, there seems often to be an expectation that they, the senior managers, should have a different sort of relationship with non-teachers than with teachers; the expectation is that non-teaching staff are going to be more difficult to manage. We found senior managers who seemed afraid to manage their non-teaching staff, while they did not shrink from their management of teachers. Examples include:

- a Head who avoided the Caretaker, communicating only through a Deputy;
- a Head who had been putting off a tightening up of caretaking work until after the imminent retirement of the incumbent;
- a Head who was aware of the problems caused by the abrasive style of the Bursar but would not do anything about it;
- a Head of Science who had issued a technician's job description 'so general as to be meaningless' and found it difficult to motivate the person he had appointed;
- a Deputy Head tackling a specific complaint about one member of the office staff by giving all four a 'pep talk'.

We also found examples of a more casual neglect of responsibility towards and a lack of valuing of non-teaching staff:

- a School Nurse whose knowledge of solvent abuse problems was not made available to the staff;
- a senior laboratory technician who had been caused unnecessary anxiety because she had been included in a general discussion about reorganising the work done by other female ancillary staff without it being explained to her that her own work was not to be considered, she was merely being kept informed;
- more generally, a too-easy acceptance of lost breaks and unpaid overtime (try getting the same from a new employee who has no loyalties to your institution);

There seem to be some important generalisations about the differences between teaching and non-teaching staff which explain why there are distinctions to be made between the contributions of each group to a school and between the considerations for management.

First, non-teaching staff identify with their particular school, not with teaching as a professional activity; there is no career path leading to other schools as there is for teachers, so we should expect non-teaching staff to stay longer. The benefits of stability and specialist knowledge are easy to applaud; it is less easy to act against resistance to change, especially if jobs are at risk.

Second, with the special exception of parents' evenings, visitors to a school are more likely to see non-teaching staff at work than they are to see teachers. We have already noted that non-teaching staff are a very important bridge between a school and its catchment community. But the impression they make when the community comes in is also important; efficiently helpful work in office and telephone reception, care with printing school publications, attention to the needs of an outside booking, and so on can all improve the image of a school. These examples may seem superficial, but in getting them right, a school will probably have set up a strong underlying system of supportive supervision.

Third, in many schools the management is drawn exclusively from teaching staff whose working and supervisory experiences have largely been with other teachers. Managers who have been, and still are, teachers have sets of assumptions shared with most of the teachers they supervise. Such managers need to discover the sets of assumptions which they can share with non-teaching staff. For example, time horizons need to be shortened from the term or year to the day or week.

The structure of non-teaching staff in two schools

In many cases, the balance and nature of non-teaching staff provision seemed to us to be a matter of accident, past history and what has always been, rather than a conscious decision. We encountered little discussion about the structure and balance of non-teaching staff. We discovered very different staffing of laboratories and libraries, even within the same local authority as the following two examples show, but did not discover particular reasons why such differences existed.

Table 9 shows the structures of two schools' staff. William Barnes, a Group 11 school with just over 1,000 pupils, has the same number of clerical and technical staff as Summerfield High, a Group 10 school with 800 pupils. However, it is in the number of hours per week where the difference appears, owing to the balance between full-time and part-time staff. We took full-time to be staff who worked 37, 36 or 35 hours per week. The figures for the two schools were 68 per cent full-time for William Barnes but only 40 per cent full-time for Summerfield High. They accordingly had a different number of total hours per week worked, 326 and 277.5 respectively. Other schools showed a different balance. One school we were in had as much as 87 per cent full-time hours.

Table 9: Numbers and grades of clerical and technical staff in two schools

School and Job Title	Scale	Full-Time or Part-Time (hours per week)	All Year or Term-Time Only
William Barnes (1083 pupils)			
Clerical/Office staff:			
Registrar	6	FT	AY
Head's Secretary	2	FT	TTO
Clerical Assistant	2	PT (22)	TTO
Clerical Assistant	1	PT (34)	TTO
Clerical Assistant	1	PT (11)	TTO
Clerical Assistant	1	PT (25)	TTO
Resources Technician	2	FT	TTO
Resources Technician	2	FT	TTO
Technical staff:			
Ancillary Home Economics	1	PT (12)	TTO
Lab Technician (Science)	2	FT	AY
Lab Technician	½	FT	AY
Summerfield High (800 pupils)			
Clerical/Office staff:			
Registrar	5	FT	AY
Head's Secretary	2	PT (26)	TTO
Clerical Assistant	1	PT (24)	TTO
Clerical Assistant	1	PT (18)	TTO
Resources Technician	2	FT	TTO
Resources Technician	1	PT (14)	TTO
Librarian		PT (20)	TTO
Technical Staff:			
Ancillary Home Economics	1	PT (18)	TTO
Lab Technician (Science)	2	FT	AY
Lab Technician (Science)	2	PT (26.5)	TTO
Workshop Technician	2	PT (20)	TTO

We found differences between schools of type, grades and hours of staff. There can also be a substantial variation in the balance between term-time-only and all-year staff, not only in the number, but in which type of staff are kept on during the holidays. William Barnes is staffed during the holidays by the Registrar and two Science Technicians. Summerfield High had no technical staff present. In another large school, the Registrar and Librarian were the only non-teaching staff present, but another school with only 360 pupils had five non-teaching members present during holidays, including three technicians.

William Barnes has more full-time staff, with more years of service, more clerical staff of a higher grade and a greater proportion of clerical to technical staff. This school has the better administrative support, providing effective back-up to the organisation and to the teaching staff, with good relationships and mutual respect between teaching and non-teaching staff, good working conditions and a sensible allocation of duties.

Descriptions of non-teaching staff

The following are representative examples of personnel from schools in our project.

Office staff I

In this small school of 535 pupils, there is a Scale 2 Bursar and a Scale 1 Secretary in the school office, located on an administrative corridor adjoining the Head's office and close to the staffroom. They have job descriptions drawn up by the Head, whom they see as their superior.

Although the Bursar is paid on a higher scale, many tasks are shared and both effectively regard themselves as School Secretaries. They feel their salaries are poor but do not resent the differentials between their scales and those of the teaching staff. They do resent strongly that the Laboratory Technician is paid the same as a secretary.

They are both efficient, helpful, co-operative and popular people. They are fully integrated into the life of the school and are very valuable resources for the school. The location of the office encourages good communication with staff and its small size discourages people staying overlong and so disrupting work flows.

Laboratory technician

Barbara, one of two full-time, all-year science Technicians, has been in the school for 20 years, ever since it first opened. It had 1,200 pupils then, compared with a current roll of 360. The teaching schemes and worksheets in current use mean that she knows what will be required at each lesson, supplemented by the weekly equipment request sheets filled in by the science staff. The school is well stocked with equipment, but is short of resources for the new curriculum and, she suggested, could really do with exchanging equipment with other schools. Barbara gets on well with the departmental staff and they are 'good about putting equipment back on trays and reporting missing items'. Barbara misses the aspect of actually producing things that she had at her previous job in industry and feels this job is more servile, yet she is still reasonably happy. She used to do diagrams and layouts for worksheets and expressed annoyance that the Head of Department brought in a YTS person to do them instead. She does all the orders and monitoring of equipment stocks.

Examples of good practice

Success in the management of non-teaching staff may come by accident, but four of our schools had achieved some success by working for it in rather different ways.

Churchbrook had ten technical, clerical and secretarial staff. Three of these were technicians in well defined jobs entirely within their subject specialisms; the remaining seven worked as secretaries, clerks, typists, technicians, librarian and so on. Two years before the research period, two of the seven had left and the problem of replacement had been taken as an opportunity for reorganising and clarifying duties. This was undertaken by the Head and a senior colleague (whose technician was one of the leavers). The staff were involved in individual and group discussions, after which new arrangements and job descriptions were drawn up. The senior colleague had continued to look to the welfare of this group. The care used in making the new arrangements was appreciated by the staff involved and had been rewarded by their willingness and flexibility. The attention to detail is shown in Table 10 and Figure 9.

Figure 9: Job Description of Non-teaching Assistant (Welfare and General)

The successful applicant will have a very varied job assisting in the smooth running of the school as part of a team of clerical and non-teaching staff.

The primary role of the non-teaching assistant will be:

1 To supervise the medical room and care for pupils who are ill or injured. A sound knowledge of first aid and the ability to remain calm in an emergency are therefore essential.
2 To be responsible for maintaining supplies of first-aid equipment, ensuring that each department has adequately stocked first-aid boxes; preparing first-aid kits to take on expeditions and to have available at public performances.
3 To be responsible for contacting parent, doctor, and ambulance, or for ensuring that these contacts are made should the need arise. To complete accident forms when applicable.
4 To distribute location cards to all tutors early in each school year, under the instruction of the pastoral head, and to file them when they are completed or updated. These will be available in the office at all times in case of emergency.
5 To liaise with the home economics technician with regard to school medicals and vaccinations.

6 To prepare and keep a log book of medical assistance given to pupils, to be available to other staff.

The secondary role of the non-teaching assistant will be:

1 To assist with typing of examination papers, work sheets as required. Some photo-copying and duplicating may be necessary.
2 To be responsible for ordering and distribution of stationery for departmental use.
3 To staff the general office for a short time each morning and to deal with the switchboard at that time, unless a medical emergency occurs.

Flexibility of attitude is essential as roles may change as circumstances within the school change. Full consultation would take place in this event.

At Jackson the management of the office team fell to the Registrar. Again, there seemed to be a willingness in the team members to work well and constructively with each other. Despite poor working conditions and, possibly, lower gradings for their jobs than in other authorities, the staff were generally contented. Why?

The Registrar herself made the staff feel cared for; she sorted out problems rapidly and before any grumbles could fester. She held meetings between all of them to sort out common problems, for example, relocating typewriting activity when it became clear that the financial and pupil records clerk could not work with that noise in her small room. She recognised potential, extending the work of some staff (by agreement); their willingness to accept extra responsibility, even without extra payment, confirmed our impression of the staff's contentment. She thought ahead, organising word-processor training before the machines arrived. In addition, we noted, 'she is a merry soul, her cheerfulness is infectious.' Well, it helps.

Brenda and Carol are full-time Resource Technicians who have each been in William Barnes for at least 12 years. Amongst other clerical and secretarial functions, they share between them the reprographics work of this large school, building it into a professional operation. The Head has given them much leeway in these activities, as he regards their efforts as worthwhile and as making a positive contribution to the image of the school, both internally and externally.

They were involved recently in the decision as to which type of reprographics machine to rent and visited other schools as part of their research into this. They have their own reprographic budget, out of which they purchase special tape, graphics books, special pens and sprays, mounting and binding materials, etc. They boost these funds by doing work privately for staff during any slack times or after school, such as producing and selling individualised drawing pads. This helped towards the financing of an electric stapler and guillotine.

They appreciate the fact that the Head gives them positive

Table 10: Non-teaching staff, priorities list

	Amy	Betty	Cathy	Doris	Eva	Fran	Gay	Harry	Ivy
GENERAL ADMINISTRATION									
1 Reception/appointments		1				2			
2 Switchboard		1				2			
3 Register/admissions		1			2				
4 Free meals									
5 Dinner monies	1		2						
6 Post	2	1	2						
7 Letters to parents (Senior Management Team/Heads of Year)	2		1			3			
8 Letters (Headteacher)	1		2						
9 Report writing	1		2						
10 Staffing admin	1	2							
11 Finance matters	1								
12 Stationery (office)		1							
(curriculum)						1			
RESOURCES									
1 Library				1					
2 Audio/Visual (recordings)			2	1					
3 Computers (Information Technology)			2	1					
4 Hardware maintenance (recorders/projectors/computers)			2	1					

REPROGRAPHICS						
1 Typing originals		1				
2 Operate reprographic		2		1		
3 Maintenance				1		
4 Stock control				1		
HEALTH						
1 Records					2	1
2 Organise medical/tests					2	1
3 First aid					1	
4 Contacts (doctors/hospital/parents)	2				1	
5 Minor injuries/sickness		2	2		1	2

1 = First priority for particular member of staff
2 = Second
3 = Third

encouragement by acknowledging their work, discussing it with them, criticising it and making suggestions on layout and design during his visits to their part of the school. They are motivated and enthusiastic about the work they do. They get on well with teaching staff and operate on a basis of friendly banter and mutual respect.

Cordial communications between the Caretaker and other teaching and non-teaching staff are conspicously absent in many schools. Francis Drake is an exception. The regular channels of communication between the Caretaker and the rest of the school include the yearly calendar of events, which details parents' evenings, open evenings, school meetings, and so on. He receives the weekly school bulletin, which sets out events taking place every day of the following week, so that he knows about changes to the planned schedule of events.

His knowledge of events around the school means that he knows the best time to do specific maintenance jobs which arise during term time. Staff keep him well informed of minor jobs such as replacing light bulbs. If any of his cleaners complains about conditions of specific teaching rooms, he has a word himself with the member of staff concerned, and usually the difficulty is resolved. He has meetings once or twice a year with the Area Technical Officer, the Head and the Registrar to discuss any mutal problems or developments.

In this variety of fairly simple ways the Caretaker is kept informed of events and he can take appropriate action to assist in the everyday life of the school.

Do It Yourself

Non-teaching staff need to be valued, just as teachers do. To find out whether such staff are valued in your school, ask yourself the following questions:

1 Are new administrative staff given an induction when they join?
2 Are they given their own copy of the staff handbook?
3 Is the opinion of technicians sought on the new photocopying machine or the location of the riveting machine?
4 Do all ancillary staff receive a copy of the school bulletin?
5 Do they have pigeonholes?
6 Is someone making sure their jobs make sense, and that they are not overwhelmed by or in despair over a certain task?
7 Do they have school-specific job descriptions?
8 Are the job descriptions of non-teaching staff published in the staff handbook?

9 Are the job titles of clerical, ancillary and technical staff included in the list of school staff handed to visitors and supply staff?
10 Are non-teaching staff included in staff social functions such as a Christmas lunch?
11 Are there carpets on the floor, curtains at the windows and paintings from the Art Department on the walls of the offices of non-teaching staff?
12 How many teachers know the name of the cook-supervisor?
13 Has anybody encouraged the Caretaker to leave his normal evening or Saturday duties to watch a school team playing?
14 How long is it since you talked to the Librarian about your classwork and subject curriculum?
15 Identify the issues for management attention encapsulated in the descriptions of non-teaching staff.

If you do not immediately know the answers, make an effort to find out by talking to the office and ancillary staff.

For Heads and Deputies:

1 When did you last see your Caretaker?
2 Who are your non-teaching staff?
3 For each group of non-teaching staff, which one of the senior management is responsible for them?
4 How are those responsibilities discharged? If they are shared, for example with an LEA officer or a Head of Department, how is the sharing controlled and co-ordinated?
5 When were the non-teaching staff last talked with by their supervisors within the school,
a as a group?
b individually?

6 Do you have clear ideas what role(s) is(are) taken by each of your non-teaching staff? Write them down.
7 (Where appropriate.) What is the style of supervision applied by non-teaching staff to their subordinates?
8 *a* Does the distribution of roles (Question 6) look appropriate?
b From *your* observations in this school and experience in others, is the match of roles (Question 6) to incumbents (listed in Question 7) appropriate?
c From your discussions with the incumbents, do *they* feel that the match of roles to themselves is appropriate?

9 If the answer to any part of Question 7 is *No*,

a Note details *and*
b What are you going to do about it?

References

Marland, M., *Head of Department*, Heinemann Educational, London, 1981.

Riches, Colin, 'The Management of Non-Teaching Staff in a School', Ch. 4, 6, in Goulding *et al.*, *Case Studies in Educational Management*, Harper and Row, London, 1984.

Chapter 20
Women in Management

We did not set out specifically to study the role of women, but we were struck by two aspects of women in senior posts. The first was how few there were. The second, how often women were doing different sorts of work from men. The first aspect is well established, with the DES's statistics demonstrating the case (see Table 11). The various causes and remedies are anguished over whenever selection of senior staff is taking place. The second aspect is the one we intend to discuss more fully here. Our material was collected under the old-style salary structure.

Table 11: Percentage distribution of staff (men and women) in various posts in schools in England and Wales in 1985

	Head-teachers	Deputy Head-teachers	Second Masters/ Mistresses	Senior Teachers	Scale 4	Scale 3	Scale 2	Scale 1
Men	9.6	7.8	0.83	3.4	13.6	23.5	24.1	17.1
Women	4.4	5.5	0.7	0.6	2.8	12.9	36.0	37.0
Men & Women	6.52	6.4	0.8	1.7	7.2	17.2	31.2	29.0

Based on Table B 129, London, DES, 1985.

Current practice

Table 12 gives the distribution of teaching posts by gender in the 24 schools of the project. The ratios of 1:7 for Headteachers, 3:5 for Deputies, 1:4 for Senior Teachers and 1:4 for Scale 4s speaks for itself about the imbalance. Only one school, Hall End, had more women (4:3) in the senior team. No other school had anything remotely like an even distribution across the four senior grades.

Table 12: Distribution of teaching posts by gender

	Head	Deputy Head		Senior Teacher		Scale 4		Scale 3		Scale 2		Scale 1	
		F	M	F	M	F	M	F	M	F	M	F	M
Abbey	M	1	1	0	0	1	4	6	4	4	6	4	3
Park	M	1	2	0	2	2	10	2	4	8	8	8	3
St Elmo's	M	1	1	0	0	2	6	6	3	5	9	6	0
Francis Drake	M	1	2	0	3	1	5	5	14	12	15	16	9
Francis Bacon	M	1	2	0	2	3	7	3	10	13	5	31	10
Central	M	2	1	0	1	1	5	5	14	8	3	1	0
Southern	M	1	2	0	1	0	7	8	8	6	6	3	0
Westcliffe	M	0	3	2	1	1	9	5	9	13	13	26 (7 PT)	3
Oakhill	M	2	1	0	2	2	6	4	6	8	4	3	3
Summerfield	M	1	2	0	4	2	3	3	11	6	4	12	2
William Barnes	M	0	3	1	2	1	8	7	9	10	9	9 (3 PT)	5
Hall End	M	2	1	2	1	2	5	4	6	7	5	15 (1 PT)	3
Jackson	M	1	2	1	2	2	10	6	9	10	9	14 (5 PT)	8
Montgomery	M	1	2	0	1	0	5	4	12	8	4	–	–
Hillside	F	1	1	0	0	1	5	3	4	6	6	8	0
Ridley	M	1	1	0	0	1	1	3	6	5	0	10	2
Ferndown	M	1	2	1	2	1	9	4	8	6	9	22	6
Churchbrook	M	1	1	0	2	0	2	4	9	9	4	4	3

Ridgeway	F	1	2	0	2	2	7	3	13	7	7	16 (5 PT)	5
Valley High	M	1	2	0	1	3	5	4	4	6	6	4	6
Pennine End	M	0	3	1	2	2	5	6	5	2	11	11	4
Renold	M	0	2	0	3	0	7	1	15	2	6	0	9
Lodge	F	2	0	0	1	5	1	9	3	13	0	7 (2 PT)	0
Kirkside	M	1	1	1	0	0	5	1	8	5	5	13 (7 PT)	6 (1 PT)
TOTAL	3F 21M	24	40	9	35	35	137	106	194	179	156	243	90
RATIO	1:7	3:5		1:4		1:4		1:2		1:1		3:1	
TOTAL			F 599		M 673								
RATIO				6:7									

An example of how women do two jobs – Jackson and Hall End

Figure 10 gives the distribution of Scale 4s and 3s by gender in the two schools. What is noticeable about both these schools is that women were

Figure 10: The distribution of Scale 4s and 3s in Jackson and Hall End

Jackson

	M	F
Scale 4	Maths HoD	History HoD (temporary)
	Science HoD	Art HoD and HoY 1
	Geography HoD	Home Economics HoD and TVEI Co-ordinator
	Commerce HoD	
	CDT	
	English HoD	
	HoY 5	
	Profiles	
Scale 3	2nd in Maths	2nd in English
	HoY 2	H of 6th Form
	Physics HoD	HoY 3
	Geography teacher	Modern Languages HoD and HoY 4
	PE HoD	Music (temporary)
	Commerce teacher	
	Commerce teacher	
	Performing Arts HoD	

8 women at Jackson are on Scales 3 and 4. Of these, three have two titles and two are temporary scales. 16 men are on Scales 3 and 4. No man has two titles nor is on a temporary scale.

HALL END

	M	F
Scale 4	Maths HoD	Art HoD
	Humanities HoD	Special Needs HoD and HoY 1
	Science HoD (temporary)	
	Careers	
	ACS Co-ordinator	
Scale 3	Science teacher	PE HoD
	English HoD	Home Economics HoD & HoY 4
	CDT HoD	RE and PSE (temporary)
	Social Science teacher and HoY 3	Home Economics teacher (protected)

(NB HoY 2 was Scale 2, HoY 5 ST, both M)

Six women at Hall End are on Scales 3 and 4. Of these, three have two titles, including one on a temporary scale, and one is on a protected scale.

doing something different from men by having two titles. (In one school, however, Abbey, all Scale 4 posts had a joint Head of Department/Head of Year role whether done by men or women.)

We also found that the sort of work women in posts of responsibility did often differed quite markedly from that of their male colleagues. For example, we had no women Heads of Maths in our sample and only five Heads of English.

An example of women in high places doing different work – Westcliffe

Nearly half the women were full-time teachers on Scale 1. Only two females were in Scale 3 + posts that were not pastoral. Over half the male teachers were Scale 3 or more. Scale 2 teachers were equally divided between male and female.

Those on Scale 3 and above had quite different types of job, depending on gender. Women were:

- Heads of Year
- Head of Special Education
- Heads of Schools, ie Lower/Upper

Men were:

- Heads of Faculty
- Head of Sixth Form
- Deputy Heads
- Headteacher
- One Head of Year leaving post to be Head of Outdoor Activities

The school had not promoted women or appointed women to the more senior posts to the same extent as men. We do not wish to get into the various reasons why that may be, but there does seem to be a fundamental difference in the types of work senior women and men are doing.

The male jobs of Heads of Faculty and Sixth Form are fairly discrete activities that do not require a great deal of cross-school liaison. The jobs mean ensuring the faculty has rooms, materials, staffing, and developments at an appropriate level. They are left to get on with this, and others assume they are the most appropriate people to do the job.

By contrast, the female jobs of Head of Year, Special Education and Head of Lower and Upper School require across-school liaison. They have to train teachers to run 'active tutorials' which they have not been trained for. They have to approach Heads of Faculty about members of staff who are having problems with class control, as the complaint often comes to them.

They have to persuade and influence folk to cater for the variety of different children the school has. Home Economics teachers (F) get more involved in extra outside activities and social functions, although making tea is not exactly a skilled job.

If there is a genuine difference in what men and women are good at, it seems the school is missing these cross-school, influencing and diplomacy skills from their promotion lists. Some of these skills should be represented at Deputy Headteacher/Headteacher level.

Conclusion

There were fewer women than men in posts of responsibility in our 24 schools. The women often had to do more for less by having a dual role or accepting a lower grading for similar work. See, for example, CDT Heads of Department and Home Economics Heads of Department. Perhaps most interesting of all is that women seem to do different work.

Men tend to do the high-profile, straightforward jobs that are part of the natural progression up the hierarchy. The job of Head of Department or Faculty has a clear role that everyone understands and accepts. This enables the post holder to be seen as being a manager and doing management work. The complex, cross-school jobs that women tend to do are often idiosyncratic to the particular school and require knowledge of the culture and details that are difficult to transfer. Whether they are jobs that need doing may be questioned by outsiders (see Chapter 17 on The Head of the Pastoral Team) but they are often very much valued within the school. This makes it very difficult for the post holder to be seen as being a manager and doing management work. There are various ways of explaining this. One is that women have often been promoted within the school, sometimes after a break for children. The traditional bastions of careers are blocked by men who have not taken a break, so women are encouraged to stay by taking the school-oriented jobs.

We do not want to over-emphasise the differences between men and women, but we would argue that precisely these subtle influencing and cross-school skills of women could be invaluable to senior staff in trying to manage and organise secondary schools in periods of change.

Example of good practice

Maureen was Deputy Head with responsibility for administration. She had previously been Head of English and previous to that had been an English teacher in the school. She had joined the school when it first started 20 years ago.

Maureen had set up all sorts of efficient administrative systems, such as examination entries on computer, where the results could then be entered and compared.

Most of Maureen's day was spent talking to members of staff. She deliberately talked to all visitors to the school, supply teachers and probationers every day. She made appointments, that were kept, to spend half an hour talking to individual members of staff she thought were having a lot of time off, were having difficulties, were doing something special or she had not seen for a long time.

The school had a large variety of cultures represented within the pupil population. Maureen made contacts with the community and, whilst we were there, was actively encouraging two Asian teachers to apply for vacancies at the school.

Maureen also taught a half timetable.

Do It Yourself

Make a list of the gender distribution of posts of responsibility in your school and the jobs they have in their title.

	M	F
Headteacher		
Deputy Headteacher		
E		
D		
C		
B		
A		
MPG		

Is there any difference in the numbers in the M and F columns?
Is there any difference in the type of work the two genders do for their promotion?

References

DES, *Statistics of Education, Teachers in Service, England and Wales, 1985*, HMSO.

Chapter 21
Core and Periphery Staff

In the 1980s commercial organisations have increasingly tended to have two categories of employee; a small core of staff who have the key skills and knowledge that are crucial to the business, and a wide range of peripheral people, who may or may not be direct employees (Atkinson, 1984). Members of the first group are highly regarded by the employer, well paid and involved in those activities that are unique to the firm or give it a distinctive character. They have good career prospects and offer the employer an important contribution that cannot come from elsewhere.

Those in the peripheral category are in two broad groups: first, those who have skills that are needed but which are not specific to the particular firm, like word processing, catering or driving heavy goods vehicles; second, those without highly developed skills who are likely to be engaged on short-term contracts. This core/peripheral tendency has led to the development of many agencies, consultancies and small businesses which specialise in the supply of peripheral personnel.

The reasons for this development have been the need to be flexible – having human resources to deploy when required, while not having the responsibility and expense of continuing to employ people who are no longer needed. It has been a particularly useful strategy for dealing with contraction and innovation. Probably the best-known examples are in the public sector of employment, with the privatisation of certain services like refuse collection in local authorities and cleaning in hospitals, but the general trend has been continuing for more than 20 years. In the 1960s it was usual for companies to employ their own catering and security staff. Now the majority of in-company catering is run by contractors and nearly all security personnel are supplied by specialist firms. The employer sheds responsibility for managing an activity in which there is no in-house expertise and can obtain the benefit of rapid deployment of special expertise when needed.

This practice is anathema to many people in education, especially as it seems to strike at the root of the idea of culture that we discussed at the opening of this book. There is, however, a long tradition of employing peripatetic staff in schools to deal with specialised subjects and casual staff to provide cover. There are signs that the core/periphery divide may become more common as schools seek the same types of flexibility that other undertakings have been trying to achieve.

Current practice

The three most common types of peripheral staff, both teaching and non-teaching, that we encountered were those who had temporary appointments, those who worked part-time and those who were on supply. Other peripheral groups were peripatetic staff, voluntary groups who work with the school, contract dinner people, students and advisory teachers.

Other aspects of school organisation that raise the same issues are consortium arrangements and TVEI relationships with colleges.

Hall End: An example of a school with a lot of staff on the periphery whose main loyalty is outside the school

At this school there were eight people on 'acting' points for various reasons. Some permanent staff were on secondment to the LEA as advisory teachers, two were on maternity leave and the school staff was due to contract because of falling rolls. For similar reasons there were eight basic-grade teachers on temporary appointments to the school whilst the changes took place. The school had a large number of supply teachers on most days – as many as 15 was quite normal – to cover for TVEI, illness, attendance on courses and unfilled vacancies. The school had several classes taught by college staff who were on the same site as the school. In addition, there was a rapid turnover of staff; first, because promotion was relatively easy for staff from this school as they had experience of many of the progressive aspects of education, and second, because it was a difficult setting and many staff wanted to teach in rather more salubrious areas. When asked, the Headteacher did not know how many teaching staff there were. For us sitting in the staff room, it was often unclear who was a member of staff. What was clear was who the core of full-time, permanent staff were.

This situation created particular management and organisation issues:

1 There was a need for clear instructions about the syllabus content, methodology and discipline procedures used in the school if the pupils were to receive anything consistently. This was met by a very large staff handbook and a great deal of written materials, workbooks and schemes for the pupils.

2 There was a need to recognise that the core staff, particularly

main-grade teachers, were primarily involved in assisting peripheral teachers, as it was they who were sharing the classes and doing most of the teaching. These core staff felt aggrieved because they were not recognised as having this additional work.

3 Senior staff spent a lot of time on peripheral staff; for example, the Deputy with students, a Deputy, Senior Teacher and Head of Department with supply teachers and the Headteacher and a Deputy with college staff. The core staff often felt neglected and taken-for-granted.

4 With so many acting roles and temporary points people had the opportunity to do senior work. After as many as two or three years in a temporary post, many found it difficult to return to their previous level. This has led to at least one inappropriate permanent appointment for sentimental reasons.

5 Out of 55 core staff, only 13 are neither probationers nor have extra responsibilities. These are the people ignored by the management, organisation and administration of the school. Yet they have the heaviest teaching loads and act as tutors, so they deal with peripheral staff as they are the tutor or subject specialist when talk is of individual children. This group of staff included those who were felt to be having personal, health or class-control problems. Were these the casualties of a school with high professional standards and high numbers of peripheral staff?

Ferndown School: An example of the effect of contraction

A large number of the Scale 1 (MPG) posts were only advertised and filled on a temporary and/or part-time basis. This was a deliberate strategy for coping with the predicted contraction of the school population. Only women had taken these posts, which exacerbated the distortion of privilege between men and women and between departments, as vacancies did not occur evenly across the school. Although the strategy was a logical method of dealing with the short-term problem of the school reducing in size, it had implications for the running of the school that had not perhaps been thought through. It was one of the many examples we found of management being reactive and resigned or defensive rather than taking positive initiatives to work out the best method.

Oakhill School: An example of two cultures

Oakhill School often had 20 to 30 per cent of the core staff out on courses, off sick or away for some other reason. These were covered by supply staff who were often in Oakhill three or four days a week. They were to be found in the staffroom exchanging ideas and materials for keeping the pupils amused and contained. Many were keen to get the pupils involved but were limited in their ability to do so, as often they were not teaching their own subjects. The core, permanent staff had a well developed content, methodology and ethos that was discussed in meetings and written down in such things as handbooks. The reality for the pupils was two sets of teaching staff.

Examples of good practice

At Westcliffe School there was one part-time secretary, based in the Lower School. Dora, the Registrar, started the day three mornings a week in the Lower School to ensure the secretary knew what was going on and had everything she needed. It was partly a social visit and partly business.

At William Barnes School each supply teacher was given a box in the morning which contained a map of the school, a timetable, a list of staff to contact with their extension numbers, an abbreviated staff handbook, paper, pencils and materials for the day's lessons. As one supply teacher said to us, 'I love coming here.'

At Westcliffe School subject meetings were held when the part-time staff were in school. This gave them the opportunity to contribute and understand developments.

Managing the core and the periphery

The core and peripheral staff both need managing and organising to ensure a co-ordinated use of resources. All the current indications are that the number and variety of people with a peripheral involvement in schools will increase, yet we found very few examples of any thought being given to the different type of management that is involved. We did not find a single school where supply staff were included in staff development or formal discussions. Nor did we find examples of part-time staff being timetabled so that they were in school for meetings. We certainly heard both these ideas being discussed.

Bereft of evidence from schools, we suggest ideas we have developed from other experience:

1 To make the most of skilled peripheral staff (like peripatetic and supply teachers) it is necessary to specify what is needed from them as closely as possible, but with the emphasis on output rather than input: what is required from them rather than on how they should do it. You take the 'how' for granted because they are skilled people, and you will reduce their confidence and their contribution if you specify the how rather than the what.

2 Whole jobs are better than bits and pieces. Thought can usually eliminate the baby-sitting risk of deploying supply staff only to keep children quiet, and replace the bits and pieces with a request to teach a specific part of the syllabus, assess the children's understanding at the end and leave a copy of the results. This makes it useful for the children, worthwhile for

the supply teacher, who has been able to do more than just hold the fort, and useful for the subject teacher, who does not spend 15 minutes on return from sick leave finding out what was done yesterday and making disparaging inferences about it.

3 Peripheral staff are nearly always emotionally detached from the school and do not have the same single-minded commitment that is likely from core staff. They will therefore expect to fit their contribution to your requirements, whatever their personal views about school culture, discipline and so forth. Attempts to involve them more fully may be unsuccessful as their commitment is to the job they do rather than to the school, their personal motivational needs are different from those of core staff and the nature of their potential contribution is also different.

4 Peripheral staff need clear guidance on the everyday trivialities that everyone else takes for granted: the location of the lavatories, where to get coffee, who does the washing up, local conventions on dress, which chairs are 'special' in the common room, rules on discipline and so forth.

5 Core staff are actually or potentially committed to the school and need a different type of valuing from peripheral employees. Although the core staff will have the same needs for confirmation that they are doing a good technical job, they will also need valuing as people, as we have discussed in Chapter 4, and will focus on the school as the arena for all their professional hopes and ambitions. That valuing is needed also to ensure the proper briefing of peripheral staff and the effective consolidation of their contribution. Members of the core are at all levels in the hierarchy and all of them are needed to enable the periphery to do a proper job.

6 No matter how rare and mysterious the skills to be brought in on the periphery, those in the core must have sufficient expertise to specify and manage the peripheral contribution – otherwise there is a serious risk that the tail will wag the dog. In a tight-knit culture like a school there is no place for the maverick expert.

7 Those who come in to the school, without being committed to it, also go out, taking an opinion about the school and about education. Some of those on the periphery are not professionals and may adopt a whole set of stereotyped judgements about education on the basis of a single experience. A significant proportion of students in teacher training either abandon their courses or do not enter the profession on graduation, and the main reason is that they are discouraged not by the children, but by the teachers.

Do It Yourself

1 Which staff are included in:

- department meetings;
- whole-school briefings;

- staff development;
- INSET;
- Baker days;
- appraisal procedures;
- coffee clubs;
- staff outings.

Who is not included?

2 What is your reaction to a new supply teacher or student:

a Include them?
b Assume someone else is looking after them?
c Too busy to help?

References

Atkinson, J., 'Management Strategies for Flexible Organisation', in *Personnel Management*, August, 1984.

Chapter 22

Conclusion: The Managing and Organising Balance: Collegiality, Prescription or Leadership

We found that the running of a school was invariably improved when there was a thorough and thoughtful approach to all aspects of the work of adults in the school community, with attention to aspects of both culture and structure; as these provide order, coherence and meaning for people who otherwise risk feeling overwhelmed in a hectic melée. Research on the work of general managers (Stewart, 1976; Mintzberg, 1973) has shown the fragmented nature of their working day, with an average of only nine minutes devoted to each activity. The American analyst Weick has commented:

> When organisational activity is lived in nine minute bursts, people seldom have time to reflect on what the bursts mean.
>
> (Weick, 1985, p. 389)

In many ways the life of the schoolteacher – particularly one with departmental or pastoral responsibilities – is similar to that of the general manager, with short blocks of time between teaching to deal with a range of administrative and managerial tasks. Our observations of individual teachers' days showed a number to have working patterns with very short spans indeed. For example, a Deputy had 166 activities in 352 minutes, a Senior Teacher 60 activities in 166 minutes, and a Head of Special Needs 142 activities in 260 minutes.

Many schools are better at creating a culture for adults to work together in than are many other organisations. However, this type of effectiveness, which has been built up over many years of tradition and embedding throughout the education service, is now in danger of being eroded as more 'managerial' approaches are introduced.

The schools we studied that worked best were those that had compatible culture and structures, that were braided together to create a supportive net for the adults to work in and, consequently, a suitable environment for the children to learn in. As Murgatroyd (1985) says: 'a school which fails to care for its staff is not likely to be caring effectively for its pupils.' Reid *et al.* (1987, p. 31) argue that the relationship between colleagues in schools is one of the unknowns. They also (p. 21) say that ways of achieving a favourable culture are not well documented. Our research has particularly looked at these aspects of school life.

Reynolds (1988) points out that British researchers have identified certain features of school organisation that are important in contributing to overall school effectiveness.

1 Rutter *et al.* (1979):
Outcomes as more favourable when there was a combination of firm leadership and a decision-making process in which all teachers felt that their views were represented.
2 Reynolds (1982):
Heads who devolved power.
3 Mortimore *et al.* (1988):
Purposeful leadership of the staff by the Headteacher without exerting total control.
Involving the Deputy Head and teachers in planning and decision making.
A positive climate.

As Reynolds says, the degree of commonality in the findings on organisational effectiveness is quite impressive.

The North American studies of schools summarised by Renihan and Renihan (1984) found similar factors important in creating effective organisations.

1 Leadership. Such things as assertive administration, instructional leadership, high standards, personal vision, expertise and force of character.
2 Conscious attention to climate with specific rules, regulations and guidelines understood by everyone.
3 Sense of mission shared by all with shared norms, agreed ways of doing things, clearly stated goals accepted and joint planning.

Our research has looked in detail at how these, and other, management and organisation processes are actually implemented. The schools in which we worked were all deemed by the local authority advisers to be effective in dealing with their particular situations. Indeed, this was the basis of their being selected for our study.

These 24 effective schools were not all being managed and organised in the same way. We came across different examples of good practice that represented different attitudes, cultures and histories. We also found that within the schools different faculties or departments were run in very different ways that could be equally effective.

Schools that were coping well with their various demands and challenges were not always similar. A model we have developed to explore the tensions of managing and organising within secondary schools is given in Figure 11. Effective management can be found in any of the shaded areas of the figure. The horizontal dimension represents the tension between tight central control on the one hand and group or individual autonomy on the other. This illustrates the range of ways that schools deal with, and who decides, such *structural* things as resources, finance, timetables, curriculum, staffing, job descriptions, teaching methodologies and schemes of work. A school in which all these matters are dealt with centrally would be located towards the right-hand side, but that could move progressively to the left as the number of matters and the nature of choice was moved out of the hands of the few at the centre and into the hands of more members of staff.

Figure 11: The tensions of managing secondary schools

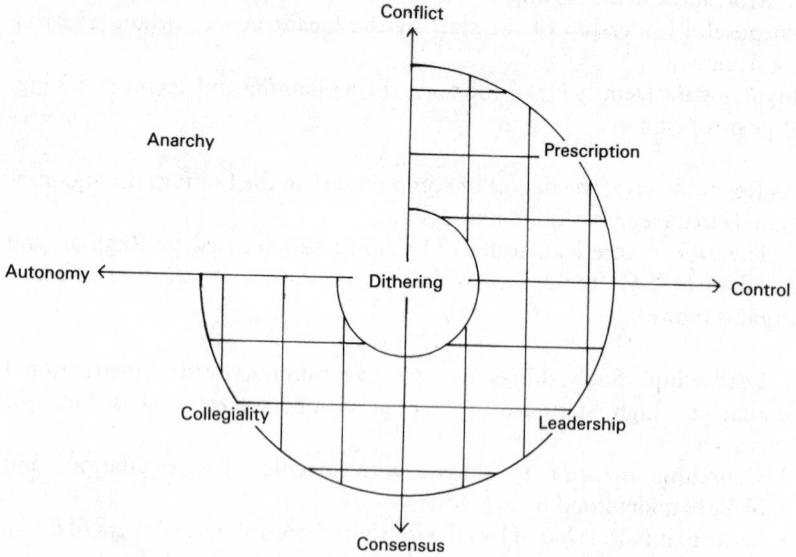

An example of practice in a school with tight central control would be Lodge School, where the timetable was devised by the Headteacher. Individual members of staff were given copies of their own timetable, but the only copy of the whole-school timetable was kept in the Head's study. An example of greater autonomy for dealing with the same feature of school organisation was Jackson School, where the Maths Department had sections of the timetable for each year blocked out for their use. Within those blocks they decided the grouping of children and the staffing of classes, with constant changes depending on the topic being taught.

The vertical dimension of the figure represents a different tension, between values of consensus and relationships of high trust at one extreme, contrasted with low trust and conflicting interests at the other. This tells us something about the *culture* of the school and represents both the assumptions people make and the behaviour in which they engage. If a significant number of people, or a small number with significant power, believe the school to be staffed by members of different groups whose interests conflict, then they will also believe that the main management and organisation task is to deal with this conflict, so their behaviour will reflect that belief. If the prevailing belief is that there are teams within the school who work together to the same ends, with the management and organisation task being to nurture this consensus, then behaviour will follow that assumption.

Summerfield School demonstrated high consensus by there being a remarkable amount of interest in each other's work shown by members of staff in different departments. It was a rare phenomenon in our experience for this degree of interest to be shown between departments, although mutual support within departments was common. At Summerfield there was further tangible evidence as staff actually offered resources to assist colleagues in other departments. In stark contrast were the more conflictual attitudes apparent at Oakhill School, where each department tended not only to be inward-looking in their concerns, but also husbanded staff, rooms, materials and finance separately from the other departments and with great secrecy. While one school was characterised by interest and reciprocity between departments, the other was characterised by mutual suspicion and a destructive narrowness in the approach to education.

Putting these two dimensions together produces four quadrants, which we have labelled anarchy, prescription, leadership and collegiality as representing the dominant management and organisational style operating. The prescription style is likely where there is a felt need for a lot of control mechanisms to manage the conflict within the school, while the leadership style is more likely when a similar felt need to control is linked with a strong consensus supporting the initiatives of the senior management team. We hold the work of Charles Handy in high regard, but the similarity between our quadrants and his organisational cultures (Handy, 1984, pp. 186–96) is a genuine coincidence, and the messages of the two sets of explanations are different.

Although we find it difficult to recommend the anarchic style for any normal school situation, each of the other three styles has both advantages and disadvantages.

The Prescriptive style imposes order, allows for a lot of co-ordination, with little duplication of effort and resources allocated on a rational basis. Hall End School had an extensive staff handbook of procedures, daily bulletins of information running to several pages distributed to each member of staff, daily senior staff meetings before school and close monitoring of individual teachers' examination results and student workbooks. However, this prescription can lead to inflexibility and a minimum contribution from staff. This was seen in the English Department at Hall End, where staff resented the close monitoring of their marking by senior staff and adopted a cautious and defensive approach to the rest of the school when whole-school issues were being discussed.

Prescription is most appropriate for dealing with matters that are routine and predictable. Such things as how to conduct fire drills and what to do about children who come late are best dealt with by clear, laid-down procedures; otherwise time is wasted and effort expended where it should not be needed. In one school, for example, there was no standard drill for the simple, routine task of collecting the registers, so that no one knew what to do and one of the Deputy Heads spent half an hour each day re-inventing how to do it, asking for information and checking what was happening.

Prescription can also be appropriate when there is a major crisis or when the identity of the school is unclear, as in the amalgamation of two or more schools during re-organisation. All organisations need some co-ordination, predictability and control; prescription is appropriate to achieve these ends when other methods have failed, are too time-consuming, or are difficult to achieve because of temporary staffing. When a school has had a strong leader as Head, the prescriptive style can be appropriate in the aftermath, as it provides an alternative structure after the collapse of the spider's web woven by the departed Head.

As a general approach to running the school, prescription can thus be appropriate for a number of temporary situations. The difficulty is to find a way of moving to some other approach to ensure the school is flexible enough to cope with changing demands. Prescription of the right things and holding back from prescribing how people should teach is a very difficult balance to achieve. In its most benign form prescription cleans up the administrative detail and minimises the routine frustrations of organisational life. It enables things to happen by removing impediments but it generates no excitement, raises no enthusiasm, makes no contribution to creativity.

There are some signs that prescription is becoming the new orthodoxy in school management and this stems from a vain hope that the world can be made stable by procedures and systems. The current and impending innovation overload for schools is such that there are many things that will be unpredictable and which need managing in other ways than by prescription.

The Leadership style can promote a sense of purpose and mission, with effort contributed willingly to this end; staff often feel valued personally and feel secure as they look up to the leader. For example, at Westcliffe many of the staff felt personally committed to the Headteacher as he had promoted them further than they had expected, as they were constantly being told by him what a good school they had and as they felt he kept them well informed of current trends in education. There is, however, the difficulty and frustration for other staff that they cannot develop without threatening the leader. This is, for example, often seen in the Deputies, who find themselves in the situation of having very little real work of their own to do because they are constantly 'working for' the Head. Westcliffe was a prime example of this, with both the Deputies and Senior Teachers, six staff in all, doing a lot of trivial administrative work.

Leadership seems particularly appropriate at the two extremes of experience: in a very stable environment and in very turbulent, life-threatening times. In stable times a leader can make control more acceptable by being a good communicator and can humanise the structures and procedures. In turbulent times, such as amalgamation, losing the Sixth Form, or getting poor press reports, a strong leader can embody what needs to be done and so help the business of creating the new purpose.

The difficulty is that the strong leader so embodies the unity of the school that it becomes almost a theological heresy to attack the leader. So flexibility, as well as uncertainty, is reduced. Not only does everyone follow the leader, they also wait for the leader and are inhibited from suggesting an appropriate route to follow.

The Collegial style emphasises collaboration and team work, enabling each member to contribute more. Methodologies and styles appropriate to different needs can be used; flexibility to meet new demands is easier to achieve and individuals can feel valued members of the school. For example, at Valley High the departments were the main organising feature and staff in departments spent a lot of time discussing curriculum and methodologies. The difficulty is really for senior staff, as they are unsure how to co-ordinate this activity and are unsure what their role should be; also some groups may become self-seeking at others' expense. At Valley High this problem was avoided by the senior staff reinforcing the central values of the school. They did this by taking the chair at meetings, especially those of high profile, and encouraging those present to make their contribution and to develop the ideas of their colleagues. Not only was this an unusually healthy mode of conducting meetings, it also provided a means of constantly encouraging members of staff to get involved in the fullness of school life. At Jackson, however, the senior staff were quite unsure what their role was and so made sure they appeared 'busy' at all times, often on quite trivial activities.

Collegiality is in many ways the opposite of prescription. It is particularly appropriate for dealing with technical matters such as how and what to teach, to whom. It is needed in situations where a staff contribution that goes beyond simple compliance with instructions is required, as the person in charge can perhaps specify *what* is to be done ('More imaginative teaching of French, please'), but can rarely specify *how* the goal is to be reached. Collegiality is the better way of managing and organising in novel situations where no one is quite sure what the required performance actually is, such as the introduction of GCSE, or the national curriculum, where each individual teacher has to make it happen.

Collegiality has such an obvious appeal that it is tempting to regard it as the 'best way' to run a school. However, where there is a shortage of competent people, a high percentage of temporary staff, a high turnover of staff, a lot of inexperienced staff or conflicting loyalties, the school will be poorly served by collegial managing and organising. It is a flexible way of organising where there is sufficient stability of personnel for continuity.

The Anarchic style seeks to meet the ideal of individual rights to self-expression and development of potential free from the constraints of control mechanisms or the discipline of conforming to group norms. We had no examples of this type of school in our sample. It is associated with such schools as Summerhill, Dartington and William Tyndale, but each of these had a strong leader as founding father. The disadvantage of this style is persuading others that this individuality is what schools should be about.

Figure 12 shows the distribution of our 24 schools on the model. The differences in position are intended to suggest that generally one school has more or less of the attribute on an axis than another school. For example, Lodge has more central controlling of structures than Westcliffe but Westcliffe has slightly more assumptions of consensus than Lodge and both have more 'control' and 'consensus' than Jackson. We do not intend this model as a precise measuring device but we found it relatively easy to rank order our schools on the axes. Within each of our schools there are parts which fit each of the paradigms. We have only used the general, whole-school management and organisation style to locate individual schools. Certainly different locations might be appropriate at different times and when considering different issues. These, indeed, might be the more interesting points for discussion within a school. However, by labelling the general management and organising style, we feel it is helpful to see whether the culture and structure of the school are congruent and woven together sufficiently to provide a supportive environment for the adults to work in and, consequently, for the children to learn in.

So what would we recommend? We would argue that none of the styles can be pursued to their extremes without creating serious organisational difficulties. Equally, we would argue that dithering in the centre with no clear view, unless there is inspired pragmatism, leads to loss of identity, direction and confidence.

Each of the three main styles is appropriate for particular situations. Prescription is appropriate where consistency is important. Leadership is helpful when there is uncertainty that can and should be dealt with quickly. Collegiality is useful when the full commitment of individuals is necessary. All schools have all these in different proportions at different

Figure 12

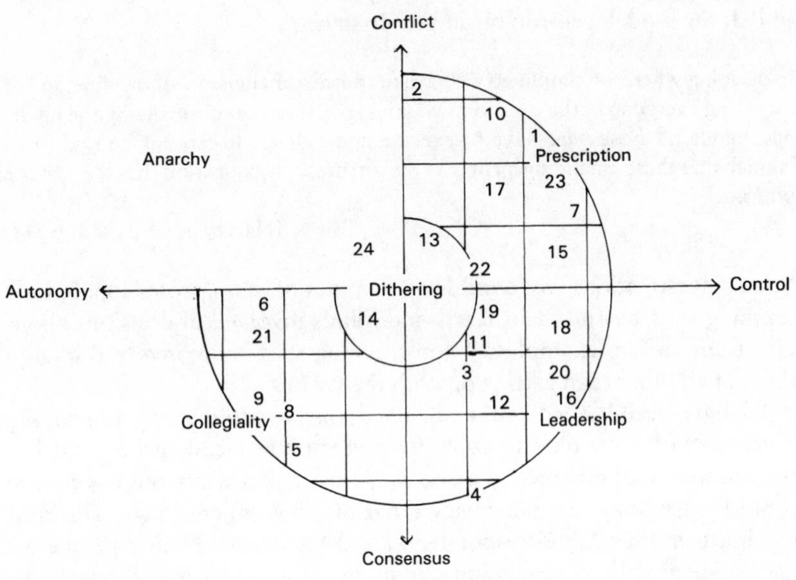

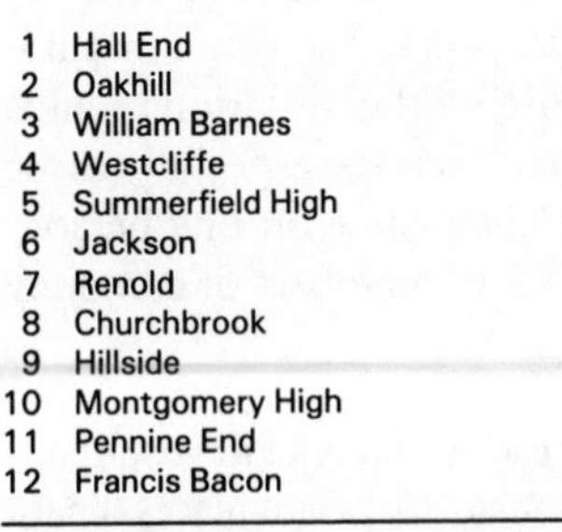
1 Hall End
2 Oakhill
3 William Barnes
4 Westcliffe
5 Summerfield High
6 Jackson
7 Renold
8 Churchbrook
9 Hillside
10 Montgomery High
11 Pennine End
12 Francis Bacon

13 Ridley
14 Francis Drake
15 St Elmo's
16 Lodge
17 Park
18 Abbey
19 Kirkside
20 The Ridgeway
21 Valley High
22 Central High
23 Southern High
24 Ferndown

times. The balance between them is the clever art of finding the appropriate management and organisation for the particular school.

Drawing lessons from industrial practice to inform methods of running schools is dangerous, as commercial organisations are driven by competitiveness in a way that is quite inappropriate for schools, and the general situations faced by industrial managers of instability, international operations, organisational size and the dominance of expedience make it difficult to draw sound conclusions. There are, nonetheless, interesting points of comparison.

We find the extent to which adults are taken for granted in schools to be unusual when looking at other organisations, where *core* employees are increasingly being nurtured and developed with heavy investment in programmes of training in communication and consultation. These efforts are viewed with scepticism by some observers, who view them as manipulative and divisive, as many are told but few are consulted, but the need for such involvement is widely accepted. Before retiring to write his best-selling book *Making It Happen*, John Harvey-Jones was Chairman of ICI, the model well-run business. He says:

> In deciding where we should go we have to transfer 'ownership' of the direction of involving everyone in the decision. Making it happen means involving the hearts and minds of those who have to execute and deliver. It can not be said often enough that these are not the people at the top of the organization, but those at the bottom.
>
> (Harvey-Jones, 1988, p. 48)

In our investigations we found few examples of main professional-grade teaching staff having their hearts and minds involved in decisions about direction, and no examples of non-teaching staff being involved in anything at all other than getting on with their work.

We have been baffled by the universal, unshakeable conviction among everyone we have spoken to about the power of the Headteacher, who has organisational dominance to a degree almost unknown in our experience of studying management in a wide range of other undertakings. The ideal of almost all our 1,065 respondents, and hundreds of other people we have spoken with in discussing our findings, is the Leadership style we have described in this paper. Although appropriate for some circumstances, we find this severely limited for most of the situations which schools now face, and all too often teachers themselves – especially those in senior posts – perpetuate this dangerous dependence on one person. Harvey-Jones makes an interesting comment about members of company boards:

> . . . clear responsibility for the company rests with each member of the board in a collegiate sense . . . It is a sad commentary that in many cases and places, board members have failed to observe their responsibilities and powerful chief executives have, to a large extent, hijacked their boards . . . no board member can be hijacked unless he or she is a willing and compliant conspirator.
>
> (Harvey-Jones, p. 26)

It would be foolish to suggest that Deputy Heads and Senior Teachers have the same legal authority and responsibility as company directors, but the general validity of the comment holds. There are many willing and compliant conspirators.

References

Handy, C.B., *Taken for Granted: Understanding Schools as Organisations*, Longman/Schools Council, York, 1984.

Harvey-Jones, J., *Making It Happen*, Collins, London, 1988.

Mintzberg, H., *The Nature of Managerial Work*, Harper and Row, New York, 1973.
Mortimore, P., Sammons, P., Ecob, R. and Stoll, L., *School Matters: The Junior Years*, Open Books, Salisbury, 1988.
Murgatroyd, S., 'Management Teams and the Promotion of Well-being', in *School Organisation*, Vol. 6, No. 1, 1985.
Reid, K., Hopkins, D. and Holby, P., *Towards the Effective School*, Blackwell, Oxford, 1987.
Renihan, F.I. and Renihan, P.J., 'Effective Schools, Effective Administration and Effective Leadership', *The Canadian Administrator*, Vol. 24, No. 3, pp. 1–6, 1984.
Reynolds, D., 'The Search for Effective Schools', *School Organisation*, Vol. 2, No. 3, pp. 215–37, 1982.
Reynolds, D., 'Research on School and Organisational Effectiveness: The End of the Beginning', BEMAS Conference, Cardiff, April, 1988.
Rutter *et al.*, *Fifteen Thousand Hours*, Open Books, London, 1979.
Stewart, R., *Contrasts in Management*, McGraw-Hill, Maidenhead, 1976.
Weick, K.E., 'The Significance of Corporate Culture', in P.J. Frost *et al.*, *Organisational Culture*, Sage Publications, California, pp. 381–8, 1985.

Appendix
Pen Portraits of Our Schools

1 Hall End
2 Oakhill
3 William Barnes
4 Westcliffe
5 Summerfield High
6 Jackson
7 Renold
8 Churchbrook
9 Hillside
10 Montgomery High
11 Pennine End
12 Francis Bacon
13 Ridley
14 Francis Drake
15 St Elmo's
16 Lodge
17 Park
18 Abbey
19 Kirkside
20 The Ridgeway
21 Valley High
22 Central High
23 Southern High
24 Ferndown

1 Hall End

Catchment area

Inner-city, EPA, run-down terraces, council housing, small factories. 95 per cent of the children having dinners have free dinners. Most are from poor white or immigrant backgrounds.

In October 1985 21 per cent were of Asian origin, 8 per cent Afro-Caribbean origin and 3.6 per cent of Chinese origin.

In October 1986, out of 146 First Years, 14 scored over 100 on the Richmond Tests (100 = norm SD = 15); that is, entrance is below average on academic assessment. Many were from single-parent homes. Two out of the five feeder primary schools were mainly black, and two were mainly white. Integration has to be established in the first year.

Some materials for parents were published in two languages, English and Urdu, with translations into Punjabi, Bengali, Hindu, Cantonese and Vietnamese also available.

There were ten children in wheelchairs.

History

Established in 1973 as part of Community Centre. There was no separate School Head, Heads of Department, etc. In 1982 the LEA reorganised to 11-16 plus Sixth Form College. There was a change of staff with many not committed to Centre-based view. The Head of School laid out new structure. In 1986 the school separated from the Community Centre with its own governors and Headteacher.

2 *Oakhill*

Inner-city location, surrounded by late 1960s/early 1970s prefabricated concrete blocks of council flats and road schemes. It has a desolate look of grey, open-access flats, scruffy shopping centres and mud. The area is currently the focus of local, national and EEC money for special attention. There are, therefore, lots of 'projects'. It is the drugs, prostitution and murder centre of the city. Relations with police are sensitive, if not non-existent. There are lots of community groups, leaders and centres run by agencies, both voluntary and authority. Many children are from hostels for homeless and battered women. 50 per cent of the children are of Afro-Caribbean origin. Most children received free meals (only 20 paid for meals per day).

The school is one large building with the hall in the centre. It had parquet floors on the ground floor and a pannelled hall with a stage. It was built for 1,400 children and opened in 1967. It now has only 360 children. The school feels empty and reduced staff have to lock doors into the hall to prevent circulation. Also, other corridors are locked on occasion. Some classrooms are never used. All teachers have their own classrooms except Special Needs, who chose not to, and I/C who share First and Second Years but have their own classrooms for other work.

3 *William Barnes*

Situated on the outskirts of a northern industrial town surrounded by estates of council houses, many of which have been sold off judging by customising of porches, stone facades, different-coloured doors and windows. The catchment area also includes executive estates.

The school itself is a long building made up of a former boys' school and girls' school joined by a long new building in the early seventies. It stands in very extensive grounds going down to a brook. The conservation people were planting hundreds of trees whilst we were there.

Inside, the school's extremities are rather tatty and in serious need of painting. The middle is quite smart. There is quite a lot of graffiti around (especially outside) and staff do not seem to remove it. There are frequent incidents of windows being broken. The only art work on show was in in the foyer and corridor, and was not changed during the two months of our attachment. Other displays in the entrance hall were, however, changed several times, for example, design, enterprise, etc.

4 *Westcliffe*

Westcliffe is a large, split-site school which was reorganised as a comprehensive 12 years ago. In the early years it had to compete with a nearby ex-grammar school, and has successfully built up a good reputation in the area. It is situated in pleasant verdant suburbs, with a catchment area which includes a wide variety of housing, including large, gracious, detached houses, mill terraces and some established council estates.

After reorganisation, the senior management remained the same seven people for seven years, with some drafting in of new blood subsequently. The age profile of teachers in the school is fairly high, with no one under the age of 25. Four members of the Senior Management Team are over 50.

Despite its earlier successes, the school has not kept totally abreast of recent developments in education, with initiatives such as TVEI, ACS or IC taking place. It has a large Sixth Form, with approximately one third of pupils staying on. In September of 1988 it will have its last normal intake into the First Year before being run down in preparation for becoming the area Sixth Form College in three years' time.

There is a sense of frustration in the school, not with the lack of change, but with the style of management of the school. The Headteacher believes strongly in the merits of a participative style of management, but this seems to have developed over time into a somewhat paternalistic and patronising leadership style, which takes great care of the individuals in the school, but somewhat neglects the task and the team. The Heads of Department are given a fair amount of autonomy on curriculum issues and appear to appreciate this. However, the effectiveness of the Senior

Management Group is severely reduced by a lack of definition of senior management roles and by a Headteacher who is off-site a lot but who has devolved to the group very little decision-making power. There is no sense of excitement in the school.

5 *Summerfield High*

The school is on the outskirts of an industrial town, close to attractive rural countryside. Surrounding the school are 1930s housing estates, mostly council, but with some private houses. The catchment area also includes small villages and farms with a sprinkling of executive, commuter-belt families.

The school facilities include the local sports centre and village hall so, in some senses, it acts as a Community School. The school's buildings are two adjoining quadrangles built in the 1930s as the boys' and girls' schools. To this new Science, Art and Sports facilities have been added. Connecting the sports hall to the old building is a most attractive hall and dining room. The quadrangles are filled with flowering shrubs and the playgrounds and fields are well-kept.

The overwhelming impression of Summerfield High is now friendly both adults and children are, to each other and outsiders.

6 *Jackson*

The school is essentially one building with a large demountable for the Maths Department. It is set in large playing fields, looking over a valley towards a major suburban centre.

The immediate area is small, privately owned, semi-detached houses and light industry. Nearby are council estates and executive estates. The school is approximately five miles from the city centre. There are no black children in the school and one Asian teacher.

7 *Renold*

The school was founded in 1569. It became a voluntary aided ('Christian Faith') school after the Education Act 1944 and provided grammar school education for boys. In September 1980 the school was reorganised to become a 13-18 Boys' Upper School, as part of the three-tier comprehensive system introduced for the catchment area.

Renold School is a Group 11 school with approximately 700 boys on the roll, some 130 of them in the Sixth Form. Numbers are projected to fall to below 600 by 1990, however, with a consequent loss of staff.

Subject teaching is organised on a departmental basis. There are two Deputy Heads and Year Heads for the Third, Fourth and Fifth Years, plus a Head of Sixth Form. There is also a vertical House system which is used principally for Sport, Music and Drama.

There is a boarding house for boys in the age range 11–18; this is located in the town and has places for about 38 pupils. 11- and 12-year-old boys attend one of the contributory middle schools. Some three-quarters of these places are allocated by the LEA to boys for whom a boarding education is clearly desirable. The remainder are allocated by the governors. The boarders come from a wide variety of backgrounds, the majority from families connected with the armed services or with overseas commercial enterprises.

There is a strong Combined Cadet Force at the school on which the governors place considerable emphasis as providing an excellent introduction to outward-bound-type activities.

Rugby, soccer, cricket, athletics, hockey and cross-country running flourish and the school maintains strong fixture lists with teams at all levels and continues with its tradition of Saturday sport. These team activities are supplemented by encouragement of many individual sports such as golf and sailing. The playing fields adjoin the school. There is a heated open-air swimming pool, an all-weather hockey pitch and a large, well-equipped sports hall. The latter is fully used by the community as part of the school's involvement in the life of the town. The governors view this as a vital part of the school's contribution to the town and the surrounding area.

The governors have been responsible for much recent building. The facilities include a kitchen–dining room, drama studio, a suite of rooms for remedial teaching, two rooms for technical and engineering drawing, three additional science laboratories (making nine in all), a greenhouse and animal house, seven integrated rooms for art, wood and metal work, printing and photography, as well as the sports hall. In addition, the governors have provided a new music block and the hard-play hockey pitch. Extra classroom provision has also been made for the English, Classics and History departments and Heads of Department have their own departmental rooms. Two years ago there was intalled a computer laboratory equipped with an ECONET network system of 16 BBC microcomputers served by a common printer and disk facilities, with linkage to a number of teaching classrooms and laboratories.

8 Churchbrook

The buildings and grounds

Disparities of style and state of repair reflect the fact that this is not a purpose-built unit. The school grew out of the old secondary modern on the site and the three-storey block of Science and Home Economics rooms, the CDT and Art rooms and the Adult Centre (see below) are all obviously older than the rest. 'Antediluvian' would be a better word than 'antiquated' for the Science rooms now that most of the taps cannot be used for fear of their effects on floors below. The newer part of the school is of CLEAPSE construction dating from the mid-1970s. Manholes (exuding off-odours at times) in various places, including the staffroom, show how the planners put the new buildings over the drains for the old. Most of the newer part is single-storey and pleasantly laid out, with broad corridors and good window provision. In this part the fabric is taking the strain well and, at least early in the school year, is looking quite smart.

The Adult Centre, despite being in an older part of the buildings, is very spruce. New funding, painting and no children make a difference.

The approach to the school is through a turning area for buses surrounded by trees and shrubs and across a car park bordered by a rock garden. This creates a good impression. There are extensive playing fields at the back of the school and these are surrounded by (and interspersed with) trees and bushes. In the long Indian summer, this was beautiful.

Catchment area

Formerly a market town, the town now has one important factory and several small light-engineering works. It has become a dormitory town for the nearby city, while the same change has affected the surrounding villages and hamlet. The school's former status as a secondary modern has continued to concern many local parents who send their children on ten-mile bus journeys to neighbouring 11–18 schools. In the early 1980s an HMI report stated that the HMI had not to that date found a school nationally which had lost more of its potential catchment than Churchbrook was losing. A Sunday newspaper report on 'The most unpopular school in the country' could not have helped staff morale. The pupils, for the most part, seem polite, well behaved and well turned out. The persistent offenders we witnessed being disciplined have, more often than not, been pupils moved into the school from outside its catchment area. Less than 10 per cent of pupils are in receipt of free school meals and less than 15 per cent of the pupils are deemed 'remedial' in the application of the LEA staffing formula.

Brief history

In 1971 the school was opened as a comprehensive and the secondary modern curriculum was phased out over the next four years. The present Head was appointed in 1975 and the senior Deputy shortly afterwards. Several of the staff have served in the school since before the 1971 conversion. From 1982 to 1985 the school was the subject of an HMI longitudinal study. This commented favourably on the long-term planning, to meet 'falling' rolls, which had begun in the school. As part of that planning and also in response to the HMI criticism of pupil behaviour and over-didactic teaching, the Lower School Unit was set up. This is a major 'plus' for the school and, because it seems to be working well, it is attracting attention from within the LEA and without, for example CSCS. The Head is active in the development of 'adult' or 'continuing' education in the town and it is possible that the school will become a 'Community School' in the near future.

9 *Hillside*

Hillside School is an 11–16 mixed comprehensive school, currently with 4–5 forms of entry. It is situated on the northern edge of the town in an open, residential position with easy access to the motorway system.

The school was built as a girls' grammar school on its present site in 1964 and became comprehensive ten years later. Facilities are good. The main building is on three floors.

The catchment area is very mixed, including private and council housing. Children are drawn mainly from four primary schools, two nearby and two serving an area from where children are bussed.

Many pupils are socially and educationally disadvantaged and the school has made much progress in offering a curriculum suited to their needs.

10 *Montgomery High*

Montgomery High school is an 11–18 co-educational comprehensive school of about 1,100 pupils, situated about two miles from the town centre just off the main road. It opened in the mid-sixties.

It is not a split-site school but consists of six separate buildings on one site with no covered walkways. The site is green and pleasant in good weather, hostile in bad. The Head's and Deputies rooms and the school office are all together in one gatehouse-like block at one end of the site. The staffroom is spacious but drab and staff facilities are very basic.

Pastoral organisation is on a Year basis.

Montgomery has a significant proportion of pupils with special educational needs. These include physically handicapped pupils, ethnic minority pupils and an approximate 20 per cent of pupils who have some learning difficulties in basic language, literacy and numeracy. The school makes a big investment in Special Needs, with 14 staff, a Scale 4 Head of Department, a Scale 3 second in the department, and a Scale 2 Head of ESL.

In general, despite the poor socio-economic background of most of the pupils and the high proportion of pupils with special needs, the school seems to be, to a great extent, successful in its aim 'to foster the development of responsible, tolerant and caring people . . .'. It must be said that academic attainment, as indicated by external examination results, is not high.

A feature of the staffing of Montgomery High is its low turnover in recent years; it is possible that this stability of staffing has contributed to the atmosphere of calm and order which generally reigns in what was in the seventies, by common consent, a very difficult school to teach in.

The present Head, Mr Higson, has been in post for three years; for much of the time the school has been affected by union action over salaries. He thinks that his staff have been the most militant of any local secondary schools and he has felt unable to bring about many significant changes in policy or practice during this period. The school has not stood still, however. As well as its deliberate involvement in integrating a number of physically disabled pupils, there has been much innovative work in information technology, both in the curriculum and in school administration.

With the long-term prospect of falling rolls, the school is in direct competition for pupils with three other nearby schools and much effort on Mr Higson's part goes into bolstering the school's image. Whilst many staff support Mr Higson's initiatives in marketing the school and respect his efforts at obtaining resources for the school, in his management style he is regarded by many staff as insensitive and unnecessarily autocatic. Following the end of the long period of union action, Mr Higson had drawn up a new consultative structure and an agenda to begin to address the school's needs as he sees them, operative from September 1986.

11 Pennine End

Prior to 1976 Pennine End School was a mixed grammar school of approximately 600 pupils serving the 'leafy suburbs' of an industrial town and some dormitory villages. When it was reorganised as a comprehensive school in that year it retained its predominant middle-class catchment but more or less doubled in size. It now has 1,201 pupils on roll with 178 in the Sixth Form.

Very little purpose-built accommodation has been provided to cater for the increased numbers. As a result the school has come to rely on a number of semi-permanent 'terrapins' for a large proportion of its teaching spaces. In many ways the school is a victim of its own success. There are, for example, severe pressure on space, overcrowding and large classes in the main academic subjects. Many of the teaching areas seem to be in a poor state of repair due, in the main, to constant use. There is no evidence of any graffiti or wilful damage.

12 Francis Bacon

This school is one of the town's new comprehensives, set up by the County LEA (which took over from the City when the County was reorganised) in

1979. Much of the city is still subject to eleven-plus exams and grammar schools, in spite of several recent attempts by the authority to reorganise, and Francis Bacon, since it was opened, has felt a need to prove to the city that the comprehensive system can deliver quality. Quality is seen as a strict uniform policy (every pupil in Year One to Five wears a maroon blazer, cost £19); there are good exam results, plenty of homework and no interruptions to the school calendar for activities weeks, residential experience or other frippery.

The catchment area is outer-suburb, private housing estates, laid out in attractive curves with shrubs and trees. Because the buildings are new and the Head publicises his school aggressively, the school has acquired a high reputation and there are more appeals made by parents to the LEA for admission to Francis Bacon than for any other school in the County. The school is full; the Head can confidently threaten parents who have struggled to get their children in with something close to expulsion if he has any problems.

Because the present Head set up the school, he has had an enviable opportunity to appoint teachers; a few of the present staff come from schools closing in the city, but many are young, Scale 1 teachers who have never worked in any other school.

13 Ridley (Voluntary Aided)

The school

The school site is small and comprises a group of buildings scattered round the edges of a tarmac playground area. There are no playing fields. The original straggling school building, comprising hall, gym, kitchen, library, staffroom, offices, four laboratories and nine classrooms, has been augmented over the years by 'The New Block' of two kitchen – dining areas and eight classrooms, a CDT block and two 'huts' providing four classrooms. There is nineteenth-century terraced accommodation on three sides of the site and the fourth side is occupied by the denominational church and primary school. Symbols of Christianity are common, but the open areas of the school lack pupils' work displays. The older part of the school has a rather 'heavy' feel to it, with dark corridors, the walls of which need decoration. The newer parts are architecturally lighter but the walls need plaster as well as paint.

The denominational community in the town is relatively large and strong. The staff includes many who have had long service in the school. Into this, the present Head accepted appointment three and a half years before the study. He is educationally 'on the ball', keen on self-development (judging by his accumulation of qualifications) but not a good mixer. He still felt himself to be an outsider. The Head and the union representative interviewed blamed each other for the way actions during the pay dispute had led to the continuing ill feeling between the Head and many of the staff. Morale in the school had been further lowered by the LEA's unexpected action of including the school in its planning for secondary reorganisation in the area. This came at a late stage of the planning and the decision to include the school was seen as threatening because it was unexplained.

There was not a requirement for staff to belong to the particular Christian denomination, but they had to satisfy the governors that they would contribute to the 'Christian ethos' of the school.

The catchment area

Geographically, the catchment area was the town and its neighbouring communities. Much of the housing is stone-built terraces, now being bought by first-time buyers, often moving out from the nearby large city. Another large section of the housing is in relatively modern estates. These larger 'family houses' are often occupied as dormitory accommodation for the city. There is a large 'overspill' estate towards the edge of the catchment.

More important than the geography is the fact that Ridley is a denominational school. This makes it subtly selective even though it does not refuse other admissions. For most of the catchment area, any one of three non-denominational schools would be more convenient. Parents who are prepared to accept (and make their children accept) the inconvenience of attending the denominational school may well be altogether more concerned for their children's education (it is known from baptismal records that some children of this particular denomination go to other schools). Further, the children of other denominations are selected; the school has more such applications than it can accept. Again the caring parent is likely to be more supportive of their child's school.

Employment in the area, formerly strong in textiles, light engineering and metallurgy, has become less easily available and many local people travel outside for work. The school has never had a Sixth Form; most of those who seek 'A' level courses go to the nearest Christian school with a Sixth Form. Very few go to the neighbouring non-denominational schools where, for several reasons, the Sixth Forms have shrunk rapidly as their pupils have also sought places at Sixth Form Colleges out of the area.

14 Francis Drake

This school is one of the best established schools in the County. It was founded in 1928 and the unusual architecture of the main buildings (built in the 1970s) suggest that some care and imagination went into its planning. The first Headteacher left three years ago to become the

Secretary of one of the Heads' Associations, his influence and reputation are still spoken of often by present staff.

The school is on three sites, each adjacent to the other. It takes about five minutes to walk between any of the three sets of buildings. The Lower School is in a red-brick 1930s building, mainly based on a red-brick courtyard block, with a collection of temporary classrooms, many of them in a poor state of repair. The Main School is in a more recent building, the front section of which is impressive in its design. The buildings at the rear are based, like the Lower School, on two courtyards and they are windswept and bleak in the winter. The Upper School is for the Sixth Form and is in a large Victorian house set in trees and parkland on a hill above the rest of the school. Unfortunately, the collection of temporary classrooms around it, and the poor maintenance of the interior of the building, means that much of the aura of grace and opulence has been lost; it is little better than seedy.

The school is in a wealthy town – an ancient place, with a castle and several old churches. In the past 50 years, the local Trust, set up by a rich and liberal American couple, has transformed the estate on the edge of the town – now the School, College of Arts, and Centre for Teachers bring a regular flow of educated people into the area. This part of the County is also, for some reason, the area to which people come for unconventional life-styles, living off the land or alternative living (there are two Rudolf Steiner Institutions within five miles of the town). The town has a larger percentage than normal of health-food shops, bookshops and craft shops.

The effect on the school is noticeable. The children are well-dressed but not conventionally dressed. There are sculptures in one school courtyard. The exam results are above average, and the Parents' Association is active and enthusiastic. There is a steady income for the school from ancient foundations in the town, and staff are all obviously aware of pressure from parents for high-quality education. The school has a regular intake of pupils from about six miles away, where there is one of the diminishing number of areas in the country with a grammar-school system.

Staff are inclined to come to Francis Drake and stay. Although housing is expensive, teachers, once in the school, find much around them pleasant and are less inclined than some to look for posts elsewhere. The age structure is older than average.

15 St Elmo's

The school has 720 pupils between the ages of 12 and 16. It occupies a compact group of buildings close to the leafy suburbs of the city, although denser, lower-quality housing and council flats are close by between the school and the city centre. There are five high schools in the city and several large private schools. In a recent reorganisation the Church of

England High School combined with a former grammar school to create a neighbouring school and extensive new building was provided. It is important to know that this new school can be clearly seen from St Elmo's. It is on a hill less than half a mile away and it is the most popular choice of parents in the northern part of the city. St Elmo's exists very much in its shadow – almost literally – and teachers at St Elmo's feel they have succeeded if they have a higher proportion of second choices than other schools – they know that the other school will be the first choice of so many that that school will be over-subscribed.

The buildings are mainly of brick, with small courtyards and a collection of temporary classrooms – four of them brand new, funded by TVEI. The grounds slope to the south and are extensive.

The entrance hall is large and bright and there is an impressive display of indoor plants on a high shelf opposite the wide main entrance. The administration corridor is off this hall and comprises the offices of the Head and two Deputies, the office shared by the two secretaries and a small office equipment store. At the end of this corridor is the staffroom. The men's toilets are here, but the women's are across the entrance hall by the main hall. There is a new block at the far end of the school from the main entrance. It looks considerably less attractive than the rest of the school and, in spite of its youth, it has suffered a lot from wear and tear.

There are two staffrooms. One of them, in the new block, is little used, apart from a group who lunch there and the teachers who teach nearby who use it at break. The main staffroom is not large, but it faces south and is always warm and bright. The pigeonholes are just enough for the staff and the extras such as students who are attached to the school. There is a telephone extension, four noticeboards and a sink with water-urn for coffee. The chairs are arranged in rows without a great deal of thought.

16 Lodge

Lodge is a comprehensive Upper School for girls aged between 13 and 18. In September 1986 it had 606 on roll, 119 of whom were in the Sixth Form. The present staffing establishment is 42, but falling rolls will reduce this to 37 or 38 by 1990. The school admits girls from three Middle Schools.

Secondary education in the area was reorganised in 1980 and the school, in its present form, dates from then. It occupies the site formerly occupied by a secondary modern school, which was improved and extended to provide excellent facilities. These include a room for Art and CDT, Home Economics and Needlework rooms, a new central library, a Sixth Form commonroom and study area, two rooms for Typing and Commercial Studies and a newly equipped Music suite. The administration area is light and spacious. Altogether, the school provides a most pleasant environment which is enhanced by magnificent views across the playing field to the ramparts of a Romano-British fortification.

Academic organisation

Subjects are organised on a faculty basis as follows:

- Communication
- Social and Commercial Studies
- Recreational and Creative Arts
- Mathematics and Sciences

The Heads of Faculty are members of the Senior Management Group which meets every Monday lunchtime with the Head, the Deputies and the Heads of House. They are also given a sum of money out of capitation, this year amounting to £1,000 each, which they can allocate to their departments at their discretion.

Third Year pupils are banded, mainly on the basis of their Middle School records, into 'M', ie the most able; 'V', ie those of average ability; and 'S' ie those needing remedial help. Within the 'M' and 'V' bands teaching groups are mainly of mixed ability.

In the Fourth Year there is a common core of subjects and an open options system, except that the less able pupils are 'guided' into a largely pre-vocational programme.

There is an open-access Sixth Form, offering both one- and two-year courses.

Pastoral organisation

The school is divided vertically into three Houses and the Heads of House are responsible for the pastoral care and academic progress of their girls, including Sixth Formers. Tutor groups in each year are on a House basis.

17 Park

The school is an 11–16 mixed comprehensive, increasingly receiving an inner-city intake.

The school was formed in 1973 by the merger of a large boys' grammar school and a smaller girls' grammar school on an adjoining site.

Initially the school attracted a high intake but numbers have declined dramatically from a peak of 1,400 to the present roll of 758. The present figures available predict that this decline will continue.

One of the main problems is the split site. For all that numbers have declined, it is still necessary to use the old building. Over half of the building is so decayed that it is unsafe for use and the other half is in a very poor state of repair. As a move is planned to the main building for

September, only vital repairs are carried out. The fact that the main body of the building is protected under listed building status makes for further complications.

Much structural work is needed in the main building to allow all years to be successfully accommodated and, as no start has been made to date, it seems extremely unlikely that the present difficulties will be resolved by the start of the new school year.

The school enjoys a local reputation as a progressive, forward-looking institution. It is certainly involved in many initiatives, some of which are known to the staff and some only known to senior staff initially.

The Head is a character of considerable local reputation.

18 *Abbey*

The school is a small, mixed, 11–16 comprehensive which caters for the Christian community in the most prosperous area of town.

Most of the pupils come from the four primary schools that serve the four parishes of the area. Children from other schools and parishes are admitted on parental request and with the agreement of the governors.

Prior to comprehensive reorganisation it had always enjoyed a reputation as a very tightly run and well ordered secondary school. Parents have continued their support for the school and this has enabled the establishment of a popular small comprehensive school which attracts pupils from further afield and allows for an element of selection of the intake.

The church influence in the running of the schools seems to be less evident in formal routines and practices and more apparent in the general familial and caring ethos that exists.

Teachers are appointed on merit, irrespective of denomination, to all posts up to the level of Deputy Headship.

The present Head, appointed four years ago, succeeded a husband-and-wife-team of Headteacher and Deputy who ran the school with as little consultation as possible. The development of the school is particularly interesting.

19 *Kirkside*

The school was set up in 1970. It is one of three 11–16 comprehensives in the area. Kirkside was originally a secondary modern school and still suffers from this image, particularly in comparison with its neighbour, which was the old grammar school. Certainly its intake is less good, both academically and socially, than the other two schools, and this is reflected in its examination results.

It is situated on the edge of a large council estate from which it draws a significant proportion of its intake. Many of the children are difficult to motivate and both pupil and parental expectations are low. Only about a quarter of the leavers go into further education. There is a higher than average percentage of pupils who experience learning difficulties (about 20 per cent) which is recognised by the County to the tune of a staffing bonus of 0.5.

Falling rolls will affect both Kirkside and its neighbour. The latter takes about half its intake from the surrounding areas of the neighbouring LEA, which makes it particularly vulnerable to any changes in County policy, leading to the removal of any or all of these children. Room would thus become available to take pupils from Kirkside's catchment area. Already there has been some movement, which amounted to 17 last year. All these pupils come from the best part of the catchment area. If this movement gathers pace, Kirkside's problems will be exacerbated. Much will depend on the LEA policy on planned admission limits and parental choice, for even without the loss of pupils to the neighbouring LEA, the school will drop to a four-form entry next year. (It has in the past been seven-form entry.) It will also be de-grouped from 10 to 9 in the next triennial review. Clearly, there is a need for the whole question of the provision of secondary education in the area to be re-assessed by the County, but the indications are that it intends to maintain the three schools.

The school itself consists of a main teaching block (the old secondary modern school); a ROSLA block, which houses the administration area, the staffroom, two science laboratories and the library; and four other units. There are decent playing fields on site, together with an indoor swimming pool which can only be used for half the year because the school cannot afford the high cost of heating. Kirkside had a 'dipstick' inspection and the HMI commented on the poor state of decoration of parts of the school but congratulated the school on the absence of graffiti and vandalism and on the system of dealing with litter. These comments still apply.

There are 40 full-time staff and eight part-timers. Of the 16 staff on Scale 3 or above, eight have been there 20 years or more and another six have been there ten years or more. Thus, there have been few opportunities for internal promotion, which has led to a loss of some good young staff. Since 1982 there have been 12 cases of staff exercising their rights to take maternity leave, with the consequent difficulty of finding suitable replacements to maintain continuity of teaching, particularly if the leave has extended over two academic years.

Falling rolls will certainly lead to a loss of staff next year. Two staff have already been granted early retirement and another one is almost definitely resigning to go to Bible College. Although this will help the overall staffing situation, the curriculum might well suffer in the Science and Humanities areas.

Therefore, the future of the school is not rosy and the staff are having to rethink the whole curriculum. One bright spot is the area of pupil profiling, where the school is amongst the leaders in the LEA.

The staff decided some years ago that teaching timetables should be equal for all those below Deputy Head level and the present Head has continued this policy. The accepted load is 28/29 periods out of a 35-period week. Although this seems fair, it does mean that Year Heads have no time to carry out their pastoral responsibilities properly, which means that the Deputies have to sweep up many of the Year Head tasks.

20 The Ridgeway

The Ridgeway was formed from the amalgamation of a small grammar school and a larger secondary modern in 1981. It is situated on the site of the secondary modern school on the edge of a small industrial town. The socially mixed intake comes from both the town and country which surrounds it. The school has 1,174 pupils on roll with 65 in the Sixth Form.

Years 1, 2 and 3 are accommodated in the buildings vacated by the secondary modern school. These original buildings are a short distance from the new accommodation which has been built to house the Upper School classrooms, CDT areas, Science Labs and Sixth Form Centre. The new buildings are very clean, well maintained and show few signs of wear and tear. The school has a good reputation in the locality and is constantly under pressure to take children from out of catchment. As a result the classes tend to be large and, in certain areas of the school, over-crowded.

21 Valley High

Valley High School was established in 1576 as an Endowed Grammar School. It is situated in a small country town which earns its living mainly through quarrying. The school serves both the town and the villages which surround it. When it went comprehensive in 1965 it acquired some extensive new buildings which enabled it to expand. It did so until about 1983, since when it has been hit hard by falling rolls. At the present moment it is struggling to keep its numbers from falling below 600 after peaking at nearly 900. It has a very small Sixth Form, since most 16+ students choose to continue their education at an FE College in a town some 12 miles away. The problem of falling rolls has been exacerbated by a tendency for some of the 'village' parents to send their children to a new comprehensive school in an adjacent town. The school sees itself as playing a central role in the community and has, over the past few years, developed a forward-looking Community Education Programme.

Much of the accommodation at the school is showing signs of wear and tear, partly because of its use as a Community Centre and Youth Club but also because parts of the school are open to pupils at break and lunchtime.

This applies to the middle floor of the 1965 accommodation, which was designed so that it could be used as the dining and assembling areas for the vertical Houses which characterise the pastoral organisation of the school.

22 Central High

Central is an 11–18 comprehensive founded in the sixties, built on a single site near the town centre. It has about 1,100 pupils. Pastoral organisation is on a Year basis.

Following its foundation, the majority of the children coming to Central were white middle- and working-class with a small intake of pupils of Asian origin. Under the first Head, a very single-minded, authoritarian figure, Central established a well-justified reputation as an academically successful school, attracting pupils from throughout the borough to its central location, both at 11 + and 16 + (not all local schools had Sixth Forms at this time). Its ethos was one of stern discipline, hard work, uniform and high expectations for the pupils in the top ability band and the Sixth Form.

Since about 1980, so many things have changed for the staff at Central:

The Head: the present Head, Mr Byrne, favours a non-directive, consensual, conflict-avoidance approach, which many senior staff, accustomed to the totalitarian approach of his predecessor, are prone to interpret as weakness and lack of firm direction.

The intake: now over 50 per cent Asian, mainly poor Bangladeshi, with considerable English-language problems and special needs; fewer pupils from white middle-class backgrounds, many more pupils from very poor white inner-city backgrounds; cut-off of supply of able Sixth Formers from other local schools.

Plus: the usual catalogue of changes and pressures that have affected so many schools in the state sector to some extent in the last few years, such as too much innovation in too short a time, teacher union action, anxiety over falling school rolls, uncertainty about what the future holds.

Many staff, particularly at Head of Department/Pastoral Head level, have been at the school for over ten years and had their attitudes formed during what now seems to them to have been a period of optimism, stability and success in the seventies. Many of these middle-management figures look back on the great simplicities of the school's successful seventies past with considerable nostalgia.

It is conceivable that these Golden Age myths are now hampering the school's ability to adapt to the changed circumstances. There is a tendency to stereotype and scapegoat and to ascribe simple or single causes and solutions to complex problems. At different times, you can hear the Head, the LEA, the Asians, the ESL Department, the Special Needs Department, the LEA's Multicultural Language service and the government each blamed for the fact that the school is no longer what it was in its hey day. The present Head in particular comes in for a lot of muted criticism from staff at all levels; he is felt to be wonderfully sympathetic at a personal level, but there is a widespread feeling that 'there should be more lead from the top.' His appointment to the Headship coincided with the deterioration of the 'steady state'; perhaps, not surprisingly, some long-standing staff see a causal relationship in this. Although most staff would not wish to go back to the days of his macho predecessor, there is a feeling that perhaps the school was in more secure hands then.

The staffroom is among the best we visited and tea and coffee are prepared for the staff each break and the pots washed up for them. Relationships seem most civil, but formal rather than warm, and there seems to be a taboo against 'talking shop' in the staffroom. There is a separate staff work area.

From the outside the school still looks modern and well equipped. The entrance hall of the school is bright and welcoming, but the corridors and most classrooms are drab; apart from specialist areas such as craft and science, few staff have their own teaching-rooms or areas.

Although much staff dissatisfaction and anxiety goes unexpressed, attempts are being made to address some problem areas identified by a staff questionnaire put out by the recently appointed Staff Development Tutor, by forming working parties.

The school's future is felt by staff to be uncertain; the LEA is discussing plans to reorganise post 16. We sensed that many staff are withholding commitment in view of this uncertainty. While many staff claimed to be, and indeed appeared to be, working very hard on a day-to-day basis, morale seems to be low. There is a lack of excitement in the school and an understandable reluctance to invest time and effort in long-term initiatives.

23 Southern High

Southern is an 11–18 co-educational comprehensive school of about 1,000 pupils, situated about a mile from the town centre. The present building opened in the fifties as a technical high school.

Foundation, decline and fall

The school seems to have soon acquired a good reputation in the town. In the mid-sixties the LEA reorganised its secondary schools on comprehensive lines and its reputation began a period of decline. The school was first reorganised as a 14–18, with a separate local feeder school (11–13); then in the late seventies there was a further upheaval as its feeder school closed and Southern became 11–18. All the staff had to re-apply for jobs and staff were redeployed from the feeder school. By this time the school's reputation was very poor indeed; very few parents would put down Southern as their first-choice school. Relations between the Head and the staff were very poor and there was unfavourable publicity in the local press. Staff turnover began to haemorrhage.

Drastic Action

The LEA sent the Head on secondment and put in a chief adviser to take over the Headship of the newly reorganised school. Mr Pattle seems to have managed to turn the school round in a remarkably short time, at least as far as the image of the school is concerned – it could be argued that the reality has not quite caught up with the improved image even yet, particularly in the areas of multicultural education and academic results.

Improvement

What were the main ingredients of the turn round? On a formal level, Mr Pattle set up a Faculty structure. It is not clear whether Mr Pattle chose this because he was convinced of its merits as a structure; the Staff Handbook says: 'Our thinking was greatly influenced by the Green Paper of 1977, which argued that there is an urgent need for more co-ordination in the curriculum.' Many staff are of the opinion that Mr Pattle used this as a means of promoting certain staff at the expense of others. Either way, the effect was to set up four faculties, alongside a pastoral system based on Heads of Year.

There were also innovations in the curriculum; new integrated courses, Mode Threes, mixed-ability classes in the Lower School, all encouraged by Mr Pattle with the aim of providing more appropriate and stimulating courses for the sort of pupils that Southern High had to deal with.

Although not universally popular, Mr Pattle remains in the minds of most of the staff interviewed as an excellent manager. The present Head, Mr Broad, was one of Mr Pattle's Deputies at this time. General opinion is that they complemented each other very well. Mr Pattle was excellent at relationships and public relations, Mr Broad was an efficient administrator. Staff began to feel that they were in good hands. They talk of a common sense of purpose at this time, of excitement even. The redeployed staff seem to have made an important contribution. Staff turnover slowed down. Mr Pattle made a virtue of necessity and instituted pioneering work in multicultural education and ESL, in recognition of the school's now large ethnic-minority intake.

Mr Pattle cleverly exploited the press to build a positive new image for the reorganised school and, within a year or two, most of the First Year intake were coming as 'first-choices'. Many staff interviewed made remarks such as 'Mr Pattle always made you feel important, that you had something to contribute.' Others note that Mr Pattle was clever, they knew he was manipulative, yet 'he always listened to you, made you feel that he considered what you had to say as important, even if in the end he disregarded it.' When asked to be more precise, staff say it was just 'little things', such as being both accessible and visible, even going round to hand out all the pay envelopes every month – this might have seemed condescending but somehow did not.

The present regime

Mr Broad was appointed to Southern as Deputy in 1978. He left in 1982 to take up the Headship of another local school, but returned to Southern as Head in 1984. He has had to steer the school through the recent difficult period of industrial action. Recently the school has begun to hum again, with the school's involvement as a pilot for the Northern Partnership for Records of Achievement (NPRA) scheme. There is widespread use of microcomputers in school administration. Southern shows some of the features of a community school, with shared school/community use of a splendid sports complex on site.

The Southern culture

The staff like to think that pupils experience Southern as a unified, caring school, but the culture that the staff themselves experience is rather different. Despite a very mature staff, much recent decision making and innovation seems to have been top-down, for instance, the decision to pilot NPRA at the school. There seems a real gulf between the mass of ordinary staff and Mr Broad, although there is a weekly staff briefing meeting and attempts have been made to improve communications. Staff want the Head to do well for the school, but are not entirely happy with the path he wants the school to go down, or his style of management.

There is evidence of a mismatch of cultures. Mr Broad and the first Deputy show an administrative, rather bureaucratic emphasis; for instance, their staff handbook is very detailed and explicit and particularly emphasises the monitoring and controlling roles of all the management positions. Yet the middle and bottom show little penetration by the top culture; there are many committed and hard-working staff, but staff relationships are on the whole more collegial than hierarchical, symbolised by the appallingly dingy and ill-equipped staffroom, with its almost war-time camaraderie.

24 Ferndown

The school opened as a comprehensive in 1965 to serve the town and its surrounding area. Built in phases it is, in effect, one huge complex of almost uniform style. Although there are places, particularly the long, often dark corridors, where the scale is threatening, it is generally attractive inside. For example, the two entrance areas are used to good effect to display high-quality pupil work, there are two large general-purpose halls, a large sports hall and two gymnasia. Much of the furniture dates from the school's opening (and shows it).

The school is set in a residential area; two sides of its site being occupied by large inter-war semis, the third by large detached houses about 90 years old. One of these has been converted into an LEA Special School. There is some playing-field accommodation on this site, but the major games area is on a waterlogged and windswept hillside about a kilometre away (and 100 metres higher). The school also uses an old building and games area, associated with the replaced grammar school, on a closer but still detached site.

The catchment area is as described in Ridley, except that the area is split with a smaller, neighbouring, comprehensive school. The LEA has a 'parental choice' policy so, although parents of 'top juniors' are advised which of the comprehensive schools their children can expect to go to (by location of dwelling and/or primary school), there is a measure of selection.

At one point during the study, both comprehensive schools were told that 49 requests for admission to Ferndown School had been made on behalf of pupils originally destined for the other school. If all these requests were approved, the other school's intake would be reduced by 45 per cent while Ferndown School's would be raised by 30 per cent, well above its admission number.

Folk Myths of Ferndown School

The School was built to admit children from an area of rapidly expanding population. Major estates of private dwellings and a major city overspill estate were being erected. To cope with the numbers, the second school was built to open seven years after Ferndown School. The school had employed many of the staff and gained some of the aura of the grammar school it had subsumed. The new school was an entirely new creation.

The LEA's intention had been that each school should take a balanced share of the children from all new estates, but the new school opened with a disproportionate share of low-ability pupils, including some transferred from Ferndown. Early exam results reflected this and, given also that the first Head of the new school is remembered as progressive rather than disciplinarian and the second had to resign on psychiatric grounds, the relative standing of the two schools has become well fixed in the minds of many parents.

Thoughtful, supportive (ambitious) parents have sought to send their children to Ferndown, while the other has never really 'taken off' in the way intended. Recently, pupils of Sixth Form age have drifted away for their 'A' levels as well as for vocational courses. The staff at Ferndown have been criticised for their complacency in not spotting this trend early enough to take effective action. Sixth Form numbers have been below DES guidelines for four years (despite a good provision for repeating 16 + exams and a generous allocation of staffing) and the school is being considered, along with its maintained and voluntary-aided neighbours, in reorganisation talks.

Author Index

Subject Index